The Maverick Spirit

Wilbur S. Shepperson Series in History and Humanities

The Maverick Spirit

Building the New Nevada

EDITED BY RICHARD O. DAVIES

UNIVERSITY OF NEVADA PRESS ▲▲ RENO, LAS VEGAS

Wilbur S. Shepperson Series in History and Humanities Editor:
Jerome E. Edwards

University of Nevada Press, Reno, Nevada 89557 USA
Copyright © 1999 by University of Nevada Press
Photograph of Molly Knudtsen by Don Dondero; photograph of
Robert Laxalt by John Ries; photograph of Sue Wagner by
Photography by Karen, Inc.; all other photographs courtesy
of the *Las Vegas Review-Journal.*
Manufactured in the United States of America
Design by Carrie Nelson House
Library of Congress Cataloging-in-Publication Data
The maverick spirit : building the new Nevada / edited by
Richard O. Davies.
    p. cm. — (Wilbur S. Shepperson series in history and
humanities)
    Includes bibliographical references (p.   ) and index.
    ISBN 0-87417-327-2 (pbk. : alk. paper)
    1. Nevada—History—20th century. 2. Nevada—Biography.
I. Davies, Richard O., 1937–   . II. Series: Wilbur S. Shepperson
series in history and humanities (Unnumbered)
F845.M39 1998   98-21144
979.3—dc21   CIP

The paper used in this book meets the requirements of American
National Standard for Information Sciences—Permanence of
Paper for Printed Library Materials, ANSI Z39.48–1984. Binding
materials were selected for strength and durability.

First Printing
07 06 05 04 03 02 01 00 99 98   5 4 3 2 1

To the pioneering scholars who blazed the trail:

Russell Elliott and Wilbur Shepperson

Contents

Acknowledgments

This collection of original essays is the result of the contributions of many individuals. The thirteen scholars who joined with me in producing this anthology have contributed substantially to an enhanced understanding of contemporary Nevada history. As the following essays demonstrate, the history of the last half-century of Nevada history is one that deserves careful attention. The emergence of the New Nevada during the turbulent years of World War II and its aftermath constitutes a major watershed in the history of Nevada, and the fourteen individuals whose lives are described and interpreted in these pages provide unique perspectives that help us understand and appreciate that major event.

Some readers will be disappointed that many prominent persons were not included, but it was imperative to limit the number of subjects to a manageable size. I believe that those fourteen individuals who were selected provide an instructive overview of Nevada's recent past. Inevitably, individuals who made major contributions had to be excluded. An informal group of scholars and public leaders with whom I consulted argued persuasively for the inclusion of such leaders as United States senators Patrick McCarran, Howard Cannon, Richard Bryan, and Harry Reid; governors Mike O'Callaghan and Charles Russell; legislative lobbyist Jim Joyce; educators Joe Crowley, Kenny Guinn, and Robert Maxson; university regents Silas Ross and Fred Anderson; media giant Donald W. Reynolds; jurists Bruce Thompson and Roger Foley; congresswoman Barbara Vucanovich; gaming entrepreneurs Benny Binion, Howard Hughes, Warren Nelson, Harold Smith, Kirk Kerkorian, and John Ascuaga (to name but a few); and a covey of legislative leaders, including James Gibson, Joe Dini, Mary Gojack, Thomas "Spike" Wilson, Floyd Lamb, and Carl Dodge. I received other intriguing suggestions as well, including entertainers Frank Sinatra, Wayne Newton, Liberace, and Sammy Davis Jr., mobster Bugsy Siegel, and brothel magnate Joe Conforte.

The purpose of the selection process—for which I alone am ultimately responsible—was to identify individuals who, taken as a composite, have had a substantial impact upon the economic, cultural, social, and political development of the New Nevada. Although the fourteen individuals came from strikingly diverse backgrounds, a few unifying themes are evident. Postwar Nevada—small, growing, fluid, and lacking an entrenched political or economic elite—provided unusual opportunities for ambitious individuals to rise quickly to positions of leadership and power in their chosen fields. Each, in a major way, affected the course of some major aspect of Nevada life in the half-century following World War II.

I gratefully acknowledge the assistance of several individuals with whom I consulted as this project took shape, especially David Hoy, Rollan Melton, Eugene Moehring, Joe Crowley, Sharon Lowe, Myrick Land, Jerome Edwards, William Rowley, John Findlay, Elizabeth Raymond, Gary Elliott, and Alan Balboni. Thomas Radko, former director of the University of Nevada Press, was enthusiastic from the outset and provided several practical suggestions, along with much-needed encouragement.

The thirteen individuals who agreed to join with me in this project willingly set aside other tasks to meet ambitious deadlines. The contributors bring to their work many perspectives and were encouraged to pursue their subjects with minimal editorial guidelines and restraints. No specific format was imposed upon them, and they were given wide latitude in presenting their narratives and reaching their conclusions. The essays reflect such academic disciplines as political science, anthropology, literature, and history, and such professions as the law, public administration, and education. The reader will encounter distinctly contrasting points of view and occasional differences in emphasis or interpretation. The collection is, I think, much richer because of the diversity of the perspectives brought to this collective project by the individual authors. Together they have helped describe the richness and complexity of the New Nevada.

The production of this book has been supported by a generous grant from the University of Nevada, Reno, Foundation. The editor and the contributors gratefully express their appreciation to the foundation and its officers for their support. This book recognizes two superb teachers and scholars who came before us—Russell Elliott and Wilbur Shepperson. These two men devoted their lives to the serious study of Nevada history and established a tradition of excellence that we hope to have approached.

Richard O. Davies
University of Nevada, Reno

The Maverick Spirit

Sagebrush and Cities

The Emergence of the New Nevada

BY RICHARD O. DAVIES

Nevada gained admission to the Union in 1864, but more than 130 years later it remains a youthful state. For much of its first century Nevada was isolated and largely ignored, its minuscule population and stunted economy often the target of ridicule. Not until the 1940s did the outlines of the dynamic society of contemporary Nevada begin to appear. Although remnants of earlier eras are readily evident—depleted copper and silver mines, dusty ghost towns, sprawling ranches, rustic small towns struggling mightily to survive—the New Nevada that emerged from the galvanizing force of World War II is a much different sort of place. It is this New Nevada, one that is largely urban and urbane, high tech and high profile, glamorous and glitzy, that is the focus of this book.

In his harsh critique of Nevada as a "great rotten borough," the historian Gilman Ostrander emphasized that Nevada was prematurely granted statehood in 1864 only because of the exigencies created by the Civil War. Under normal circumstances Nevada's tiny population would have made it the last of the contiguous forty-eight states to enter the Union, but the lightly populated territory afforded President Abraham Lincoln political advantages he could not ignore: two Republican votes in the United States Senate, three electoral votes in the 1864 presidential election, and additional votes to ensure that his plan for Reconstruction would not be overturned by the vengeful Radical Republicans.

Once prematurely admitted to the Union, Nevada promptly languished. Its modest ranching economy proved unable to support sustained growth, while its boom-and-bust mining industry created periods of optimism and growth only to be followed by decades of atrophy. A territorial census in 1861 placed Nevada's population at just 16,000, but the mining boom on the Comstock pushed that figure to an estimated 35,000 to 40,000 by the time Nevada was admitted to the Union. In 1870, the Bureau of the Census counted 42,491 residents. Although the mining boom brought the number of

[handwritten margin notes: 1864 / Admission to the Union]

[handwritten margin notes: focus of book: "New Nevada" urban, high tech, high profile, glamorous, glitzy]

1

residents to more than 60,000 in 1880, the subsequent collapse left the Silver State with just 42,335 residents in 1900. For a time Nevada faced the ignominious possibility of having its statehood revoked by an unsympathetic Congress and being returned to the status of a territory.

That did not happen, of course; but during the first forty years of the twentieth century, Nevada witnessed only modest growth as the state's economy continued to depend upon mining and ranching. The Great Depression of the 1930s hit Nevada especially hard, and even the legalization of gambling in 1931 had no immediate impact. Nevada remained a poor state, muddling along in the back eddies of American life. That reality was abruptly changed by the powerful economic forces unleashed by the Second World War. If there ever was a watershed in the history of the State of Nevada—a time of substantial and lasting change—it occurred during the 1940s. Nevada may have been "Battle Born" during the Civil War, as the state's motto proudly proclaims, but the foundation for the bustling, dynamic, diverse, and expanding Nevada that we know today was established during that decade.

In 1941 Nevada's population stood at just 110,000, much of it concentrated in the Carson-Truckee region. The small city of Reno, with a population of only 21,000, possessed enormous influence statewide, its power brokers ruthlessly controlling and manipulating Nevada's political and economic systems. His self-righteous indignation notwithstanding, Ostrander essentially got it right: Nevada was indeed a "rotten borough," using the power to be derived from two votes in the United States Senate to secure an often disproportionate share of federal funds and other benefits. Throughout its early history Nevada might have been victimized by the imperial corporate whims of Phelps Dodge or Central Pacific, but it also leveraged its small congressional delegation to great advantage. In 1902 Congressman Francis Newlands secured passage of his Reclamation Act, which made federal funds available for reclamation projects. The first project funded under this legislation was the provision of a reliable water supply to support agricultural development within the Carson-Truckee basin. During the 1930s and 1940s the dominant conservative political machine, controlled by the portly, often meanspirited Patrick McCarran, wielded a power in Washington on behalf of the Silver State substantially disproportionate to its limited population. Utilizing the power inherent in the congressional seniority system, senators such as McCarran and Key Pittman made it their primary mission to keep the price of silver artificially high and the cost of leasing federal grazing lands inordinately cheap.

McCarran's bipartisan and highly personalized political machine demonstrated only occasional interest in the state's yet-unrecognized future as a gambling mecca. In 1940 Las Vegas, with just 8,400 residents, took a back seat to the bosses in Reno. The second-class status that McCarran and his minions callously assigned to Clark County would not last long as modern casino gambling shattered traditional political alliances and allegiances. By the time McCarran dropped dead of a heart attack in 1954 while giving a speech in Hawthorne, the rapid rise of gambling had already begun to tip the balance of power toward the south.

It was not Nevada's cities, however, that took on considerable importance to American military planners during the early days of the Second World War. Rather, they looked with anticipation toward Nevada's enormous expanse of uninhabited desert. Nevada's leadership, smelling a bonanza in the swirling winds of war, unabashedly encouraged that interest. Located relatively close to the Pacific Ocean, but secure from Japanese attacks, Nevada provided the obvious location for new military bases. Its desert climate and clear skies invited the establishment of pilot training bases, and enormous infusions of federal capital quickly produced air bases near Las Vegas, Reno, Wendover, Tonopah, and Fallon. The hydroelectric power being generated at the recently completed dam at Boulder City—yet another major federal investment in the infrastructure of the Silver State—made possible the construction of the huge Basic Magnesium Plant to produce a strategic metal that had multiple military uses. By 1943 the hastily constructed magnesium processing plant in Henderson employed more workers than had any single mining operation in the history of Nevada. A new era of Nevada history was quickly taking shape.

The influx of thousands of military personnel and civilian wartime workers jolted the state's traditional sleepy equilibrium. The near-moribund economy of the Great Depression changed to one of unprecedented boom, setting off a sustained period of growth that eclipsed in size and scope that which swept the Comstock during the 1860s and 1870s. Construction workers and their families scrambled to locate housing, and businessmen and real estate developers found themselves in the midst of a huge, federally induced economic expansion.

The somewhat casual decision by state legislators in 1931 to legalize gambling now took on profound significance. Off-duty military personnel and workers flocked to the tiny storefront gambling emporiums for recreation, producing an economic boomlet that attracted the attention of out-of-state investors, many of whom had close ties with organized crime syndicates in such distant urban outposts as Cleveland, Detroit, and New York City. The arrival of pioneering gambling visionaries, like Benjamin "Bugsy" Siegel and Moe Dalitz, at war's end set in motion a transformation of the small and dingy gambling dens into the mega resorts of contemporary Las Vegas, Laughlin, South Lake Tahoe, and Reno. Siegel provided a sneak preview of the New Nevada when he opened the Flamingo on December 26, 1946, along the two-lane highway leading toward Los Angeles. During the next few years a bevy of well-financed veterans of illegal eastern and midwestern gambling emporiums made their way westward to the new promised land. The once sleepy railroad town of Las Vegas was transformed by the construction, in rapid succession, of the Thunderbird (1948), Desert Inn (1950), Sands and Sahara (1952), the Dunes, Riviera, an expanded and refurbished New Frontier (1955), and the Stardust (1958).

Jump-started by massive infusions of federal and mob money, the city of Las Vegas prospered tremendously. The population of Clark County increased twelvefold by 1960 (to 127,000) and never looked back. In 1960 a stunned Reno establishment contemplated the dire implications of a census report that indicated Clark County contained more residents than traditionally dominant Washoe County. Las Vegas and its several new suburbs continued to grow at a rate that exceeded even the most optimistic of projections. By 1990 Clark County contained nearly 70 percent of the state's population, and the Bureau of the Census reported in late 1995 that the county's population exceeded 1 million.

Although Reno also moved into the gambling business during this formative period, it did so with more caution and on a more modest scale. Reno prided itself on its family ambience—"a community of churches," as one long-running public relations campaign put it. Local politics dictated that gambling (and related enterprises like prostitution), however lucrative, nonetheless be kept under wraps. This meant confinement of gambling establishments to a narrow corridor in the downtown sector. Raymond I. Smith's Harolds Club set the cautious tenor in Reno with a traditional western decor, although it did launch an extravagant national highway-billboard advertising program (even with one sign planted in Antarctica). Entrepreneur William Harrah soon established a new industry standard for quality service and amenities in his Reno hotel-casino. By 1960 the long era of economic and political dominance by "the biggest little city" was coming to an end, overwhelmed by the casino boom occurring in Clark County.

Reno lacked three important ingredients that its southern rival happily exploited: an ample supply of water provided by the Colorado River, proximity to the burgeoning population of Southern California, and, especially, a community leadership willing to take high-stakes risks on casino gambling. These risks included giving the new casino moguls, who arrived with dubious reputations but much-needed management expertise and venture capital, a wide berth when it came to state controls and taxes. Thus did Las Vegas accommodate itself to the potentials of tourism and gambling in a much more nimble way than the stodgy folks up north. While Reno leaders pursued restrictive planning policies intended to prevent the casinos from dominating their community, Las Vegas and Clark County planners, politicians, and business leaders openly and happily worked to attain that very objective. Planners facilitated the development of the automobile-friendly suburban "Strip," an attractive feature to clientele from Southern California. By emulating the glitzy imagery of Hollywood, by warmly welcoming the emissaries from eastern gambling circles, by adeptly accommodating to the realities of the age of the automobile, and by exploiting water from the Colorado River, Las Vegas quickly outdistanced its stunned, and hopelessly outmaneuvered, northern rival.

The history of the New Nevada is intimately tied to the rise of Las Vegas as a major American metropolis. The stunning growth rate in Clark County not only undergirded the amazing reversal of the state's once dismal economic fortunes but restructured the political and cultural life of the Silver State as well. Las Vegas has become, students of American popular culture and urbanization contend, the harbinger of things to come in postmodern, postindustrial America. The unique sprawling, glitzy metropolis that blossomed in the sun-baked desert of southern Nevada has become one of the most dynamic, indeed fascinating, cities in all the world.

The rise of the modern casino industry provided the powerful economic engine that changed Nevada forever. But one important vestige of the Old Nevada remained: the state continued to benefit from large and regular infusions of federal dollars. Throughout its history, as Ostrander pointedly observed, Nevada's small but determined congressional delegations succeeded in securing a disproportionate share of the federal largesse. Whether Republican or Democratic, Nevada's conservative political establishment—and its equally conservative voters—ironically continued to view the federal government as a primary source of essential revenue. The tradition of keeping state taxes low while condemning wasteful federal spending has long been a staple of Nevada political rhetoric; the truth is, however, that not until very recent times have Nevadans seen a federal dollar they did not eagerly grab.

It was in this hallowed tradition of importing federal funds for financing expensive local needs that vast areas of Nevada's empty expanses of fragile desert became essential components of America's bristling military establishment during the early, frigid years of the Cold War. An enormous swath of land in central Nevada became home for navy pilots learning to drop their bombs with electronically precise accuracy. Enormous deposits of ordnance filled seemingly endless rows of earthen bunkers around Hawthorne, and most American jet fighter pilots learned the essentials of their craft at Nellis Air Force Base, located just north of Las Vegas. Supersecret military aviation innovations were tested at isolated bases near Tonopah and Rachel. In 1951 Yucca Flat, located some eighty miles north of Las Vegas, hosted its first atomic bomb tests as giddy residents of Las Vegas held celebratory, early morning parties. By 1955 forty-five above-ground tests had been detonated, some of them so powerful that the flash of light was visible five hundred miles away. Although national security considerations mandated that no financial figures be made public, the hundreds of millions of dollars expended at the sprawling Nevada Test Site contributed mightily to the spectacular growth of nearby Las Vegas.

The great majority of Nevadans and their elected officials, in Carson City as well as those dispatched to Washington, D.C., welcomed federal dollars—including the Nevada Test Site, and the Nuclear Dump at Beatty, and the gargantuan Southern Nevada Water Project that by the 1990s provided some 260 million acre feet of water annually for burgeoning Las Vegas. This mindset lasted at least until the 1980s, when Nevadans began to have second thoughts about the inherent goodness of federal dollars as they began to contemplate the enormous, and heretofore largely unrecognized, social, environmental, and cultural costs that often accompanied those funds.

It took the absurdities of the MX proposal to create the first backlash against federal spending in Nevada. The MX would have converted enormous chunks of western Utah and eastern Nevada into an armed nuclear camp of gigantic vehicles continuously moving long-range missiles from one launch silo to another along a 500-mile "race track" in an effort to confuse and confound Soviet missile launch commanders. Although the MX promised to eclipse easily the cost of building and operating the Nevada Test Site, the social and environmental costs seemed much too high. Even such conservative leaders as Senator Paul Laxalt subtly joined forces with outspoken environmentalists to fend off the MX.

Overwhelming grassroots opposition to the MX proposal stands as a major fault line in contemporary Nevada history, marking the first time the state willingly rejected substantial amounts of federal dollars. A few years later the proposal by the Department of Energy to establish a nuclear repository for the entire nation at Yucca Flat produced an even greater outcry of protest. In quick order there emerged a broad coalition of Nevadans of all political persuasions determined to fend off what would be the greatest federal investment, in terms of dollar amounts, in the history of the state. For once the residents of Clark and Washoe Counties found themselves in full agreement.

The outcome of that fierce battle remains to be determined as this book enters production, but it is clear that Nevadans are overwhelmingly and adamantly opposed to having their state treated as a nuclear landfill by the federal government, massive economic windfalls notwithstanding.

The pervasive influence of the federal government within Nevada provides a unifying theme in the pages that follow. Over 85 percent of all land in Nevada is owned by the federal government, a fact to which periodic eruptions of the Sagebrush Rebellion readily attest. It is not surprising to learn that federal policies have fundamentally shaped policies and events in Nevada, including such aspects of Nevada life as water use and development, the condition and status of Native Americans, the multiple use of forests and rangeland, the location and construction of highways, regulation of mining, cultural resource management, environmental protection, voting and representation, urban planning and development, criminal justice, social policy, and education. Important policy decisions impinging directly upon Nevada's recent past have often been shaped by unknown or remote administrators, operating out of such agencies as the Atomic Energy Commission, the Bureau of Land Management, the Department of Defense, the Bureau of Indian Affairs, the Department of Agriculture, and the Department of Interior.

Although the fourteen individuals whose lives are examined in the pages that follow came from strikingly diverse backgrounds, a few similar themes are evident. Postwar Nevada—small, growing, and lacking an entrenched political or economic elite—provided many opportunities for ambitious individuals to rise quickly to positions of leadership and power in their chosen fields. It is noteworthy, for example, that the egalitarian nature of Nevada's society made it possible for two brothers, Robert and Paul Laxalt, born to immigrant Basque parents, to achieve national recognition in such disparate fields as literature and politics. Similarly, Nevada provided the grandson of Italian immigrants, Bill Raggio, an opportunity to become a dominant force over three decades in the Nevada legislature, and afforded opportunities for women like Maude Frazier, Molly Knudtsen, and Sue Wagner to make important contributions to education, ranching, cultural resource management, and politics, as well as women's rights. The political career of the product of the small northern Nevada towns of Lovelock and Fallon, Alan Bible, is particularly instructive for the relationship of Nevada's growth to federal funding of massive water projects. Bible aptly epitomizes the essential, enduring truth of Nevada politics: If at all possible, let the Feds pay for it!

The fluid social and political climate of Las Vegas proved ideal for tempestuous journalist Hank Greenspun, whose privately owned *Las Vegas Sun* stands out as one of the last of an old breed of independent American newspapers. The impassioned editorial crusades that characterized Greenspun's career have largely disappeared from the land, muffled by the cautious, bottom-line corporate mentality of the media conglomerates of the present day. Las Vegas not only enabled a Jewish man from the streets of Brooklyn to become a powerful, if controversial, community voice, even a candidate for governor, but also provided a courageous black man like James McMillan, born in Mississippi and raised in Detroit, a venue to demonstrate that Nevada, despite a checkered record on matters of race and racism, would not resist new initiatives in the civil rights movement of the 1960s.

Probably the most widely recognized individual featured in this book is Jerry Tarkanian, an intensely driven man who found in Las Vegas a community desperately seeking national recognition at a time when it was routinely being flailed from the outside by many critics for its unique lifestyle. The mercurial coaching career of this son of Armenian immigrants provides a lively context for examining the sharply divergent viewpoints that emerged as Las Vegans, and indeed all Nevadans, grappled with the vagaries of their community's and state's image through the troubling questions that hovered around his powerful Runnin' Rebels basketball program.

While Tarkanian received an abundance of statewide and national media attention, state senator Bill Raggio exemplified the influence and power that could be accumulated within the legislative chambers in Carson City. The image of rogue celebrity that was Tarkanian and the image of the consummate insider that Raggio epitomized were far removed from the Nevada that novelist and essayist Robert Laxalt projected to critical reading audiences. Robert Laxalt's Nevada lay far from the glitz of Las Vegas or the smoke-filled rooms in Carson City. This introspective man found his special Nevada in the solitude of the mountains, hills, and sagebrush-dotted desert. His simple but eloquent prose probed deeply into the heart of the American Dream as he wrote of the Basque culture that flourished in the rugged Sierra Nevada, a special place of solitude where the head of the family could quietly tend his sheep in much the same manner as did his ancestors in the mountains of Europe. Robert Laxalt provided Nevadans a spiritual compass, connecting them to enduring values of land, family, and country during a time of rapid change.

As several essays make clear, the New Nevada offered a friendly tax and regulatory climate that made possible the spectacular emergence of casino gambling. This essential topic is examined in several essays, most directly in the contrasting careers of casino entrepreneurs Moe Dalitz, Bill Harrah, and Steve Wynn. Governor Grant Sawyer ensured that the pioneering gaming regulatory efforts of his predecessor, Charles Russell, would not be lost; he also provided courageous leadership by insisting that Nevadans confront the new realities of the civil rights movement. Although Paul Laxalt's friendship with President Ronald Reagan thrust him into the national spotlight in the 1980s, it was as governor that he made his most important contribution when he intuitively recognized the potentials of corporate gaming. His delicate negotiations with the reclusive Howard Hughes ultimately led to a new era in gaming, making possible, among other things, a business and political environment that encouraged the emergence during the 1980s and 1990s of the multibillion-dollar corporate empire headed by Steve Wynn.

The careers of these fourteen leaders illuminate many of the central themes of contemporary Nevada history: the growth and maturation of the gaming industry, the quest for adequate water supplies, the acquisition of vital federal funding, the spectacular growth of Las Vegas and the relative decline of Reno as a power center, the push by minorities and women for equal opportunity, the intense and sometimes destructive regional rivalry between "the North" and "the South," the development of educational and other social service systems to support a growing and increasingly modern society, and the constant struggle for external acceptance by a state whose reputation was sullied by negative impressions regarding not only its major industry but also relics from an earlier era: legalized prostitution, quickie marriages, and speedy divorces.

All of these essays touch upon the effort of Nevada to become a reasonably self-sustaining society, free from its historical status as a colony of external railroad and mining corporations and the federal government, proud of its uniqueness and stubborn individuality. What emerges in the pages that follow is the fascinating story of a small, fragile, and dependent state—a "rotten borough," if you will—striving to assume control of its own destiny, and doing so in its own, distinctly maverick sort of way.

14 leaders   themes:
growth of gaming industry
water supplies
federal money
growth of Las Vegas
decline of Reno
push by minorities & women
for equal opportunities
rivalry betw. N & S
legalized prostitution
quick marriage & divorce

Maude Frazier

Pioneering Educator and Lawmaker

BY JAMES W. HULSE

Although Maude Frazier has become a legendary figure in Nevada history, the shadow that she has projected since her death in 1963 does not do justice to her tangible record. One problem is that the written legacy of her service is quite vague, partly as a result of her own choices. Frazier either underrated her own accomplishments or looked upon her civic achievements so casually that she saw little reason to comment on them. Much of what she said about her career was anecdotal and light-hearted; she accepted with genuine modesty the honors that were showered upon her. Moreover, she covered her tracks across the Nevada landscape in a most curious manner.

Frazier was a more important figure on the Nevada political and social scene than she allowed us to believe. She left her mark on the state from the time she arrived in 1906 until her eighty-third year, after she had served for more than a decade in the state legislature and briefly as Nevada's lieutenant governor. The record of her accomplishments is not merely sequential; it is cumulative.

The basic facts of her life are easily summarized. Born in the farming country of southern Wisconsin on April 4, 1881, she attended the Wisconsin normal school at Stevens Point (with her father's disapproval) and taught in Wisconsin iron-mining towns. In at least one job the school board demanded that teachers promise not to dance or play cards, either in the town where they taught or anywhere else.

Soon after the turn of the century, Frazier began to hear stories of the new gold rush in the West. She listened to engineers in the Wisconsin mining towns tell stories about Jim Butler and his burro, who are given credit for the discovery of the rich silver veins at Tonopah in 1901. Frazier apparently became as excited by these tales as any aspiring gold seeker, and, her restlessness stirred, she began to send applications to several frontier regions, including Alaska. She eventually turned down a job offer in Juneau because it would have been too costly to travel that far. But in 1906, she received a contract

in Nevada

1906 - 1963

Born 1881

2

from the school board in the small community of Genoa, Nevada, located near the state capital of Carson City. She resigned from her teaching job in Wisconsin and caught a train westward, again without the approval of her parents. Her mother displayed a "bewildered does-this-wild-gypsy-belong-to-me-look" in her eye when Maude announced her intentions.

What the family may not have known was that young Maude had spent summer days in the hot attic of their home reading her grandfather's papers about his own migration into the old Northwest Territory two generations earlier. The yearning to go West was not determined by time or gender; she was ready to follow the call of the frontier that so many had heeded earlier.

From 1906 to 1961, Frazier served for about fifteen years as teacher and/or principal in rural Nevada schools, six years as deputy superintendent of public instruction in southern Nevada, nineteen as superintendent of the Las Vegas Union School District, twelve as an influential state legislator, many seasons as a tenacious promoter of higher education in southern Nevada, and a few months as lieutenant governor. No person during these years traversed the spectrum of Nevada education and civic responsibility more completely than she.

Writing near the end of her life about the turn-of-the-century period when her career began, Frazier said, "At that time there were three sexes—male, female, and teachers, the last named supposedly comprising the weak women of the two established with the coming of Adam and Eve."

Readers of the later twentieth century may be tempted to read more into this witty remark than she intended when she wrote it. Miss Frazier (as most of us who knew and respected her called her) was a model of propriety and dignified authority. The essence of her life's story is that by her service she claimed higher status for the female schoolteacher and administrator in Nevada and in the process raised the consciousness of her fellow citizens about the importance of public education. She was not a feminist or an advocate of women's rights in the contemporary sense of those terms, but she was an activist who had no doubt that she could perform any of the important social and political work traditionally assigned to men.

About the time she retired as superintendent of schools in Las Vegas in the mid-1940s, Frazier wrote or dictated an "autobiography." In it, she disguised (but not very thoroughly) the names of towns and localities in which she had lived and served as a teacher or administrator. It is not clear why Frazier camouflaged these names. She also omitted the names of most individuals with whom she had worked and offered only the vaguest of clues about what she had done professionally and socially.

In her memoirs, Frazier told of beginning her career in "Gold Creek" (apparently Genoa) for a year, of learning to handle a horse and riding the range with cowboys for summer activity. She followed a mining rush to "Dinero Gorge" (the camp of Seven Troughs in the Stone House Mountains about thirty miles west of Lovelock), where her classroom consisted of a tent with no books or supplies except those she carried with her. "A good school is a thing of the mind and spirit," she wrote later, "and not a thing of gadgets." While pastoral Genoa had some agricultural features that would have been familiar to her from her Wisconsin childhood, Seven Troughs was among the most basic of mining camps. State records show that Frazier was paid $75 per month in Genoa and $100 per month during her years in Seven Troughs.

Genoa

During World War I, Frazier taught in "Joshua Orchard," a larger town easily identified as the illustrious mining camp of Goldfield, which only a few years earlier had produced the richest "jewelry ore" in the West. It was past its peak as a boomtown by the time she taught there.

Goldfield

She attended summer school at the University of Nevada in 1918, 1919, and 1920. Her name appeared in the university register in the first year as a resident of Goldfield and in the latter two years as a resident of Sparks, the young railroad town in the eastern Truckee Meadows. Because of her performance in the classroom, she received a recommendation by the dean for a job as principal at a junior high school in Sparks. (New quarters for education classes—in the building known as Thompson Student Services in the 1990s—opened during her time there).

Sparks

In 1921, she applied for and won a job in "Desert Oasis" (Las Vegas), which remained her home for the next forty-two years, the last half of her life. She was appointed deputy superintendent of public instruction for the southern district of Nevada, an area embracing about forty thousand square miles in Clark, Lincoln, and most of Nye Counties. It was highly unusual for a woman to be appointed to such a position; in fact, there was no precedent for it in the state. One may infer that men with similar qualifications did not aspire to it. Frazier's fifteen years of teaching in Nevada had been an apprenticeship for this place—a dusty railroad town of 2,500 citizens—and its hinterland. She wrote: "Desert Oasis was the most unprepossessing place I had ever seen, and nobody at that time could have convinced me that I would ever come to love it as I eventually did. It became dearer to me than any other spot on earth."

Las Vegas

It is obvious from her writing that Frazier developed a passionate love not only for Las Vegas but also for the arid land beyond it. She found the desert terrain and its residents friendly, and she devoted some of her best prose to the joy of watching the light and shadows on the mountains and the desert fauna. As Frazier performed her duties of riding the circuit and inspecting the schools in her district, she drove an old Dodge named "Teddy" in honor of

Theodore Roosevelt, because it was a "rough rider." She had been warned that people would be hostile, but she found the opposite to be true. In her later years she enjoyed relating anecdotes about being stuck in ruts and befriended by prospectors, bootleggers, and other isolated denizens of the desert. She had no fear of traveling on the outback roads of Nevada, because there was a code of honor operating that protected one in her situation.

It is possible to supplement her blurry, impressionistic account about her work with the official reports that she filed with the office of the superintendent of public instruction in Carson City. Within her jurisdiction in 1922 were 39 local school districts, with 2,346 students and 131 teachers—29 men and 102 women. The state's educational system had endured a severe teacher shortage for several years; the problem had been especially severe in southern Nevada because no direct railroad connections or improved roads linked Clark or Lincoln Counties to Reno and other northern towns. Those teachers who received normal school diplomas at the University of Nevada typically took jobs in the communities nearer the state's population center in the north. Southern Nevada drew most of its teachers, when it could hire them, from California and Utah.

The authority of the deputy superintendent to effect improvements in the local schools was minimal. State law placed ultimate responsibility for establishing and maintaining each school in the hands of a locally elected school board, and nearly every school had its own board. Some did not operate for the full academic year because funding was erratic.

Judging from her reports, Frazier took a special interest in the remote rural schools, where one or two teachers were required to teach a broad spectrum of subjects. She wrote in 1922:

> The best trained teachers should be in the rural school districts because:
>
> 1. Rural school districts have less supervision than most town schools.
>
> 2. A rural-school teacher must teach all subjects and handle children of all ages and grades. This requires superior ability.
>
> 3. The rural community needs the teacher as a social factor more than does the town. The school must furnish the social life for the country children. This requires a many-sided ability on the part of the teacher.

Even thirty years later, while serving in the Nevada legislature, Frazier was an eloquent advocate of the needs and interests of the small rural schools. In 1957, she made memorable remarks on the floor of the assembly to the effect

that a child in Goldfield—by then a tiny town in an impoverished county—
had as much right to a good education as one in Reno or Las Vegas.

In her report for 1923–1924, Frazier recommended the establishment of a
"good standard state normal school . . . in the southern part of the State." She
was thus one of the first to envision and advocate an institution of higher
learning for that region. By the time she wrote her last report as deputy
superintendent in 1926, she took satisfaction from the fact that more students
from southern Nevada were attending the university in Reno than all comparable out-of-state institutions. That had been far from true when she arrived
in the region.

recommended state schools of higher ed.

At times, when she observed a promising student in a local high school,
she would encourage that student to attend college during a summer session
and enroll in the basic classes in order to obtain a temporary Nevada teaching
credential, and promise to find that individual a job in a rural school in the
coming school year.

Frazier's second car, after "Teddy" could no longer be coaxed along the
unimproved roads, was christened "Bobby" in recognition of Wisconsin senator Robert LaFollette, because it had a muffler cutout that made an awful
roar. That she named two of her automobiles for leaders of the Progressive
movement may offer a clue to her political preferences, but in general she
kept her political sentiments to herself.

The superintendent of public instruction under whom Frazier served was
W. J. Hunting, whom she obviously respected. He was defeated in the 1926
general election by Walter W. Anderson in a close race. Frazier tried to assist
Hunting in his political campaign in her district and lost her job in the
political shuffle that followed his defeat. She referred to this event with some
emotion in her memoirs.

Writing her final report as deputy superintendent a few weeks after the
election, Frazier made several recommendations for the improvement of
schools and the administrative structure of the state Department of Education. She was obviously disappointed that her mentor had lost his office, and
this apparently prompted her to reflect more broadly on the future of education in Nevada. She was in the process of expanding her interests from
pedagogy to politics.

First, she argued, the state superintendent's office should be appointive
rather than elective. A nonpartisan board, either the Board of Regents of the
state university or a board of education with broader authority, should appoint the superintendent and the deputies. In addition, she wrote, deputy
superintendents should have their powers and duties more fully defined.

Frazier also commented on the excessive number of school boards and districts, suggesting that in some counties only a single board for all schools would be more efficient. She also recommended some control over itinerant salesmen who peddled school supplies and a cost-control study to be made by an authority from outside the state, one who had nothing to gain or lose by the findings, one who would give a square deal to the children as well as the taxpayers. Many of the central features of her recommendations found their way thirty years later into the Peabody Report, which led to a dramatic renovation of the Nevada educational establishment, when Frazier was an influential member of the state legislature.

Shortly after Frazier lost her position as deputy superintendent, two members of the Clark County school board told her that the office of the city superintendent of schools would soon be available and encouraged her to apply. Once again she was challenged to accept a job that had previously been filled by men in all parts of the state. She knew the "educational eyes" would be on her and that she would have to "do more work and better work than the men if I were to prove myself." With her typical zeal, Frazier took charge. Finding the school buildings in bad repair and dangerous, she planned and led the community drive for improvements. With the federal government preparing to build the huge dam and hydroelectric plant thirty miles away on the Colorado River, she designed a new high school building for five hundred students, which her critics said was an extravagant number.

As the industrial base of the Las Vegas area grew in the 1940s with the addition of the Basic Magnesium Plant at Henderson, she recognized that many children who arrived with their families from the Deep South were poorly prepared for school and that this affected the way in which the local schools could operate. Her experience in accommodating disadvantaged children from the South into the Las Vegas schools convinced her that education was a national, as well as a local, responsibility.

Frazier had a reputation as a firm administrator. According to Elbert Edwards, a longtime Boulder City educator who greatly admired her, Frazier was known to stroll the hallways when she visited a school, and if there seemed to be too much inappropriate noise emerging from a classroom, she would simply jangle her keys. Order would be restored immediately.

On several occasions, according to Edwards, candidates who sought election to the school board talked about the need to replace Frazier as chief administrative officer of the school district. Some of them were elected, but once they took their seats on the board, they came to respect her work.

As the years passed, Frazier raised her voice more often on a variety of social issues. Las Vegas had been a city notorious for prostitution during the period of the construction of Hoover Dam, but during World War II, with the opening of the U.S. army air base (later Nellis), federal authorities successfully pressed the local authorities to close the bordellos. When efforts were made to reopen them following the war, Frazier spoke out publicly in favor of continuing the ban.

against legalized prostitution

Although she retired as superintendent in 1946 at age sixty-three, Frazier was still vigorous. She served as a consultant to the school district for a year after leaving her post. Her tall, lean figure and desert-weathered face had become one of the best known in southern Nevada; she was ready for her next career.

She was subsequently elected six times to the Nevada assembly and served as chair of the Education Committee in every legislative session from 1951 through 1961. The first time she ran for the assembly in 1948, she lost. Two years later, she led the ticket in the eight-candidate race in the Las Vegas district from which four members were selected. Las Vegas was then in an early stage of its post–World War II growth explosion; the population of the city in 1950 (the year of her first successful candidacy) was 24,624—approximately ten times as large as it had been when she had arrived in "Desert Oasis" as deputy superintendent of schools in 1921.

elected 6 times to Nev. assembly

Frazier became more effective in the legislature as she gained experience, just as she had done as deputy superintendent of the southern Nevada district thirty years earlier. The first session of the legislature in which she participated (1951) ignored the growing school enrollment crisis, especially in Las Vegas. Frazier lamented that oversight but acknowledged that limited state government revenues did not allow larger appropriations to be made for education.

In short order, she became part of a small movement to redesign not only the state school system but also the fiscal structure to support it. In her second legislative session (1953), Frazier participated in an effort to gain a substantial increase in school support funds beyond those suggested in the budget proposal of the superintendent of public instruction. The legislature managed a modest increase during that session without raising taxes, amid growing recognition that future improvement in school financing depended on finding new sources of tax revenue. In the autumn of 1953, R. Guild Gray, superintendent of schools in Las Vegas, reported that many children in his district were forced to attend half-day schools in dilapidated buildings. School budgeting was based on the previous year's enrollment, and Las Vegas had experienced an increase of more than 25 percent in its student population in a single year.

By the beginning of 1954, school crowding was so acute in the state's urban areas that Governor Charles Russell called a special session of the legislature to address the problem. The legislature established an interim School Survey Committee and appropriated $25,000 to enable it to employ out-of-state consultants to study the problems—a tactic that Frazier had recommended in her final report as deputy superintendent twenty-eight years earlier. The School Survey Committee engaged the George Peabody College for Teachers, a Tennessee institution, to conduct a study and make recommendations to the 1955 legislature.

The Peabody Report recommended the most complete overhaul of the state's educational system in its ninety-year history, and the essence of it embraced basic ideas that Frazier had contemplated in the 1920s. It advocated a consolidation of more than two hundred scattered school districts into seventeen districts governed by countywide boards, one for each county. It also encouraged the improvement and standardization of teacher salaries and facilities to provide equal opportunities for children—goals that Frazier had proposed in almost four decades as a teacher and administrator. Even though Frazier was a Democrat and Governor Russell a Republican, he respected her as much as he did any member of the legislature on educational matters, and her advice to him was an important factor in shaping his agenda. The 1955 session enacted most of the Peabody recommendations into law without significant opposition.

By the middle 1950s, Frazier had become one of the most influential members of the Nevada legislature in the field of education, playing vital roles not only in the enactment of significant school reorganization legislation in 1955 but also in passing a 2 percent state retail sales tax to enhance the financing of schools. The same session of the legislature recommended that the position of the state superintendent of public instruction be filled by appointment rather than by election and submitted the question to the voters, who approved the proposal in the 1956 election. Thus Frazier had the satisfaction of seeing another of the reforms she had proposed in the 1920s implemented in the 1950s.

No member of the legislature was more effective in promoting the opening of a university branch in Las Vegas than Frazier. She was one of the prime organizers of a "porch light campaign" to rally public support in 1955 for a $100,000 fund drive to assist with opening the Las Vegas campus. She devoted innumerable hours to meeting with civic leaders and assembling and distributing information on the school system that she had guided for so long. When the time came to break ground on the acreage that had been purchased on Maryland Parkway for a campus, the Board of Regents chose Frazier to turn the first shovel of earth, and it named the first building, erected in 1957, Maude Frazier Hall.

The range of Frazier's interests in government was impressive. During some of her years of service in the assembly she sat on the Ways and Means Committee and became involved in significant budgeting decisions. When one of the earliest civil rights bills was introduced in the Nevada legislature in 1959, her name appeared as the first sponsor. When Grant Sawyer became governor in 1959 and found the executive mansion to be dark, gloomy, and in a poor state of repair, his wife, Bette, invited a few key legislators over for tea. Frazier was among them, and according to Sawyer's memoirs, she became one of the leaders in helping to raise money to refurbish the old official residence.

Civil Rights

refurbish Gov. mansion

In the last few pages of her "autobiography," Frazier's mood becomes solemn. Rather suddenly the text takes on a nostalgic tone, reflecting on the era through which she had lived. One suspects that she may have added this portion to her memoirs late in life. She remembered her bucolic childhood home and closely knit family as a self-sustaining unit and a veritable factory, with its vegetable garden and barnyard that provided most of the food, an industrious grandmother who made clothing, and children who wore shoes only on Sunday to save the leather. Then she wondered solemnly about the contemporary age, with its synthetics, its prepackaged products, and its households in which children come home to no parents, about longer lives and expanded leisure time, and about the perils of the atomic age. Her sense of compassion and social responsibility emerged frequently during those last few pages.

As she wrote this delicate series of late reflections, her thoughts turned to contemporary children and how they might be more effectively prepared for the rapidly changing world around them. Nevada needs more nonconformists, she ventured, possibly thinking of her own unusual career. "We must develop our sociological frontiers," she wrote. "When the world is composed of two armed camps, each with the means of destroying the other, we may not be here to enjoy the material progress we have made. We have succeeded in inventions and gadgets, but we have fallen down pitifully in our human relationships." Her educational philosophy was direct and simple: The children of a community are the most important asset of society. She would have embraced the message of Marian Wright Edelman, the contemporary leader of the Children's Defense Fund: "We must leave no child behind."

Frazier's lifetime constitutes a condensed and personalized pilgrimage through the history of Nevada. Genoa, where she began her career, is the state's oldest town, and when she arrived as a teacher in 1906 it was little changed from the pioneer era of a half-century earlier. In her moves to Seven Troughs in Pershing County and Goldfield in Esmeralda County, she followed in the wake of the mining migrations that shaped the state's society and economy for the first sixty years after statehood. When she settled in Sparks she became a participant in the railroad frontier in its early phase, and her move to Las Vegas in 1921 foreshadowed the later migrations to that city. There she shared in the educational decisions that prepared this small town for its future growth. Her career overlapped with that of Helen Stewart, the pioneer woman who had owned the Las Vegas Ranch since the 1880s. Frazier mastered the horseless carriage and back roads of the southern deserts along with the earliest artisans of that craft; she referred to herself later as an "embryo mechanic." After her quarter century of service as a school administrator in the fastest growing part of Nevada came her six terms as a state legislator and her brief tenure as the first woman lieutenant governor—which took her occasionally back to Carson City, near where she had begun her Nevada odyssey in Genoa a half century earlier.

When Governor Sawyer appointed her to fill a vacancy in the office of lieutenant governor in 1962, he said he had no doubt she could perform any responsibilities that might be required of her. When interviewed by the press, Frazier agreed, and no Nevadan who knew her believed otherwise, although she was frail and largely confined to her home. She was the first woman to hold that office. There was no special political significance to the appointment; she had earned the recognition that went with the appointment. Only about six months remained in the unexpired term, and no heavy duties were assigned to the office at that time. The appointment was an honorary acknowledgment that she had served her adopted state with distinction and was a token of the widespread respect for her across the state.

Miss Frazier died at her home in Las Vegas on June 20, 1963, in her eighty-third year.

Moe Dalitz

Controversial Founding Father of Modern Las Vegas

BY ALAN BALBONI

Mr. Las Vegas. The mob's man in Las Vegas. An associate of organized crime figures. These were the terms commonly used by journalists to describe Moe Dalitz. Which was he? Some of each, and more. Certainly, he was the foremost of the men with shady pasts who created modern Las Vegas. Yet throughout his lifetime, and even after his death, the Las Vegas community remained ambivalent about his business and philanthropic achievements, praising him as a civic leader and entrepreneur while never forgetting or forgiving him for his cozy relationships with organized crime.

Morris Barney Dalitz was born of Eastern European Jewish immigrant parents in Boston on Christmas Day 1899. The modest circumstances of his birth, as well as his religious and ethnic background, were typical of the entrepreneurs who founded and operated the hotels and casinos on the Las Vegas Strip in the 1940s and 1950s. Most were either born in the Austro-Hungarian or Russian empires or were the sons of parents recently arrived from Eastern Europe. A few of the founders, and many of the casino managers and hidden investors, were of Southern Italian birth or ancestry. Like Dalitz, these men grew up in ethnic enclaves in the cities of the Northeast and the Midwest. Also like Dalitz, while trying to realize the American Dream, they did not hesitate to violate America's social taboos—prohibitions on prostitution, alcohol, and gambling—that the dominant Anglo-Saxon Protestants converted into law.

The Dalitz family moved several times in their efforts to achieve financial stability. Soon after Morris's birth they relocated to Ann Arbor, Michigan, and opened a laundry. His parents apparently achieved at least modest success, helping keep the students and professors of the University of Michigan in clean attire; they remained in Ann Arbor for several years before opening a laundry in Detroit. While Moe Dalitz never endured severe poverty, he observed that his parents, like so many other immigrants who operated small businesses,

3

had to work long hours under difficult conditions just to survive. His early life and exposure to the rigors of demanding labor undoubtedly served as a powerful motivating force in a life that would be devoted to seeking wealth and power.

Dalitz was one of thousands of young men of immigrant Italian or Jewish background who dropped out of high school to make money on the streets as a way of avoiding numbing labor in the factories, on construction projects, and, indeed, with the small businesses of early twentieth-century American cities. Arrested at least twice on misdemeanor charges during adolescence, Dalitz, like so many of his contemporaries, quickly perceived Prohibition as a great opportunity. A relatively small group of well-organized men and women, people unfamiliar to Dalitz and others like him, had imposed their morality on the heterogeneous American population. The Eighteenth Amendment and the federal and state legislation that provided criminal penalties for possession and distribution of alcohol appeared particularly absurd to first-generation Americans of Italian or Jewish ancestry. Moderate use of alcohol was part of their cultures. A young man who made or distributed liquor had a chance not only to get rich quickly but also to gain respect in his community. Bootlegging, rum-running, or whatever one called it was far more acceptable than violent crimes, even violence directed at outsiders.

Dalitz encountered competition when he began rum-running on Lakes Ontario and Saint Clair. Charley Resnik, also a rumrunner as well as a founding father of the Las Vegas Strip, recalled that Dalitz had a serious dispute in the mid-1920s with some Italian American competitors. Dalitz sought assistance from Resnik and other members of Detroit's Purple Gang, who advised him to pursue his activities in another city. Dalitz first went to Akron, Ohio, where he met Sam Tucker, another young entrepreneur of Eastern European Jewish ancestry. Dalitz soon moved to Cleveland, the city that would serve as both his home and the center of his initially illegitimate, although increasingly legitimate, business enterprises.

Dalitz and Tucker joined with two Cleveland bootleggers and business-men, Morris Kleinman and Louis Rothkopf, to operate a variety of profitable enterprises. In addition to extensive bootlegging—ranging from smuggling whiskey across the Great Lakes to manufacturing and distributing alcohol throughout Ohio, western Pennsylvania, and Kentucky—they also invested in such legitimate and mundane commercial enterprises as poultry wholesal-ing and laundries. Realizing that the end of Prohibition was near, Dalitz and his associates broadened their investments to include catering services and supper clubs. They also established cooperative business relationships, both legitimate and illegitimate, with Italian Americans and, less frequently, with others. Many of the Italian Americans, most notably Pete Licavoli, Joe Massei, the Milano brothers, and Chuck and Al Polizzi, were often referred to as Mafiosi when that term captured the fascination of newspaper reports and readers in the late 1950s and beyond.

Dalitz, Tucker, Kleinman, and Rothkopf had amassed considerable wealth by the mid-1930s, and they did not escape the scrutiny of the Internal Revenue Service. Kleinman served almost a year in a federal penitentiary for income-tax evasion, while Rothkopf was sentenced on June 9, 1937, to four years for the same crime. Almost a year later a federal court of appeals ruled that the evidence used to convict him had been seized in violation of the Fourth Amendment, and Rothkopf was released from prison. Although Dalitz was frequently investigated, he was indicted only once. Charges for rum-running in Buffalo were dropped.

"Hard times make hard people" was the reply Moe Dalitz often gave when Las Vegas newspaper and television reporters queried him about his past involvement with organized crime. Dalitz knew not only the hard times of a family working long hours six or even seven days a week but also the hard times of seeing close friends and associates say good-bye to loved ones as they began lengthy prison terms. Moe Dalitz refused to be judgmental about the strategies that others adopted to achieve wealth and power; he understood that luck alone had kept him out of jail during decades of supplying Americans with the vices denied them by the dominant Anglo-Saxon culture.

By the late 1920s Dalitz and his longtime associates Tucker and Kleinman had joined with experienced gamblers Ruby Kolod and Frank Rosen to operate casinos throughout Ohio and Kentucky. The most successful was the Beverly Hills in Newport, Kentucky, just across the Ohio River from Cincinnati, which openly featured nationally renowned entertainers. He learned in northern Kentucky the benefits of making certain that local law enforcement agents and elected officials benefited financially from tolerating the popular, but illegal, casinos. It was a practice that he would continue in Las Vegas. Dalitz and his associates brought to Las Vegas in the 1950s an understanding of both how to gain the support of local officials and the importance of cooperation among men of different ethnic backgrounds.

Dalitz's success in finding legitimate outlets for profits gained in illegal enterprises, even more than his own achievements as a bootlegger, gained him the respect of prominent organized-crime leaders throughout the country. His attendance at an unpublicized Atlantic City bootleggers' convention in 1929 reflected his success in that field. Other Jewish American and Italian American racketeers who gathered at the Hotel President included King

Solomon from Boston; Joe Bernstein, who was a founder of Detroit's Purple Gang along with Charley Resnik; Max Hoff of Philadelphia; a large delegation from the greater New York City area that included Meyer Lansky, Joe Adonis, Longie Zwillman, and Charley Luciano; and, of course, Al Capone from Chicago. Lansky, the alleged mastermind of organized-crime finance, respected Dalitz's business acumen enough to invest (using his brother, Jake, and his father-in-law, Moses Citron, as the fronts) in Molaska Inc., a company Dalitz and his associates founded. While supposedly making powdered molasses, the employees actually ran an illegal distillery. A decade later, Dalitz had major investments not only in Midwest commercial real estate, Detroit and Cleveland laundries, and Ohio supper clubs, but also in a linen supply company and two Detroit-based steel companies. He was clearly a man who knew how to invest ill-gotten gains wisely and, equally important, to keep quiet about hidden partners.

Dalitz's financial success allowed him to travel, an activity he enjoyed all his life. He occasionally found time for hunting and horseback riding in both the Midwest and in the desert Southwest. He made at least two trips to Arizona and New Mexico in the late 1920s. Dalitz spent several weeks camping, hunting deer and mountain lions, and riding through desert and mountain terrain. Allard Roen, Frank Rosen's son, recalled that although Dalitz once fell from his horse, lay in the desert sun for several hours, and suffered damage to a kidney as a result, the experience did not dampen his enthusiasm for the outdoors. Business associates from Ohio and Michigan often accompanied him to the Southwest. Often Dalitz's companion was Pete Licavoli, probably the first Italian American organized-crime leader to discover the potential of the desert Southwest for legitimate and illegitimate business investments.

Dalitz was less successful in his three marriages than in his investments. His first marriage lasted only a few years. After military service in the Second World War, Dalitz, whom former associates remember for his keen appreciation of beautiful women, married Toni, an exceptionally attractive former Cleveland model. Las Vegas attorney Louis Wiener recalled that they divorced shortly after Dalitz arrived in Las Vegas in 1951. An adopted son, Drew, later died when a plane he was piloting crashed. Although not regarded as a womanizer, Dalitz also never lacked for female companionship between marriages or after the termination of his third marriage.

Dalitz always expressed an appreciation for the opportunities America gave him and other children of immigrants. Too old for the draft when World War II began, he enlisted in the army in June 1943. His extensive knowledge of industrial laundries helped him gain an officer's commission. Lieutenant

Morris Dalitz had the good fortune to reside at the Hotel Savoy-Plaza in New York City while managing a quartermaster laundry, where he renewed acquaintances with East Coast gambling entrepreneurs and presumably exchanged information on the potential of the desert Southwest, an area that had a growing population as a result of the establishment of military bases and defense industries. Always the entrepreneur, Dalitz served his country even as he investigated new business opportunities.

The most entrepreneurial of the mobsters—syndicate leaders, gangsters, men with shady pasts, investors from this or that city (whatever term was used in the press)—recognized the potential of the rapidly growing West. They began looking for both legitimate and illegitimate business opportunities during World War II. While Benjamin Siegel and former Chicago mobster Willie Bioff initially sought opportunities in the movie industry, Dalitz and associates from Cleveland and Detroit bought land in Tucson, Arizona, and the Tucson Steam Laundry. Others made investments in Reno casinos, which were legal, and in Phoenix bookie joints, which were not.

By the late 1940s, Las Vegas offered the greatest potential of all. The dusty desert city, with a population less than 25,000 in a state of only 150,000, had much to offer: a warm and dry climate, lovely desert vistas, proximity to the rapidly growing Southern California population as a result of the rise in automobile ownership, and, of course, the only legalized gambling in the United States. Additionally, the booming U.S. economy provided the great majority of adult Americans with discretionary personal income. These factors alone ensured more than a reasonable return on investment for experienced gambling entrepreneurs.

Because gambling was legal in Nevada, achieving social respectability was a reasonable goal for those formerly involved in bootlegging, labor racketeering, and hijacking. Las Vegas's reputation as a frontier town with a focus on the future rather than the past made this goal seem even more attainable. Political influence was less expensive in Nevada than in the states of the Northeast or Midwest, where political relationships were often clouded by larger populations and a multiplicity of conflicting interest groups. Mobsters from New York, Chicago, Cleveland, and elsewhere were bringing significant capital to Las Vegas, a city with a population smaller than some ethnic neighborhoods of such cities as Boston, Cleveland, or Chicago; and local and state officials seldom asked questions about the sources of the capital that directly or indirectly provided jobs for a large segment of working adults.

Pioneer casino owner Benjamin "Bugsy" Siegel had been unable to shake his image as a violent mobster, and his well-publicized execution in 1947 reaffirmed that image. Other founding fathers of the Las Vegas Strip were

more successful. Moe Sedway, Siegel's junior partner in Las Vegas investments, served as chairman of the Las Vegas United Jewish Appeal in 1946.
Five years later Jake Kozloff, a former Pennsylvania bootlegger and gambling
entrepreneur, assumed the same position. In 1952, Gus Greenbaum, well
respected among the Italian and Jewish leaders in American and Cuban
gambling enterprises, succeeded Kozloff. Indeed, Greenbaum, whom the
mobsters investing in the Flamingo chose to operate the casino immediately
following Siegel's execution, took a leadership role in thwarting efforts by the
city of Las Vegas to incorporate the Strip. Greenbaum's notorious past did not
interfere with his becoming the unofficial mayor of Paradise, the artificial
political entity created to preclude incorporation by Las Vegas and higher
taxes on Strip gaming properties.

Organized-crime leaders declared postwar Las Vegas an open city. Dalitz,
as well as his longtime associates, rushed to invest their considerable capital in
the Las Vegas Strip. They were not alone. Later, in the mid-1950s, with most
of the new Strip resorts either open or under construction, both natives and
tourists had no hesitation in proclaiming that the Chicago mob operated this
casino and the Detroit mob that casino, and the New York Mafia families
operated still another, and so on. These popular perceptions were not far
from reality, although sometimes more than one organized-crime group undertook a joint skimming operation on the same property. Often the front
men for the new hotels were described in the local press as "Miami hotel-
men." This meant, to the discerning reader, that they enjoyed the confidence
of Miami-based mobster Meyer Lansky, who discretely coordinated a substantial part of the mob investment in the Strip.

The good citizens of Las Vegas did not rise up in righteous indignation.
The casinos introduced a new lucrative lifestyle. The general standard of
living was rapidly rising; particularly well-off were the dealers and cocktail
waitresses, who did not report their tip income to the IRS. Frank Modica, a
longtime gaming executive, was asked at the time of his retirement in 1995
what aspect of Las Vegas had changed most since he was a dealer in the early
1950s. He responded that no longer did casino employees live in big homes,
own two cars and, often, a boat. A much publicized IRS crackdown on
unreported tip income that began in the late 1970s put an end to the boats,
and sometimes the second car. Yet, as many a Las Vegan will attest, it was
great while it lasted. The good citizens also felt safe; street crime was broadly
perceived as minimal when "the boys" were in town.

Dalitz, Kleinman, Tucker, and initially less-visible associates such as Tom
McGinty, Louis Rothkopf, and Ruby Kolod, found their big opportunity
when Wilbur Clark exhausted his capital before the Desert Inn on the Strip

was finished. In addition to Clark's wealth of experience as a card dealer and a manager in illegal gambling enterprises, including Tony Cornero's well-publicized gambling ships anchored off the California coast, he was an excellent front man because he had never been convicted of a crime. Dalitz, Kleinman, and Tucker, though they were investors in the Desert Inn and had to apply for a gaming license from the Nevada Tax Commission, initially downplayed the extent of their roles at that casino. McGinty, Rothkopf, and Kolod initially stayed even further in the background as lenders to their Cleveland investor associates.

Thus, the name in lights when the Desert Inn opened on April 24, 1950, was that of Wilbur Clark, not Morris Dalitz. This was to the satisfaction of all concerned, particularly as the Kefauver Committee (more formally, the U.S. Senate Special Committee to Investigate Organized Crime in Interstate Commerce) was conducting highly publicized hearings on organized crime in cities across the country. Ironically, one effect of the committee's investigations was to increase Las Vegas's appeal to mobsters with money to invest. As other localities elected reform administrations pledging to wipe out illegal gambling, Nevada and Las Vegas attracted even more of the capital and the expertise of investors who knew how to run successful casinos. Adding to the attraction was the inability of the Nevada Tax Commission and Clark County authorities to investigate thoroughly the backgrounds of gaming-license applicants, or indeed to even identify and reveal the major investors in the casinos.

Dalitz and his longtime associates, however, did not escape the scrutiny of the Kefauver Committee. While none was anxious to receive the scrutiny that inevitably came with testifying, Dalitz was the most effective communicator. When Senator Estes Kefauver suggested that Dalitz had amassed a considerable fortune from his early rum-running ventures, Dalitz replied, "Well, I didn't inherit any money, Senator." This caustic response captured much of the underlying tension of the committee hearings. Inheritances were virtually unknown among the men whose business dealings were investigated, but they were common among the ranks of the investigators. Kleinman and Rothkopf, convicted felons, chose not to engage in the verbal sparring as had Dalitz, Moe Sedway, and the reputed New York City underworld boss Frank Costello (né Franco Costiglia). Their Fifth Amendment right to silence was confirmed by a federal-district-court judge after they were cited for contempt of Congress.

The Kefauver Committee hearings created only a few ripples of concern in Las Vegas. This was not surprising, as Patrick McCarran, longtime U.S. senator from Nevada, blocked Kefauver's efforts to establish a 10 percent tax on gambling profits. New hotels were opening on the Strip, older casinos in the downtown area were expanding, personal income was rapidly on the rise, and money from the men with shady pasts was filling the coffers of both political and local charitable campaigns. Some of the locals did not like to deal with the Jews and Italians who dominated the gaming industry, but they seldom voiced their concerns beyond their own circles of friends. They, too, benefited from the capital and expertise that the foreign born or their children brought to Las Vegas.

Dalitz clearly saw the tremendous potential of Las Vegas, but he proceeded with caution. He initially let the lights shine on Wilbur Clark. Dalitz's Detroit and Cleveland associates—not only his coinvestors Kleinman and Tucker, but also Pete Licavoli, Joe Massei, and Frank Milano—attended opening night at the Desert Inn. All maintained a low profile. Always concerned about conveying the image of professionalism, Dalitz recruited as hotel executives Allard Roen and Bernie Rothkopf (Louis Rothkopf's nephew), younger men who, while they had learned both the rudiments of managing casinos and the importance of never speaking publicly of others who engaged in illegal activities, had avoided any brushes with the law. Roen had graduated from Duke University, making him almost certainly the only casino executive on the Strip in the 1950s possessing a bachelor's degree.

Even before Dalitz, along with Kleinman and Tucker, bought out Wilbur Clark in 1953, he demonstrated his belief that Las Vegas had the potential to become a resort city, not just a gambling center. He challenged the conventional wisdom that the more time Las Vegas visitors spent in the casinos, the better for casino owners in both the short and long runs. Roen recalled in a 1995 interview that Dalitz convened a meeting of Strip entrepreneurs and proposed building a golf course adjacent to the Desert Inn, with an entrance on Paradise Road, the street just east of the Strip, so that other existing and planned Strip hotels might participate. After much debate the hotel owners and executives rejected this radical, though not totally novel, idea, with Gus Greenbaum leading the opposition. Undeterred, Dalitz developed a golf course at the Desert Inn that attracted gamblers as well as the best of the nation's golfers. He organized a Tournament of Champions that eventually brought Sam Snead, Arnold Palmer, and Jack Nicklaus to Las Vegas, and with them a high-profile acceptance.

Roen, Merv Adelson, and Irwin Molasky, Dalitz's partners in purchasing the International (later Las Vegas) Country Club from an out-of-state corporation in the late 1960s, remembered Dalitz's commitment to selling memberships to Las Vegas residents at a price that did not cover costs, because he believed a family-based country club would enhance Las Vegas's growth potential. They also recalled in the early 1960s, when Dalitz was the leading investor in the Stardust, finding land a few miles west of the Strip to set up a track for the Stardust Grand Prix. Dalitz, the hotel owner, brought new entertainment attractions to Las Vegas to help fill the rooms of his properties. Moe Dalitz, the entrepreneur, saw the appearance of famous singers and movie stars as contributing to Las Vegas's emergence as the premier resort city in the Sunbelt.

Dalitz's contributions to Las Vegas's development were many and diverse. When Nevada Southern University (soon to be renamed the University of Nevada, Las Vegas) officials needed $100,000 to field a football team, he gave $1,000 and helped round up ninety-nine other donors. He served as chairman of the Las Vegas United Jewish Appeal in 1956. David Goldwater, Dalitz's attorney in many business and personal matters, said that fundraisers for virtually every charity knew Dalitz would not only contribute but also urge others to do so. Another longtime Las Vegas attorney, Louis Wiener, echoed Goldwater's comments, adding that if any well-connected Las Vegan needed to raise money for a good cause, he or she started with Moe Dalitz. Goldwater and Roen mentioned the financial support, land, and encouragement that Dalitz and Joe Bock, the Yiddish-speaking food-and-beverage director at the Desert Inn, gave to Roman Catholic leaders so that they might build the Guardian Angel Cathedral adjacent to the Desert Inn as an example of both the nonsectarian nature of Dalitz's generosity and his vision of Las Vegas as a resort city. They agreed that Dalitz's favorite charity over the decades was the Variety Club, which raised funds for handicapped children.

In the same manner that Dalitz filled hotel rooms while enhancing the appeal of Las Vegas as a resort city, he made money as an investor while providing housing, shopping malls, and medical care for Las Vegans. Impressed by the plans of Merv Adelson and Irwin Molasky, whose families had come to Las Vegas in the 1940s to pursue grocery and motel businesses respectively, Dalitz became a major investor in the Paradise Development Company in 1957. Adelson and Molasky had the same faith in Las Vegas's potential for growth as Dalitz, but much less access to capital. Dalitz, along with some other Desert Inn investors, including Allard Roen, provided some of their own capital. More important, Dalitz recruited investors who had long respected his financial acumen. Jimmy Hoffa and other officials of the Teamsters union's regional pension funds made the key investment in 1959 with a $1 million loan that provided funding to continue construction of Adelson's and Molasky's first major project, Sunrise Hospital. This was only one of the first of many loans that officials of the Teamsters union's regional pension funds, particularly the Central States fund, made to Las Vegas entrepreneurs over the next fifteen years. Adelson and Molasky went on to become the premier residential and commercial developers of southern Nevada in the 1960s. Later, they founded one of the largest entertainment companies in the world, Lorimar Productions. Dalitz was not involved in all their projects, yet he always encouraged them to think positively about Las Vegas's future.

In spite of long workdays, Dalitz found time to relax in the sunny climate of Las Vegas and the wide-open spaces of southern Nevada and Utah. Shortly after assuming a highly visible role at the Desert Inn in 1954, he married a stunningly attractive woman many years his junior. The Houston-born-and-raised Averille had been a secretary to Jake Friedman, a Texas gambling entrepreneur who was the front man at the Sands for several investors with backgrounds similar to those of Dalitz and his associates. For the several years of her marriage to Dalitz, Averille joined Allard Roen's wife in coordinating a variety of social and charitable functions at the Desert Inn. Well-trained in the use of a shotgun for bird hunting from her childhood, she enthusiastically joined her husband on hunting and camping trips on the Shivwit Indian Reservation near St. George, Utah. On one occasion, the society page of the *Las Vegas Review-Journal* featured a picture of Averille standing over a forked-horn deer she had bagged. In 1955 Dalitz purchased a large ranch near the reservation, began raising cattle, and built a hunting lodge.

Dalitz was reluctant to openly display his leadership talents. He always had the respect of most of the other founding fathers of the Las Vegas Strip, and by both his philanthropy and his boosting of Las Vegas as a resort city he gained the respect of many civic leaders. Equally important, the Desert Inn was the centerpiece of the Strip, the classiest casino in Las Vegas, in the words of locals as well as visitors. Other hotels—the Sahara, the Riviera, the Flamingo—might be bigger or taller, but none had the elegance of Moe Dalitz's place. Even when larger and more ostentatious hotels such as the Tropicana and Caesars Palace opened, the Desert Inn retained its reputation. Dalitz, too, retained his reputation as a gentleman. Goldwater and Wiener agreed that he stood out from the crowd of Strip founding fathers by always treating people—whether employees, customers, or other casino owners—with respect.

Just as he had sought new opportunities for investment of his own capital and the capital of associates in the decades before his coming to Las Vegas, Dalitz looked for new opportunities to invest in the rapidly expanding gambling industry. He was willing to take the risk of building a casino away from both the Strip and downtown. His successful bootlegging and gambling experiences in the Midwest had taught him the importance of gaining the goodwill of elected officials and respected community leaders, and so he joined with J. Kell Houssels and William Moore, downtown and Strip hotel owners, to build a new hotel, the Showboat. It was located east of the Strip and south of downtown on a highway leading toward Arizona. Dalitz engineered a complex arrangement whereby Houssels and Moore operated the hotel while Dalitz, Bernie Rothkopf, and Desert Inn casino manager Cornelius Jones ran the Showboat's casino. The new venture experienced several tough years, even though Dalitz brought in Pete Brady (né Genchi) and other experienced casino managers from the Detroit and Cleveland areas. Eventually the population growth in nearby neighborhoods and effective management by Joe Kelley, whose previous experiences included service in Hot Springs, Arkansas, casinos and aboard Tony Cornero's gambling boats, put Showboat finances in the black.

When Tony Cornero suffered a fatal heart attack on July 31, 1955, his lifelong dream, the Stardust, was still under construction. This provided Dalitz with another opportunity to demonstrate his financial acumen and managerial skills. He moved quickly to buy control. No one knew then or subsequently, with the exception of Dalitz and a few close associates, the identity of the investors in the Stardust. Almost certainly they included many with experience in illegal gambling, and probably some whose criminal activities were broader. There is no reason to think that they were a different mix than the men who opened the other Strip hotels. Dalitz, always effective at bringing together capital from diverse sources to achieve a healthy return on investment for all parties, initially worked closely with Jake Factor to finish construction of the Stardust. Factor, an associate of Chicago organized-crime figures, sold his investment before the Stardust opened.

Dalitz once again drew upon his previous experiences to run the gaudy new casino. The Stardust opened on July 2, 1958, with Silvio Petricciani as casino manager. Petricciani's family had owned a slot-machine parlor in Reno even before the Nevada legislature relegalized gambling in 1931. As a result of his experiences at the Palace Club in Reno and at such Las Vegas casinos as the El Dorado and the El Rancho Vegas, he presented solid recommendations from Ruby Kolod. Knowing well the economic advantages of having a unique attraction that would draw players to the casino tables, Dalitz hired Frank Sennes, a former associate with an excellent track record in managing nightclubs in Ohio and Kentucky, then in Southern California. He had no difficulty persuading Roen and Molasky to travel to Paris and, with Sennes, make arrangements to bring the Lido de Paris show to the Strip. It was a remarkable success, playing at the Stardust into the 1990s. Once again, Dalitz showed that he knew which attractions would increase Las Vegas's visitor volume.

During the late 1950s and 1960s allegations of involvement with mobsters were leveled at Dalitz with increasing frequency as Justice Department investigators focused on Las Vegas as the financial center of American organized crime. With Fidel Castro closing the lucrative Havana casinos and increased law enforcement attention to organized crime, particularly after the extensive media attention to the Apalachin, New York, meeting of Italian mobsters in 1957, investments in Las Vegas casinos became even more attractive. Dalitz's recruitment of so many key casino managers—pit bosses, floor men, shift bosses—at the Desert Inn and the Stardust, whose pre–Las Vegas employment had put them in contact with men reputed in the popular press to be Mafiosi orchestrating a national organized-crime network, added substance to the accusations.

Visits by well-known mobsters to the Desert Inn or the Stardust added more substance. Like his peers on the Strip, Dalitz made little apparent effort to avoid contact with mobsters, meeting several times with Sam Giancana, the rising star of the Chicago underworld. Always the gentleman, Dalitz appeared courteous, even deferential, to Giancana and his daughter, Antoinette, who sometimes accompanied her father to Las Vegas. His longtime associates Kleinman and Kolod also had considerable contact with former midwestern business partners who had not achieved the relative respectability that Las Vegans generally accorded to major casino investors. Indeed, one conversation between Kleinman and Chicago mob enforcer Marshall Caifano deteriorated into a shouting match characterized by ethnic slurs, which received national attention when Ed Reid and Ovid Demaris recounted a version of it in their popular book, *The Green Felt Jungle*.

Writing more than a decade after Moe Dalitz had sold his interests in the Stardust and the Desert Inn, Ned Day, a well-respected columnist for the *Las Vegas Review-Journal,* suggested that Dalitz and others of the Jewish founding fathers of the Las Vegas Strip could not, try as they might, separate themselves from their former Italian associates in organized crime. Dalitz probably wished that his former associates would no longer seek to establish skimming operations in his casinos. Yet he knew that no one could unilaterally terminate relationships from which he had benefited handsomely over many years. Dalitz never distanced himself from colleagues who were convicted of crimes, whether operating illegal distilleries, tax evasion, or stock manipulation. When he actively sought Teamster loans, he chose to deal with men whose illegal activities had not been confined to bootlegging and gambling.

The 1960s were characterized not only by a continuation of the rapid growth and development of Las Vegas but also by an expansion of state regulation of casino gambling, an expansion supported by key elected officials, most notably by Democratic governor Grant Sawyer and his Republican successor, Paul Laxalt. They and others responded to the very real threat that the Justice Department would seize Strip casinos, as part of an effort to strike at the heart of organized crime, by restructuring regulatory agencies and by bringing professionalism to the top ranks of gaming enforcement.

Dalitz had demonstrated throughout his career an ability to adapt quickly to changing circumstances. He did so again by completing the sale of his Stardust interests in 1969 to Albert Parvin, a close associate of Meyer Lansky. In the years that followed, the Stardust came under close scrutiny from Justice Department organized-crime investigators and Nevada gaming regulators. Indictments brought changes in ownership, which in turn brought more indictments and, in 1984, a raid by Nevada authorities that forced Dalitz's business partner, Al Sachs, to give up his ownership in the resort.

Dalitz continued to exercise influence in Las Vegas during the 1960s. He was the guiding force in the establishment of the Nevada Resort Association, the lobbying and public relations organization of the major hotels in southern Nevada. Despite the publication in 1963 of *The Green Felt Jungle* and numerous national newspaper and magazine stories that included Dalitz among the Strip founding fathers identified as mob (sometimes the term was *Mafia*) associates, Dalitz continued to enjoy the respect of most Las Vegans; neither charities nor high-profile candidates for public office turned down his donations. When he and Averille were divorced in 1964, with Averille retaining custody of their daughter, most Las Vegans expressed no concern. Easy divorce laws had drawn wealthy players to Reno and Las Vegas gambling tables for more than two decades.

In one area Moe Dalitz had no less difficulty adapting than most Americans of his generation. The civil rights movement reached Las Vegas, a distinctly Jim Crow town, in the late 1950s as several African American professionals worked with ministers to more effectively politicize and organize the community. African Americans had been settling in Las Vegas for thirty years. Particularly well represented were men and women from Arkansas and Louisiana who had responded to job opportunities during the Second World War. Although segregation was nearly absolute in housing and in the casinos, African Americans had greater economic opportunities in Las Vegas than in the rural South. Nonetheless, premier black entertainers, such as Sammy Davis Jr., who performed in the showrooms of Strip hotels in the 1950s, had to endure the indignity of spending nights at hotels on the segregated Westside. Apparently Dalitz never questioned these practices. De facto segregation had been a way of life for more than the half century he resided in the Midwest, and he apparently had no reason to question these practices.

Like most of his contemporaries, Dalitz did not initially welcome the civil rights movement and the drive toward racial integration. He was shocked when many Las Vegas African Americans, frustrated by segregation in the casinos that denied to them the opportunity to work in relatively high-paying jobs such as dealers and cocktail waitresses and to enjoy casino gambling and entertainment, threatened to demonstrate on the Strip. Dalitz told some friends that permitting nonwhites to work or play in the casinos would drive away the high rollers from Texas and other parts of the South. Fairly quickly, however, he realized that this was one more challenge to which he must adapt. As the dean of the Strip owners, he passed the message to Dr. James McMillan, leader of the group planning to lead marches on the Strip, that the policy of racial segregation in the casinos was ended. Forthwith African Americans joined European Americans and Asian Americans in losing some of their disposable income at the gambling tables. The sudden and complete end of Jim Crow practices in the casinos did not deter high-rolling oil-rich Texans, or tens of thousands of middle-class white southerners for that matter, from continuing their gambling forays to Las Vegas.

On Thanksgiving Day 1966, the reclusive, eccentric Howard Hughes surreptitiously entered Las Vegas and rented the top-floor penthouse at the Desert Inn. Dalitz's life, and that of all Las Vegans, would never be the same. Initially Dalitz and his longtime associates received Hughes's decision to stay at Las Vegas's classiest resort as a compliment. As the days passed and potential revenue from high rollers who were denied an opportunity to stay in the penthouse was lost, Dalitz and other Desert Inn executives grew concerned about Hughes's intentions, particularly as New Year's Eve was only a few weeks away.

Their inquiries produced a startling result. Hughes wanted to buy the Desert Inn. Exactly who conducted the difficult negotiations regarding the sale remains a matter of interpretation. Molasky suggested that Robert Maheu's account of the negotiations was fairly accurate. Maheu, second-in-command of Hughes's business empire, later wrote in *Next to Hughes* that Washington, D.C., attorneys of his acquaintance, including Edward Bennett Williams, contacted Jimmy Hoffa, who in turn persuaded Dalitz to let Hughes and his entourage of male nurses and sycophants remain in the suites on the top floor of the Desert Inn through New Year's Day. Then the serious negotiations on the sale began. Apparently a number of facilitators in addition to Williams and Hoffa played roles. They included Ed Morgan, another Washington attorney, who had previously assisted journalist Hank Greenspun in several of his legal battles, and Johnny Rosselli, organized crime's reputed representative and deal maker in Las Vegas. Effective March 27, 1967, ownership of the Desert Inn passed to Howard Hughes.

This transaction signaled major changes not only on the Strip but also throughout Nevada. Hughes bought several other Strip hotels and casinos and added to the thousands of undeveloped acres that he had purchased in previous decades. The extent of his political power in Nevada was reflected by the deference that Governor Paul Laxalt and his successor, Governor Mike O'Callaghan, gave him. The secretive Hughes was licensed sight unseen by the Nevada Gaming Commission, and in 1973 Governor O'Callaghan traveled to London just to confer with him regarding the arcane workings of his gambling empire. Of even greater significance, the Nevada legislature responded to Laxalt's initiatives and passed the Corporate Gaming Act, which facilitated and encouraged the entry of stockholder-owned corporations in Nevada gaming. Nevada authorities announced to the world that Howard Hughes had, if not run the hoodlums out of town, at least made them offers they could not refuse. Nevada proclaimed itself to be clean and now in the business of seeking honest corporate investors. Nevada's business and political leaders all wanted to believe that they had created a new Nevada.

Of course, many aspects of Las Vegas did not change. The mobsters— those canny survivors of internal mob struggles, law enforcement wiretapping, IRS investigations, and indictments—shrewdly adapted to the new environment. First, they incorporated: Parvin-Dohrman Corporation, Argent Corporation, Trans-Sterling, the last two operators of the Stardust, are good early examples. They even hired effective corporate front men, with Allen Glick at the Stardust providing the most publicized, if not the best, example in the 1970s. Second, they continued to skim. As Hughes's executives searched for trusted men to run their casinos effectively, the mobsters, by many accounts, enjoyed a bonanza, stealing money upon which they never paid taxes.

Moe Dalitz did not change, either. He prospered from the sale of the Desert Inn. Allard Roen recounted that, much to Dalitz's amazement, Howard Hughes refused to accept the Tournament of Champions as part of the Desert Inn package. The eccentric millionaire's sense of privacy was apparently more important than a revenue-generating golf tournament. Hughes feared that throngs of people attending the tournament would be gazing at his quarters on the top floor of the Desert Inn. Dalitz simply moved this premier golfing event to the Stardust's golf course. While Hughes protected his privacy, the Stardust reaped a bounty of additional publicity and income.

From the time of the sale of the Desert Inn until his death in 1989, Dalitz's public life reflected the love/hate relationship of Las Vegas's civic and political leaders toward the men who built the Strip. Some openly extolled Dalitz as "Mr. Las Vegas," a few denounced him as a notorious associate of organized-crime figures, and others took no position or shifted their opinions according to circumstances. In 1970, David Zenoff, a justice of the Nevada Supreme Court, chaired a testimonial dinner for Dalitz at the Dunes. An Israeli general presented Dalitz with the City of Peace award in recognition of his support for the Israel Bonds program. However, during a 1978 hearing about the licensing of an associate of Dalitz, a young accountant appointed to serve on the Nevada Gaming Control Board responded to a statement by the associate's attorney, Frank Schreck, that Dalitz had been honored by high government officials and civic leaders as man of the year. The accountant, Jeff Silver, warned, "When a person who would be on a post office wall in other communities is honored by high officials, it is a sorry, sorry case for society. This is the sickness in our society today. We pay homage to power and money."

A year later, the control board's chief investigator publicly stated that Dalitz's intention to be licensed as an owner of the Sundance Hotel would place the gaming commission (to which the control board makes licensing recommendations) in a difficult position. He explained, "On the one hand, he is Mr. Nevada, and you probably can't find anything he's done wrong in 15 years. On the other hand, he has a history of organized crime links." Four years later John Moran, the elected sheriff of Clark County, and Bill Briare, the mayor of Las Vegas, attended a community leadership banquet at the Riviera, the highlight of which was a tearful Joan Rivers presenting "Mr. Las Vegas" with the Torch of Liberty award of the Anti-Defamation League of B'Nai B'Rith. A Nevada governor, a U.S. senator, and numerous state and local officials attended other testimonials for Moe Dalitz.

Whenever Dalitz attracted the attention of the media, he invariably was referred to as an associate (or former associate) of organized-crime leaders. The rehashing of prior charges (only one of which resulted in an indictment and never a conviction) made good copy; conversely, in both his business ventures and his social activities, Dalitz repeatedly interacted with men mired in controversy. A review of the headlines of several newspaper articles that focused on Dalitz is instructive: "Hospital Group Sets Dalitz Fete"; "Investigator Says Dalitz Poses License Problem"; "Las Vegans Honor Dalitz on 80th"; "Retirement Board OKs Loan for Sundance"; "Dalitz Honored as Las

Vegas Promoter"; "Mob Links Denied by Dalitz"; "Anti-Defamation League Honors Dalitz"; "Laxalt Down Plays Links with Dalitz"; "Records Suggest Link between Laxalt, Crime Figures"; "Offers Considered for Reputed Mafia Resort."

The controversies surrounding Dalitz's involvement with the financing of the La Costa resort in Carlsbad, California, and the Sundance Hotel in downtown Las Vegas illustrated both his inability to escape guilt by past (by then a very distant past) associations and his inclination to maintain business or personal relations with men under suspicion of illegal activities. In 1969, he was part of an investment group that raised $3 million for the planning and building of a lavish oceanside resort by longtime Las Vegas business partners Adelson, Molasky, and Roen. He was widely reputed also to have played an important role in arranging for more than $90 million in Teamster loans for La Costa. In 1975 *Penthouse* ran a lengthy story by two free-lance journalists that suggested La Costa was a resort built by organized-crime (*Mafia* was the term often used) leaders as a future resort for organized-crime leaders. Dalitz, Adelson, Molasky, and Roen immediately sued in a California court for almost $500 million in libel damages. Dalitz and Roen dropped the suit when the trial judge ruled that they were public figures, thus making it difficult to prove libel.

Dalitz was eighty-two years old when he spent several days on the witness stand in this high-profile case, testifying that he had knowingly broken the law as a young man during Prohibition and in the 1930s when he entered the gambling business in Ohio and Kentucky. He denied any illegal activities in Nevada and said that he had never spoken with any Teamster officials about financing for La Costa. Louis Nizer, Dalitz's attorney, was unsuccessful in his efforts to have his client's many honors and awards introduced as evidence. The net result of the case for Adelson and Molasky was more than $5 million in legal expenses and a letter of apology from the *Penthouse* publisher that affirmed there had been no intent to link Adelson or Molasky to organized crime. Dalitz's testimony did little to resolve the speculation about his past and present roles in organized crime.

Dalitz organized a group of investors, including Al Sachs and Herb Tobman, to build the Sundance in 1980 on land that he, Tucker, Roen, and Bock had leased twenty-six years earlier. This was one more example of Dalitz's financial acumen and his faith in Las Vegas's potential for development. When it appeared that Nevada gaming regulators probably would not license Dalitz to run the casino, he demonstrated his usual talent for overcoming adversity by narrowing his role to that of landlord, with Sachs and Tobman operating the Sundance. Rumors abounded that mob interests supported by

Dalitz were skimming at the Sundance. At one point, Sachs had to state at a gaming-commission hearing that Moe Dalitz was not influencing his decisions. Predictably, Dalitz outlasted Sachs and Tobman. Nevada authorities seized control of the Sundance shortly after the 1984 raid that closed the Stardust. Dalitz sold his interest in the Sundance to Fitzgerald's, a Reno-based hotel-and-casino corporation, in 1988.

Dalitz found time for travel and philanthropy after selling the Desert Inn and the Stardust. Roen and Molasky recalled that he enjoyed visiting national parks and other scenic areas that traditionally attracted many tourists, as well as out-of-the-way, rustic places. David Goldwater said that Dalitz continued to make generous contributions to several charities, though he took a particular interest in the development of the Las Vegas YMCA and of Ner Tamid, a Reform Jewish congregation that formed in 1980. Goldwater and Mel Hecht, rabbi for the congregation in the early 1980s, recalled that Dalitz, never a religious Jew, contributed almost $750,000 in three increments to the development of a religious school, which bears his name, and a social hall. Believing that numerous investors bring strength to a project, his initial contribution of about $400,000 had the condition that the congregation must match it.

In the decade following the sale of the Stardust, Dalitz's companion at Las Vegas social events was Barbara Schick. In her forties when she and Dalitz began their relationship, Schick was intelligent, articulate, and attractive. She received a bachelor's degree in economics at the University of Nevada, Las Vegas, then gained a master's degree before directing the Center for Economic Education at UNLV for almost fifteen years. Two years after her death, in 1986, from a rare blood disease, Dalitz responded to an appeal from her successor, Robert Smith, and donated $50,000 to give the name Barbara Schick to the center.

When cancer weakened Dalitz in 1987, he was confined to his home and then the Sunrise Hospital. With a few final weeks of limited consciousness, he had time to reflect on his full life. He had learned well how to run a business from his hard-working, immigrant parents. As a young man, he had outwitted Prohibition agents and amassed a small fortune as a bootlegger. Recognized as "Mr. Las Vegas" for his many contributions to the community, and recognized as the most powerful and the most gentlemanly of the founding fathers of the Las Vegas Strip, he knew how to make money, and how to spend it. He lived well but not ostentatiously and focused his many charitable contributions on assisting young people. Often professing innocence of any crimes beyond bootlegging and gambling, he never provided law enforcement authorities with information about others. On a personal level, he divorced three wives, yet avoided acrimony and adverse publicity. His relationship with Barbara Schick was long lasting and positive. The death of his son, Drew, was a tragedy, while his reestablishment of positive relations with his daughter, Suzanne, was comforting. Before the onset of his terminal illness, he had provided trusts for his daughter, her two children, and his grandson Michael Dalitz, as well as almost $700,000 for United Way charities and additional funds for such youth-oriented charities as the Boy Scouts of America in Las Vegas, Saint Jude's Ranch, and the Hebrew Academy.

The newspaper stories immediately following his death on August 31, 1989, focused on the Moe Dalitz who was "Mr. Las Vegas," the mob's man in Las Vegas, an associate of organized-crime figures, and more. Grant Sawyer, former governor and leading advocate of effective state control of gaming, said, "Moe Dalitz was probably as responsible for the successful gaming economy in Southern Nevada as any one person," while a Metro Police official said that he considered Dalitz to be the "elder statesman of the mob." Among the more than three hundred mourners at Ner Tamid services for Dalitz were Las Vegas mayor Ron Lurie, Sheriff John Moran, former sheriff Ralph Lamb, and District Attorney Rex Bell. His daughter, Suzanne Dalitz Brown, praised his unswerving faith in Las Vegas's potential to become an internationally recognized resort city, and she concluded by saying, "In my child's eyes he was like John Wayne in a dinner jacket, more godlike than fatherlike."

James B. McMillan

The Pursuit of Equality

BY GARY E. ELLIOTT

On November 9, 1990, the Clark County School District officially dedicated the James B. McMillan Elementary School,
located at 7000 Walt Lott Drive in Las Vegas. Dr. McMillan
had been active in community affairs for nearly thirty-five
years and developed a considerable reputation for candor, but
even he was stunned when a young boy walked up to him after
the dedication ceremony and asked, "What have you done to
have a school named after you?" McMillan was more than just
a little amused by the child's unabashed honesty and replied
that he was not quite sure why they had named a school after
him. What is certain, however, is that he witnessed and participated in the monumental civil rights struggle that sim-
mered in the 1950s, then boiled over into all parts of American
life in the following decades. What is more, he had dedicated
his adult life to the political, economic, and social betterment
of black Americans.

McMillan was born on January 14, 1917, in the small town
of Aberdeen, Mississippi, to James Bates McMillan and Rosa
Lee Gay. His father, a cotton-harvest laborer, died during a flu
epidemic that swept Aberdeen when his son was only two years
old. His mother had been born April 27, 1896, the result of a
union between a former slave, Ophelia Gay, and a white plan-
tation owner, Sam Gay. The liaison produced three other offspring, all male. The relationship between Ophelia and Sam
was well known to the inhabitants of Aberdeen and seemed to
be an accepted part of the social life of the community.

Ophelia Gay and her four children lived separately from
Sam and his traditional or legally recognized family. After
Rosa and James married, they, too, lived with Ophelia, as did
James's six-year-old son from a previous marriage, Theodore
McMillan. This extended family unit was cared for and protected by Sam Gay until his health began to decline. After his
death, Rosa became embroiled in a fistfight after a white couple called her a "nigger." Blows were struck on both sides,
and within forty-eight hours, the Ku Klux Klan was at the

4

McMillan home. McMillan recalled seeing his mother forcibly taken from their home to town by hooded Klansmen, who tied her to a post, stripped her blouse down to the waist, and applied several lashes to her back. Not long afterward, Rosa and her son left Aberdeen for New York City, leaving the family behind for a new life in the North.

Rosa McMillan was always outspoken in her demand for equal treatment, a trait that she passed on to her son. Once the patronage and protection provided by Sam Gay were no longer available, Rosa had few, if any, options other than moving beyond the confines of a small southern town. Rosa soon found work in New York's garment district and a residence in Harlem. The family stayed in New York for only about eight months, when Rosa decided to move to Philadelphia.

Again, Rosa found work in the garment industry and had enough money to enroll James in a Catholic boarding school. Shortly afterward, Rosa married Emory Philpot, a cement finisher she met in Philadelphia. Economic hard times soon prompted another move, this time to Pontiac, Michigan, where Henry Ford was recruiting southern black workers for his automobile factory. But employment conditions in Pontiac were little better than those in Philadelphia, so the family relocated to Hamtramck, a Polish suburb of Detroit. Again, jobs were few, and Emory was forced to accept beans and rice from the Red Cross to feed his family.

This proved to be a turning point for the family. Emory was embarrassed by accepting charity and refused to stand in line for food. Instead, he enthusiastically embraced the underground economy—the numbers racket. He established his own route, which provided the family with a good income, even during the depression. Meanwhile, Rosa had become active in Democratic Party politics, which paid off in a spoils position in the welfare department after the Democrats took control of city government. By the time McMillan entered high school, the family could afford better housing in another neighborhood of Hamtramck.

But when the family moved to their new home, some neighborhood kids wrote on the house, "Nigger move out." McMillan recalled that he had to fight nearly every day to survive in this Polish-dominated neighborhood, and it was no different in high school, where he initially fell in with a rowdy group. He began to hang out on the streets, and had little direction, desire, or ambition, until he attended a pep rally before a scheduled football game during his freshman year. The star player was a black youngster who was being hugged by the girls and cheered on by the crowd. From that moment on, McMillan wanted to be a star athlete.

McMillan excelled in football and track, winning All State honors and twelve varsity letters, serving as cocaptain on the football team, and receiving scholarship offers from major universities. It was athletics that drove his academic studies to a B average. Although a professional career in football was not an option when he graduated from high school in 1936, McMillan decided to use football to launch a career in the medical field. Medicine paid substantially better than being a lawyer, teacher, preacher, barber, or under- taker, which were about the only professions then open to black Americans. Another factor in his career choice was the prestige that came with being a physician, always an important consideration to McMillan because he liked being a star.

McMillan's decision to attend the University of Michigan on a football scholarship was short-lived. In a harbinger of things to come, he left in protest after only two weeks because he was assigned living quarters inferior to those provided to white athletes. He returned to Detroit and accepted a football and track scholarship to the University of Detroit. Although inelig- ible to play football his freshman year, he used his time to improve his grades, which kept him academically eligible during his sophomore and junior years when he won All American honors. However, his senior year was a different story. The college president declared him ineligible, citing declining grades. It was true that McMillan's grades had declined, but they were not below the standards set by the university. During a meeting with the president over his scholarship, the real reason for the ineligibility surfaced: McMillan's sus- pected relationship with a white girl, whose father was a major contributor to the school. Although there was no intimate relationship, the university could not afford to take a chance. Nevertheless, McMillan stayed in school and paid his expenses by working at the Ford Motor Company. He never forgot, or forgave, the president for his actions, which cost McMillan his scholarship and senior year of football eligibility.

By 1941, personality traits and life experiences had made McMillan a bru- tally frank critic of American society. While working at Ford at night and going to school during the day, he became active in union affairs as a commit- teeman. He told anyone who would listen that the army's segregationist policy was one reason black Americans should not fight in any war, or for any coun- try that practiced discrimination. He was accused of being a Communist after an incident involving the rights of black workers that resulted in the melt- down of expensive magnesium furnaces. Although cleared of the Communist charges, he remained a constant critic of discrimination in the military.

When the United States entered the Second World War, McMillan failed his army induction physical. He then entered Meharry Medical College School of Dentistry in 1941 and qualified for the army's specialized training-corps program, which paid for his tuition and books. He finished dental school in 1944, and married Dolita Moore just before he passed a qualifying physical and entered the army as a first lieutenant assigned to Barracks, Pennsylvania. His disillusionment with America continued to build when Lieutenant McMillan saw German prisoners of war treated better than black soldiers, who were segregated in local theaters and transportation facilities. In fact, McMillan became involved in a fistfight with a city bus driver who ordered him to the back of the bus, which prompted the base commander to announce that there would be no difference in the treatment of black and white servicemen, even though he was powerless to command civil authority.

Insults continued, particularly when McMillan and Dolita traveled together, because of Dolita's fair complexion. Segregated seating was common practice in southern states, invariably leading to confrontations and unpleasant exchanges. Affronts of another kind were experienced at the Fort Huachuca Medical Service pool in Arizona, where McMillan was assigned for specialized training. There were hospitals for white soldiers and separate facilities for blacks, and black dentists were prohibited from working on white soldiers. Nor did conditions improve for McMillan when he arrived at the 49th Ordnance Battalion in Calcutta, India. He soon had a confrontation with a white officer from Florida, who loudly explained that where he came from, they knew how to treat "negroes."

McMillan's war experiences only reinforced his negative image of contemporary American life. After being discharged in 1945 with the rank of captain, he returned home to Detroit to his wife and daughter, Jerri, who had been born while he was serving in India. While he built a professional career, his marriage was beyond salvaging. Dolita, who was only eighteen when she married McMillan, had grown apart from him, and he from her. After their son, James, was born in 1947, Dolita and McMillan divorced, and the two children remained with their father.

There was little stability in McMillan's life after the divorce except for his friendship with Dr. Charles West, which would eventually lead him to Las Vegas. But in the short term, caring for two children and working to establish a dental practice had taken its toll, so much so that he did not protest a return to active service during the Korean War: He simply wanted to get away and think. He was assigned to the Army Dental Corps at Fort Benjamin Harrison, Indianapolis, Indiana, and traveled between the base and Detroit to see his children, who were being cared for by a housekeeper. After being discharged in 1955 with the rank of major, McMillan's life changed suddenly and abruptly.

At the time, Charles West had relocated his practice from Detroit to Las

Vegas. Like McMillan, he was recently divorced and had moved to Nevada for a new start. What had lured West to the Silver State would soon appeal to McMillan as well: a twenty-four-hour town, live entertainment, gambling, money, and sunshine. Also, McMillan planned to marry Magnolia Rutherford, whom he had met while traveling to Detroit to visit his children. Consequently, when he received a postcard from a friend in Arizona advertising a temperature of 75 degrees, he called West and asked what the weather was like in Las Vegas. When he heard that it was hovering around 75 degrees, McMillan told his friend that he, too, would be leaving the snow and ice of Detroit for the sun and fun of Las Vegas.

In early 1955, McMillan flew to Las Vegas to meet with West. During a taxi ride from the airport, the driver asked him his destination, which was Wyatt Avenue. The driver, unfamiliar with the street, asked the dispatcher for directions and received the cryptic reply, "That's where the niggers live." The driver apologized and delivered McMillan to his destination: a small, new development amid the unpaved and dusty streets of West Las Vegas. West had purchased two houses, and he told McMillan that his practice was doing well. During the visit, West received a call to treat a patient at the newly opened Moulin Rouge Hotel on Bonanza Road. McMillan accompanied his friend to the hotel, only to discover the patient was suffering from a severe hangover. After treating him, West was told to take his fee from a stack of chips on the table, which he gladly did. Afterward, McMillan was shocked to discover that these little tokens were worth $400. McMillan told West that Las Vegas was the place for him, and he wasted little time in scheduling his qualifying exams before the Board of Dental Examiners.

McMillan then encountered an unexpected delay in learning the results of the dental examinations. Dr. Quannah McCall later told McMillan that the board had hesitated to pass him because he would have been the first "negro" to be board certified, but they had little choice because of his high scores. With board certification in hand, McMillan and Magnolia Rutherford moved to Las Vegas in 1955 and were married at the Moulin Rouge Hotel. Shortly afterward, they bought a house on Wyatt Avenue close to West, and McMillan opened a dental practice in a small building on Bonanza next to the Moulin Rouge Hotel.

When McMillan arrived in Las Vegas, he had high expectations, despite rigid segregation in public accommodations. He opened his office on the west side of Las Vegas, anticipating a clientele of mostly African Americans. But he was surprised to find at his office a substantial number of white patients who worked at the Atomic Test Site. He kept his office open late to accommodate their work schedule, which added significantly to his business.

During this time, he became disillusioned with the Democratic Party, except for President Harry Truman's executive order desegregating the armed services. Southern Democrats, Dixiecrats, and their Republican allies had first stalled, then blocked, all efforts to guarantee African Americans equal treatment and access to public accommodations. Nevada was little different from the nation as a whole, even though Assemblyman George Rudiak of Las Vegas had tried to legalize open accommodations two years before McMillan arrived in the city. Rudiak had introduced AB 248 during the 1953 legislative session, which was reported out of the judiciary committee with no recommendation and tabled when a motion to permanently reconsider passed overwhelmingly. In 1955, Rudiak was defeated for reelection, which meant that the black community lost its most outspoken white ally in the assembly.

McMillan's activism on behalf of civil rights began in 1956. He had become acquainted with the NAACP in Detroit and with Congressman Charles Diggs's work for civil rights. McMillan, West, and David Hoggard started the *Missile,* a small, weekly newspaper that was produced in a garage and reprinted many articles gleaned from other black newspapers collected from around the country. Most articles in the *Missile* concerned black issues, with a generous dose of columns on civil rights matters, including the court-ordered admissions of Autherine Lucy to the University of Alabama, the bombing of Martin Luther King Jr.'s home in Montgomery, the signing of the Southern Manifesto, the boycott of city buses in Tallahassee, Florida, and the Supreme Court's ruling in *Gayle* v. *Browder,* striking down racial segregation on buses in Montgomery. This cut-and-paste operation lasted about eighteen months, when West took it over and renamed it the *Voice.* The short-lived *Missile* had provided the west-side community with news on issues important to black people, filling the void left by the city's major publication, the *Las Vegas Review-Journal.*

McMillan despised John and Al Cahlan, who ran the *Las Vegas Review-Journal.* While not openly racist, their editorial policy most often reported black people in an unfavorable light, and they never supported black civil rights. By contrast, Hank Greenspun's *Las Vegas Sun* came out solidly on the side of civil rights legislation, the NAACP, and desegregation.

In 1956, McMillan attended a meeting of the Las Vegas chapter of the NAACP and complained bitterly about local housing conditions and particularly about the segregation of public facilities on the Strip and in downtown casinos. Segregation even extended to black performers, who were denied accommodations and forced to the west side of Las Vegas for shelter. McMillan complained so long and passionately that he was elected president, a post he held until 1961.

McMillan was a confrontational leader—outspoken, impulsive, abrasive, and uncompromising. He clashed with supporters and opponents alike. For example, the NAACP was holding a joint meeting with the Conference of Christians and Jews to work on solutions to problems in Las Vegas when McMillan found out that several members of the conference's executive board were also key executives at hotels that practiced discrimination. Characteristically, he confronted the organization's members by saying that segregation would end overnight if they simply did the right thing.

Under McMillan's leadership, the NAACP moved from dialogue to boycott, and the black churches proved to be the key to organizational success. Churches were the traditional meeting places for the black community and provided a convenient forum for disseminating information to large numbers of people. McMillan and the NAACP began modestly by calling for a boycott of milk companies that refused to hire black delivery men and of west-side casinos that would not pay black dealers the same as their white counterparts. While both boycotts resulted in additional hirings, they contributed little to the improvement of overall conditions in the city.

In 1958, McMillan and the NAACP made two key political decisions that would prove beneficial. Oran Gragson and Wendell Bunker were both running for mayor of Las Vegas, and the NAACP chose to support Bunker, whose family had a good reputation in the black community. By contrast, it was rumored that Gragson, an Arkansas native, had a black dog that he named "Nigger," an allegation that was later proved untrue. Gragson was clearly disappointed not to receive the support of the black community's leadership; but after winning the election, he set out to prove that McMillan and the NAACP had misjudged him. He went to the west side and shook hands with everyone in sight, proclaiming that he had been elected mayor of all the people. Over the years, Gragson proved to McMillan and other black leaders that he was a good mayor, fair, impartial, and without the racial prejudice that was so common in the city.

McMillan and the NAACP actively supported Grant Sawyer for governor in 1958. The two-term incumbent, Charles Russell, was no friend to the civil rights movement. McMillan proved correct in his assessment of Sawyer, who began early in his administration to dismantle all vestiges of discrimination in state government. McMillan always considered Sawyer to be on the side of civil rights, although "he was no flaming liberal." Sawyer stood apart from most state leaders, like Senators Alan Bible and Howard Cannon and Representative Walter Baring, whose condescending attitudes toward equal rights McMillan considered an affront to black people. McMillan found Sawyer "the best of the lot."

What frustrated McMillan and others were that politics, compromise, and accommodation that led to the watered-down 1957 federal Civil Rights Act and to the creation of a state Human Rights Commission, in 1961, with little money and even less power. Cosmetic changes in public policy and the avoidance of substantive progress produced bitterness that often spilled over into impolitic dialogue, particularly when McMillan became involved.

In early 1960, McMillan attended a political rally for presidential hopeful Lyndon Johnson at the Las Vegas Convention Center. A press aide to Johnson made the mistake of asking McMillan for his impressions of the senator. Without hesitation he told the stunned staffer, "He's the rottenest, filthiest, [most] bigoted bastard that I've known, and I wouldn't support him for dog catcher." McMillan's assessment was in stark contrast to those who knew Johnson and considered him fair-minded and beyond racial prejudice. Not long afterward McMillan was confronted by Johnson, who extended his hand. McMillan accepted it, only to find that Johnson would not let go until he had his say. McMillan recalled Johnson telling him that he would be the best president black people ever had.

McMillan was unimpressed and continued to support John F. Kennedy for president. But he soon realized that because Kennedy could not afford to alienate his southern friends in the Senate, he moved cautiously on civil rights. Thus, frustration and anger continued to build in the black community, and McMillan saw the lack of progress in Las Vegas as symptomatic of the nation as a whole.

A showdown in February 1960 proved to be the high-water mark in McMillan's leadership of the Las Vegas NAACP. He received a letter from the national office stating that each local chapter must do everything possible to eliminate discrimination in its area. On March 16, 1960, McMillan wrote a letter to Gragson requesting a meeting of government officials and public accommodation representatives to discuss equal access to public facilities, including hotels, motels, theaters, and casinos. He warned that unless hotels and casinos desegregated their facilities within ten days, the NAACP would launch a protest march like the sit-ins taking place across the country in support of the student demonstration in Greensboro, North Carolina, protesting segregation at Woolworth Department Store lunch counters. He took this action without consultation with, or the approval of, the executive board of the Las Vegas chapter. It was a bold move that committed the organization to action without planning or preparation, in the event the owners refused.

The issue escalated quickly. *Las Vegas Sun* reporter Alan Jarlson happened to be in the mayor's office and either was shown the letter or saw it by accident.

Jarlson telephoned McMillan and asked if he had any further comment, because he was going to publish the story. McMillan encouraged him to do so. After the *Sun* article appeared on March 17, the story was picked up by the national media, which placed additional pressure on McMillan, who had begun receiving death threats at his home. These threats were taken seriously, and the NAACP began twenty-four-hour protection around the McMillan home. Some influential members of the local NAACP encouraged McMillan to go slowly, because they feared retaliation and violence from whites.

But for McMillan there was no turning back, even though he began to wonder, as the deadline of 6 P.M. on March 26 approached, how much support he would actually get. On March 23, Gragson informed the *Las Vegas Sun* that he was unable to guarantee an end to racial discrimination in Las Vegas. On March 24, two days before the appointed time for the demonstration, Oscar Crozier, owner of the El Morocco Casino, telephoned McMillan and said that the hotel owners were meeting and were extremely concerned about the effect the march would have on their businesses. Crozier told McMillan that the owners were very serious and indicated to him that McMillan might end up at the bottom of Lake Mead. McMillan told Crozier that all he wanted to do was to improve the hotel business by allowing black people to spend their money where they wished. He added that there was no intention to injure the casino business in any way. Crozier ended the conversation by telling McMillan that he would relay the message and call him again.

Shortly before the deadline, Crozier telephoned McMillan to report that the hotel owners had agreed to integrate their facilities. Crozier instructed McMillan to telephone "Mr. Taylor" at the Desert Inn to confirm the agreement. The following day, March 25, McMillan telephoned "Mr. Taylor," whom he assumed to be speaking for Moe Dalitz and the Desert Inn. "Taylor" told McMillan that blacks could come into the Desert Inn and, in fact, all Strip hotels. Before McMillan could announce the cancellation of the demonstration, he was visited by three ministers representing west-side churches. The ministers told him that they could not support the march because of the potential for violence to African Americans. McMillan reported that they need not worry: The hotels had agreed to accept integration. The cautious clergymen were naturally elated—and relieved.

Afterward, McMillan met with Hank Greenspun, owner of the *Las Vegas Sun,* to arrange a public announcement of the settlement. They agreed to meet at the Moulin Rouge, since it was convenient and could accommodate many people, including the press. The Moulin Rouge was not selected for any particular significance attached to the cause of civil rights, at least not in

McMillan's thinking. It was simply close to his office. The announcement proved to be a political event of some significance. Governor Sawyer flew to Las Vegas to be present along with Gragson and other civil leaders.

What has become known as the Moulin Rouge Agreement was, from McMillan's perspective, simply a calculation by the hotel/casino owners of their economic self-interest. He was unaware of any behind-the-scenes political maneuvering on the part of Sawyer, Greenspun, Gragson, or others. But he was loath simply to accept public pronouncements of integration, and he moved quickly to test the owners' good faith. To his amazement, no blacks encountered any difficulty in entering Strip hotels, and most of the downtown establishments complied with the agreement as well.

The Horseshoe and Golden Gate Casinos, however, refused to admit black patrons. In a move of organizational self-interest, McMillan directed a challenge to Golden Gate policy by taking a paraplegic, Nolan Sharp, into the hotel. Sharp was a veteran, and McMillan believed no one would refuse service to a man in his condition. When he and Dave Hoggard arrived with Sharp, they were summarily shown the door and told not to return. Afterward, Sharp filed a complaint with the Nevada Equal Rights Commission. The hotel refused to honor the commission's subpoena to appear. That refusal was later upheld when the district court ruled that the E.R.C. lacked the power to command the appearance of witnesses, thereby undercutting the effectiveness of the state's civil rights machinery.

More hopeful results appeared to come from the Southern Nevada Human Relations Committee, formed as an outgrowth of the Moulin Rouge Agreement. The committee's purpose was to deal with problems resulting from desegregation, and McMillan specifically pushed for more jobs in casinos, a position that Gragson strongly supported. Despite some improvements, the gains were marginal, and the few advancements in employing blacks were confined to the lowest-paying positions.

The lack of progress in employment opportunities again moved the NAACP to threaten protest demonstrations at the convention center before the Sonny Liston–Floyd Patterson world heavyweight championship fight in 1963. The hotels and casinos again promised more jobs, and the demonstrations were canceled when seven hotels offered to meet with NAACP leaders. But nothing short of intervention by the federal government could stop the unfair employment practices of Las Vegas's major employers and labor unions.

On June 4, 1971, Bart M. Schouweiler, U.S. attorney for the District of Nevada, sued the Nevada Resort Association, the major hotels and casinos, and the local trade unions for violating Title VII of the Civil Rights Act of 1964 by engaging in racially discriminatory employment practices. A decade earlier, McMillan had clashed with Al Bramlet, head of the Culinary Workers Union. McMillan's charges of racial discrimination going back more than fifteen years were formally acknowledged when the suit was settled by a consent decree: The defendants agreed to cease their illegal activities and hire more African Americans.

McMillan has always believed that progress in the black community depended more on access to capital than on consent decrees. Integration and jobs were the first steps, but McMillan wanted to move beyond employment to create business opportunities through a black-owned bank. He moved aggressively to press the Sawyer administration to charter a bank, once $500,000 had been raised. Even though promises were made and the money committed, state bank examiners refused to grant a charter because of the extraordinarily high interest rates attached to the loan-repayment schedule. McMillan believes that the failure to obtain a bank charter, which would have allowed African Americans to have access to capital investment, is his greatest failure and, indeed, the outstanding omission in the nation's commitment to equality.

After desegregation, black-owned businesses suffered great financial loss as blacks began to spend their money in establishments that until then had been closed to them. To help promote black-owned business, McMillan led in the formation of the Black Chamber of Commerce to educate businessmen about the opportunities available through government contracts and grants. The success of the organization has been mixed, but undeniably it has fostered a commonality of interest in the black business community.

In 1961, business and personal considerations combined to induce McMillan to step down as president of the Las Vegas chapter of the NAACP. McMillan fully expected the executive board to refuse to accept his resignation and ask him to stay on as president; but to his amazement, they offered no resistance or protest. Clearly, McMillan had alienated a significant number of people on the executive board by his "shoot from the hip" approach to policy formulation. Although the resentment felt by board members was behind the scenes, many clearly and vocally disapproved of his failure to consult them on vital issues. Never again would he be president, although he remained a member of the executive board for nearly a decade after his resignation.

Outrage more than political ambition drove McMillan to challenge incumbent U.S. senator Howard Cannon in the 1964 Democratic Party primary. McMillan had never cared for Cannon. In fact, his dislike stemmed back to Cannon's position on civil rights during his time as Las Vegas city attorney, even before McMillan arrived in Las Vegas. After the assembly had defeated the Rudiak bill, Woodrow Wilson, president of the Las Vegas chapter of the NAACP and later an assemblyman himself, asked the city of Las Vegas to pass an ordinance along the lines of the failed Rudiak proposal. Cannon's legal opinion rested on the lack of authority in the city charter to enact a civil rights ordinance. Since the state constitution and statutes did not provide for integration, local government was powerless to act in the absence of specific authorization. This legal maneuvering to protect the status quo angered McMillan and made him suspicious of Cannon's dedication to equal rights. Indeed, it did seem strange to many west-side residents that integration was prohibited in hotels and casinos but not in the U.S. military, which had been desegregated since 1948.

Little in Cannon's Senate career had erased the memories of 1953. His votes on cloture—that is, a resolution to shut off debate—were inconsistent, as were his votes on the procedural issues before the final vote on the 1964 Civil Rights Act. McMillan believed Cannon wanted to add exemptions to the public-accommodations section to protect gaming establishments, for example, which again raised questions about his motives in 1953. Even though he supported the 1964 Civil Rights Act and did cast an important vote for cloture, his record would indicate that he wanted to have it both ways, particularly when it came to not antagonizing Senator Richard Russell of Georgia and the southern oligarchy that had dominated the Senate for so long.

McMillan entered the four-way Senate primary race as the civil rights candidate and was trounced, receiving only 1,717 votes compared to Cannon's 36,320. McMillan's dismal showing was not so much a reflection of civil rights support in Nevada as it was a demonstration of his political naïveté in challenging an incumbent senator and in doing so with little money and even less organization. Nevertheless, McMillan would not run for public office again for another twenty-seven years.

In the intervening years, his professional career thrived. He was appointed to the state Board of Dental Examiners, the board of directors of Health Plan of Nevada, and the Economic Opportunity Board Health Committee. He served as a community leader in many capacities, among them as a member of the Small Business Administration Advisory Council, chairman of the Governor's Commission on Minority Business Enterprises, member of the board of directors and editorial board of KVBC Television, and director of the Clark County Boys' Club.

McMillan's marriage to Magnolia Rutherford ended in 1961, a casualty partly of the stress caused by the civil rights uproar and partly of incompatibility. In 1964 he married Marie Elizabeth Daly; together they had a son, Jeffery Bates McMillan. This interracial union has survived thirty-two years of all the problems associated with the intractable issue of race in America. According to Marie, McMillan's great passion is, and has been, the betterment of his people, which accounts in part for his willingness to reenter the political arena.

In 1991, he ran for city commissioner against Frank Hawkins and three others. Hawkins, a young, good-looking graduate of the University of Nevada, Reno, an All American fullback, and a professional football star with the Los Angeles Raiders, now a black Las Vegas businessman, proved a formidable foe. While McMillan was well known, he may have been perceived as an aging warhorse whose time for political activism was past. He had failed to build a political organization with financial support, which predictably duplicated his 1964 showing: He received some 600 votes to Hawkins's near 43,600. Undaunted, McMillan again sought public office in 1992, and this time he was elected to the Clark County School Board, defeating a younger black candidate, John Rhodes, who was later elected to the North Las Vegas City Council.

In the late 1990s McMillan spends his free evenings and weekends poring over the paperwork associated with school board affairs. His living room is strewn with stacks of reports, statistical data, agendas, and other assorted pulp. When not bedeviled by school board affairs, he worries about the fate of affirmative action, integration, the imbalance in the busing of black students, the direction of the Supreme Court, and the welfare of African Americans. He is more convinced than ever that black Americans will never achieve equality unless, and until, they have access to capital to develop neighborhoods, communities, jobs, and businesses. So in the final analysis, the young man's question to McMillan on November 9, 1990, can be answered simply. What James McMillan has done to have a school named after him is to have fought all his life for a vision that has yet to be realized: racial equality in the New Nevada.

William F. Harrah

Nevada Gaming Mogul

William Fisk Harrah was a very private man. However, he had greater impact upon the development of the casino gaming industry in northern Nevada, and indeed, in Nevada, than any other individual.
—William Eadington[1]

The interminable Harrah harangues [in his oral history] documented his distorted perception of womanhood, his own mother, his seven wives, his family, his drunken driving, education, law-and-order . . . and social conventions in general.
— Ben Jordan[2]

"An anomaly" perhaps best describes the figure of William F. "Bill" Harrah: Nevada gaming pioneer, millionaire, visionary, overgrown adolescent, failed husband, and disinterested citizen. For if the public Harrah arguably set the standards for the modern casino industry, his personal life was incredibly messy—uninspired and hence uninspiring. Harrah bordered on the reclusive; had he not consented to an oral history in 1978, a few weeks before his fateful (and fatal) open-heart surgery at the Mayo Clinic, it would have been largely impossible to contemplate his life at all, except as seen through press clippings.

The Background

Nevada's modern casino industry essentially began in Reno in the aftermath of the enabling legislation of 1931. Reno-based Nevada political and business magnate George Wingfield was instrumental in its passage, apparently as one of the state's defensive measures during the Great Depression. During the 1930s, shady interests, who operated what were more dens than destination resorts, dominated gaming in Reno. The Bank Club, owned by Bill Graham and Jim McKay (and located in Wingfield's Golden Hotel), was arguably the premier establishment. Graham and McKay were also the principals in the Riverside Securities Company, which controlled "the Stockade," or Reno's houses of prostitution. The co-proprietors of the Bank Club were believed to have connections with some of the era's most notorious hoodlums, notably the Ma Barker gang and Babyface Nelson. When the government indicted Graham and McKay for mail fraud, key witness Roy Frisch disappeared before giving his testimony. In Reno it was commonly assumed that Frisch was eliminated by Nelson on the orders of his friends and benefactors.

In its own way Reno was (and still is) a conservative town that was profoundly ambivalent about its image as America's

5

gambling (and divorce) capital. Consequently, the liberal (some said libertine) legislation of the 1920s and 1930s triggered bitter debate and conflict within the city's body politic. But it was the Wingfield crowd, in part through its ability to fund and control Mayor E. E. Roberts and key city councilmen, that prevailed. For better or worse the seeds of Nevada's modern, tourist-based economy were planted, and within questionable soil, more than a decade before Bugsy Siegel even thought of moving to Las Vegas.

In retrospect, however, it is apparent that the Wingfields, Grahams, and McKays were not the founders of today's gaming industry. These early pioneers were drawn out of the state's former turn-of-the-century, mining-camp, barroom–poker table, gambling legacy—one that had continued to operate more or less openly at the margins of Nevada society once gambling had been outlawed in 1910. When the activity was again legalized in 1931, their response was to move the formerly "gray gaming" operation in the basement of the Golden Hotel up to the first floor. Its prime audience was the hard-core local player, supplemented by the bored, aspiring divorcée establishing her required six-weeks' Nevada legal residence, rather than today's "tourist" per se.

To realize the full potential of Nevada gaming required the involvement of two transitional and transformational figures: Harold Smith and William F. Harrah. Together they converted a still-somewhat-shady and myopic business into a reasonably respectable leisure-time pursuit embedded within a larger recreational complex characterized by classy surroundings, fine cuisine, and live entertainment. In short, under the aegis of the Smith family and Harrah, "gambling" became "gaming," the cornerstone of an adult-oriented, Nevada-unique tourist industry designed to appeal to the masses. While somewhat pretentious, perhaps the most graphic symbol of this new approach was the famous HAROLDS CLUB OR BUST billboards placed throughout the nation and the world as tangible evidence of Harold Smith's claim to operating "the biggest and most famous casino in the world." One can only speculate about what the more sedate casino operators in places like Monte Carlo thought (if at all) of such hoopla.

In any event, when describing the contributions of Harold Smith and Bill Harrah to the modern casino industry, *precursors* rather than *architects* is the proper operative word. With a few notable exceptions, today's gaming industry is dominated by publicly traded, multinational firms headed by former attorneys and/or accountants, whose corporate culture is decidedly antithetical to either the management style or personal flamboyance of a Harold Smith or a Bill Harrah. Indeed, neither survived the transition, nor was either in particularly good financial shape when Harolds Club disappeared into the maw of Howard Hughes's Summa Corporation and Harrah's was forced to go public to provide its founder with the financial wherewithal to support his extravagant lifestyle.

While Harrah's organization did manage to evolve into corporate gaming, Harolds Club, at this writing, is boarded up. Bill Harrah remarked in 1978, "Harolds isn't much competition—hasn't been for years, really. It's just another place; it isn't run very good [*sic*]. . . . It used to be 'Wow, Harolds Club!' "

The Friendly Rivals

There are striking parallels in the lives of Harold Smith and Bill Harrah. Each worked for his father in the carnivalesque bingo business on the margins of California society during the difficult years of the Great Depression (Smith in the summer fairs along the Russian River and Harrah in Venice). Each had his periodic scrapes with the law and local politicos and was therefore attracted to Nevada's newly established sanctuary for legal gambling operations (Smith in 1935, Harrah in 1937). Both first entered the Reno market with cottage-industry bingo operations rather than full-blown casinos. In the 1930s competition among gamblers included patronizing one another's establishments as players. Both were nightly figures on the Reno scene, developing in the process monumental drinking problems (which they subsequently overcame), gambling habits, and a reputation for carousing. In the course of their numerous affairs and marriages each had a liaison with a famous chanteuse (Smith with Kay Starr and Harrah with Bobby Gentry).

There were, to be sure, differences between the two men. Perhaps the most notable was their relationship (business and personal) with their families. While each began his gaming career working for his father, Harold never managed to crawl out from under "Pappy's" long paternal shadow. In his later fifties Harold Smith narrated his life's story in the book *I Want to Quit Winners*. (He didn't.) A psychiatrist might treat it as a cri de coeur from an exasperated son who wanted the world to know that it was he who brought the family to Reno and generally set the tone of what was, after all, *Harolds* Club. Harold Smith's problems in this regard were compounded by the involvement of his elder brother, Raymond, in the business. In contrast, when Bill, in his early twenties, had his first serious disagreement with John Harrah over their Venice operations, he simply bought out his genitor's interest. By the 1940s the senior Smith and senior Harrah were both living in Reno with their sons, but in the world's view Raymond I. Smith *was* Harolds Club, whereas no one doubted that Bill Harrah was his own man. Therefore, while Harold (born in 1910) and Bill (born in 1911) were contemporaries, when dealing with the Smiths even Harrah tended to relate to Pappy.

And relate to Pappy he did. While neither Harold's book nor Bill's oral history discusses their relationship in depth, what is stated (as well as what is not) suggests that they were rivals. Harrah, as an avid car collector and prime mover of northern Nevada's Horseless Carriage Club, began to organize outings of antique car bugs that included a parade though downtown Reno. One year Harold Smith, dressed in appropriate costume and goggles, slipped into the parade with a child's pedal car brandishing the sign HAROLD'S AUTO COLLECTION.

Certainly in the 1940s and 1950s Harolds Club was by far the better known of the two operations. Some observers have gone so far as to suggest that Harrah's establishment was successful because it was next to the famous Harolds Club and the similarity in the two names led to a public confusion that created a penumbra effect for Harrah's. The reality was considerably different and more complicated. By the mid-1940s Harrah controlled Harrah's Heart Tango on one side of Harolds Club and the Reno Club on the other—both bingo parlors. Harrah also owned the Blackout Bar two doors south of the Reno Club and adjacent to the First National Bank. Harrah approached Pappy with the proposal to cut a hole in the common walls that separated their operations. In Harrah's own words, it "was really good for both of us, because the people could run back [sic], and we're noncompetitive—they had no Bingo and a lot of slots, and we had Bingo and very few slots; and they had a bar, and we didn't have a bar. And so people really circulated."

The plan was implemented; and although their two operations were never a partnership, they were horizontally integrated to a considerable degree for a while. As the internal foot traffic flowed freely in both directions and Harrah's cocktail waitresses serviced their bingo players from Harolds' bar, the three clubs must have appeared rather seamless, from the customers' perspective, and any distinction at the ownership level somewhat academic.

Ultimately, there would be a falling out. After the war, control of the Reno Club reverted to the Aoyama family, and Harrah learned that the Smiths were negotiating with his landlord, a Dr. Chase in Los Angeles, for control of the Heart Tango property. The Smiths wanted to expand their successful operation north as far as Douglas Alley. Harrah received assurances from Chase that his tenancy was secure. However, it wasn't once the Smiths made an offer that Chase could not refuse. Bill was miffed at Pappy, but he conceded, "I'd've probably done the same thing."

For the next few years Harrah's presence on Virginia Street was reduced to a bingo parlor north of Douglas Alley and the small Blackout Bar property. In time Bill acquired the Frontier, the adjacent property to the north of the

Blackout Bar, from Joe and Pick Hobson. That combined real estate formed the initial core of what would eventually become today's Harrah's casino.

During World War II, Bill had learned another critical lesson. He entered into a frustrating partnership that included Virgil Smith, Wayne Martin, and Bill Williams. They operated a small property called John's Bar. Harrah was eager to expand the business but was thwarted by Williams's conservatism. The experience convinced him that you should have partners only when you must. In retrospect Bill was pleased that his earlier joint ventures failed, since otherwise he might not have been the sole owner of Harrah's Club after it succeeded.

For the remainder of his days Harrah placed neither credence nor confidence in business arrangements that limited his total control over his destiny. Indeed, after his personal financial needs finally required Harrah's to go public, which thereby subjected the organization to a board of directors and the rules and restrictions of the Securities and Exchange Commission, Bill Harrah failed either to realize fully or to accept the limitations that this placed upon his personal authority.

HARRAH THE BUSINESSMAN

The key question, of course, is what made Harrah so different from other operators as to warrant writing an article about him at all. In part his success was certainly conjunctural. That is, both the Smiths and Harrah ended up with prime locations on Virginia Street (Harrah after first learning the hard way with less successful storefronts for his bingo operations on Center Street and then Commercial Row). By his own account Harrah was able to acquire one of Reno's better bingo operations, Ed Howe's Heart Tango, for a song, since he had a mole who informed him that Howe was tired of the business and wanted out. When severe injuries from an automobile accident exempted him from military duty, Harrah remained on the local scene and was thereby able to profit from Reno's booming economy during the Second World War. Then, too, the property adjacent to him, Reno's most successful bingo parlor (called the Reno Club) was owned by the "Japs." While the Aoyamas, a Japanese American family, were never interned, they leased their property to Harrah for the war's duration. In short, Bill got some breaks and made others for himself. But there was more than simply luck to his success; Harrah possessed a business philosophy that ultimately set him apart from the field.

One essential characteristic of Bill Harrah's makeup was his integrity at a time when honesty was rare in the business. He noted, disdainfully, that with the possible exception of the Bank and Palace Clubs, all of the gambling joints in Reno cheated the player in one way or another. Without being overly moralistic about it, he believed that cheating (or hoodwinking the public through shilling and contrived promotions that failed to deliver what they promised) was simply bad for business in the long run. Thus, he refused to play by the slipshod, informal rules of Reno's gambling fraternity and welcomed state regulation of the industry in the mid-1940s as good for Nevada's image when few other operators concurred. He was particularly critical of the perceived predatory attitude prevalent in Las Vegas, and he had a policy against hiring help from there. According to Harrah, "Generally the operators in northern Nevada are far superior to the operators in southern Nevada. Southern Nevada is just take the money and run. . . . Not repeat business, just bring in another bus load, another plane load and . . . get their money and get 'em out, and another, another, which is kind of the Vegas philosophy."

Another peculiar twist was Harrah's approach to politics. At a time when Reno's political establishment was beholden to the Wingfield machine, Harrah remained largely aloof. The reasons are not altogether clear. His personality certainly did not lend itself to hobnobbing or personal lobbying, which may account in part for his reticence. Then, too, he may have felt either insignificant as a potential player or simply protected adequately as a gambler by the obvious machinations of the Wingfield crowd. There are, however, other intriguing clues in his oral history. He gives us glimpses of the demimonde of Venice politics, where his father served as mayor before becoming engaged in gray gaming. He notes that their bingo operations were most likely to be raided and closed down at the start of each racing season, inferring that they were probably denounced by the Santa Anita Racetrack management as a way of removing competition for the wagered dollar. So Harrah possibly harbored a deep-seated aversion to the strategy of currying political favor, not to mention the outright greasing of the palms of corrupt officials. Regarding gray gaming, he said: "I just hate to operate [it]. I've done that in California with our Bingo games—under subterfuge, and you have to look people in the eye and tell 'em . . . two and two is nine—it's not fun."

The critical feature in Harrah's business philosophy was his relentless pursuit of good customer service and a propensity to innovate to achieve it. "I like our customers to be treated as I would like to be treated," said Harrah. "When I go to the men's room, I like it clean, and I like toilet paper and towels and soap and a good light. . . . [A]nd then the restaurant, I like . . . this chair to be comfortable and the things clean and the menu not dog-eared, and just on and on and on."

Harrah grew up in a relatively affluent family in Venice and, later, Hollywood. His father, John, doted on him and told him that he could have whatever he wanted (as long as the family could afford it). Indeed, Bill could have whatever he wanted whenever he wanted it, since gift-giving occasions like Christmas and birthdays were "mostly for your mother and your sister." So Bill got a hot car at an early age. When he was regularly hauled into court for speeding (nearly weekly), his exasperated lawyer-father berated the police and court system rather than his own son.

Bill Harrah was a demanding traveler, most critical of his surroundings and treatment. He was a keen observer of systems and a firm believer in usurping good ideas rather than reinventing wheels. When, for example, he was planning the first stage of Harrah's he was mightily impressed by the work of a young Beverly Hills architect who had designed an attractive and functional bar in a tiny Hollywood location. Harrah looked him up and hired him. In short, when it came to running his properties Harrah embraced the perspective of the consummate and critical consumer rather than that of the complacent operator. In retrospect, given a playing field in which Nevada held a monopoly on casino-gaming and given that his competition, in northern Nevada, was not overly concerned about customer comforts, Harrah's obsession in this regard was as much the personal predilection of an avowed perfectionist as driven by business necessity.

In the process of establishing his businesses, he set a new standard. If Harrah was somewhat oblivious to his local competitors, over time they could scarcely afford to be so regarding Harrah's. Arguably, when MGM constructed Reno's largest property in 1978, it considered Harrah's to be its most serious foil, just as Caesars or Harvey's had to contemplate Bill's standard when planning their subsequent Lake Tahoe projects. It also seems evident that, to at least some degree, the Harrah's standard has influenced the architectural design of casino construction throughout the nation and beyond, whether implemented directly by its present holding company or not.

Probably the least fathomable aspect of Harrah's management style was his handling of his employees and customers. Harrah clearly preferred being a lone wolf. According to Mead Dixon, the key executives at Harrah's (excepting himself) were toadies who feared for their jobs if they crossed the boss. In this view Bob Ring, Harrah's trusted sidekick from his Venice days, was the King Toady, who never ceased reminding the others that "this is not Harrah's Club; it's *Bill* Harrah's Club." According to Dixon, when Harrah announced that he had given up drinking, Ring quit drinking; when Harrah took another drink fifteen years later, so did Ring. Ring's oral history is essentially an accolade to Bill Harrah:

Mr. Harrah thinks big, he thinks very big, and I've likened him to Cecil B. De Mille of the movies. Many times, some of us have considered things—maybe Mr. Harrah might bring them up, or maybe we might bring them up, but we thought maybe the fact that they were quite costly, we'd think that they were prohibitive, which would react very negatively to Mr. Bill Harrah, because he didn't feel that *we* were the ones to decide it was prohibitive. *He* should decide whether it's prohibitive. Consequently, he's had many of us think big, but not quite as big as he thinks, however.

Dixon is highly critical of Harrah's personal management style, which brooked no criticism and produced the kind of paranoia that had key executives roaming the property, endlessly searching for burned-out lightbulbs before they were discovered by the boss during his ceaseless prowlings. Then there were draconian measures, such as the requirement that each executive weigh in (literally) each day, since Bill had an aversion to fat people, or the not-so-subtle free provisioning of Binaca mouthwash to the executive staff. There is, however, a sense in which Harrah was less arbitrary and hands-on than such examples might suggest. Once he became comfortable with a key employee he extended him latitude, particularly since most came up through the ranks. To a considerable degree Ring, Maurice Sheppard, Lloyd Dyer, Rome Andreotti, and Dixon defined their own duties within the boundaries of their designated roles. Harrah commented, "One thing about being successful, and many people can't do that, is delegation, and I've always been real good at that." Indeed, this was the flip side of Harrah's aversion to meetings and general lack of people skills. The boss was much more comfortable reading his daily computer printouts and helping out in the counting room than engaging in face-to-face encounters with his managers. Over time Harrah's developed an extensive policy manual—a document that Harrah endorsed and Dixon judged to be "as thick as the Manhattan telephone directory," "overkill," and "cumbersome to use." One can argue that a detailed policy manual is in keeping with the personality of a man who eschewed meaningful human interaction.

By Harrah's own admission this personal style extended to his dealings with customers. Harrah positively loathed glad-handing and, unlike many casino operators, shunned the role of host. In his oral history Harrah attempts to justify this in good business terms, arguing that it is better and more credible for a key employee, rather than the owner, to console an unhappy loser. He further noted that by making yourself scarce you create an air of mystery that makes your next appearance a real event and your greeting special. In reality, these were the rationalizations of a man who cherished privacy and who, after the Prospectors' Club was installed in Harrah's and he had little choice but to join, constructed his own private dining room next to it, complete with a separate entrance accessible only from the executive office. Thereafter Harrah took his lunch in that private room, rather than run the daily gauntlet of customers in his public restaurants or Reno's establishment in the businessmen's club.

There is evidence that Harrah was not averse to taking advice. He commissioned outside consultants, such as the Stanford Research Institute, to examine his organization and make suggestions. This was both expensive and visionary at the time. Considerable thought and care went into the room design before construction of the hotels at Harrah's Reno and Harrah's Tahoe. Ring proudly displayed the maquettes of the room layouts in his office. Harrah's obsession with systems that improved customer service prompted him to hire the George S. May Company for "an unheard-of sum" just to do an engineering study on how to keep the Harrah's properties clean. Such exercises did have their limits, however. When the Arthur Little firm was commissioned to study Harrah's Lake Tahoe property and issued a highly critical report of management's expansion plans, it was not only tabled but also tabooed within the organization.

Above all, Harrah was an innovator. Harrah's slot department "invented" many of their machines by modifying the standard manufactured product. Harrah's devised the "rabbit ears" system for selecting the balls used in today's keno (as a security measure for protecting the game). To enhance customer satisfaction, Harrah's was the first to install a change light on its slot machines. Harrah's employees were required to wear name badges to make them more approachable. Harrah's management placed great emphasis upon proper temperature control in the public areas.

Harrah's pioneered the use of marketing studies in the industry. Bill was an early believer in providing liberal slots to combat the imagery of the "one-armed bandit." When the business at Harrah's Tahoe proved to be more seasonal than expected, Bill Harrah instituted the first massive Nevada-casino bus program out of northern California. At one point the run to Harrah's entailed one hundred Greyhound buses daily, making Harrah's the bus company's second biggest client (after the U.S. armed forces). Harrah's was also a leader in billboard advertising.

Harrah's own words best sum up his management philosophy: "Like they say, the ideal form of government—and I agree with it—is a benevolent dictatorship 'cause they just do what's right and do it right now, and not a lot of waste effort and not a lot of waste money."

One might have expected that such thinking would lead to confrontations with the employees. This was simply not the case. By the early 1950s, and in the aftermath of the strike of 1949, Harrah's had an organized work force, and Bill decided to try to decertify the Culinary Workers Union. Despite his aversion to public speaking he addressed his employees and was able to convince a majority to vote for decertification. Harrah later noted, "If everyone had treated their employees as they would like to be treated themselves over the years, there'd be no unions, but so many companies have asked for it. And they deserve it."

In Harrah's view the key to success in labor relations was to ensure employees against arbitrary termination and to remain ahead of the union's curve in offering proper salary and benefits. By the early 1970s Harrah's employees enjoyed good health benefits, counseling services, an employee cafeteria and lounge area, clothing allowances, and an in-house newsletter. All available openings were first advertised within the organization and dealers' schools, and training programs were established to enable employees seeking advancement to acquire the necessary skills. In the early 1980s Harrah's constructed employee housing in Reno. Bill Harrah's standard in this regard remains exemplary within the industry. Arguably, to this day Harrah's enjoys an enviable degree of employee loyalty at all levels of the organization.

Harrah had the capacity to attract and befriend top-name entertainers. Headliners such as Sammy Davis Jr., Liza Minnelli, and Bill Cosby regularly performed at both Harrah's Reno and Harrah's Lake Tahoe, and at rates considerably below those paid by Las Vegas establishments. Lower pay scales notwithstanding, many famous entertainers regarded Harrah's as *the* class place to perform. They were always accorded VIP treatment, including transportation in a Harrah's private jet, a limousine pickup on arrival at the airport, and dinner with the boss and his current wife. Clearly, when motivated to do so, Bill Harrah could be a thoughtful and charming host. However, this charm did not come easy, since Harrah oftentimes "dreaded" having dinner with a new entertainer. But, as Harrah recalled,

then you go up and they come in—and I'm sure they feel the same way. But you sit and have a drink and look at each other for two hours and tell stories back and forth and problems you've had in your life and fun you've had, and Europe, and old cars, and new cars, and airplanes, and Australia, on and on. And when you part, why, everyone seems to have had an excellent time; I know I always do, have a wonderful time. Then afterwards I think, "Why did I not want to do that? That was *fun!*"— you know. You get so much inside stuff, you know.

His performers seemed genuinely fond of Bill. Jim Nabors once hosted a surprise party in Hollywood for Harrah that was attended by most of the stars who had ever worked at Harrah's.

Viewed from the perspective of Harrah's, Bill Harrah was alternatively autocratic and reclusive; but there were other ways in which he distanced himself from his properties. Idaho became his sanctuary, and Bill spent as much time there as possible. He acquired the Middle Fork Lodge, a wilderness property on the Salmon River. He fell in love with the tiny town of Stanley. Before he was through he had constructed a sumptuous residence there and owned the gas station, the grocery store, and a restaurant. While in Stanley he would frequently drive the sixty miles to the Sun Valley–Ketchum area. Eventually, he purchased the finest house there and acquired an automobile agency (Jeep, Volkswagen, Audi, Porsche) and a general store as well. He also bought a cabin on Pettit Lake (halfway between Stanley and Ketchum), although he scarcely used it. In short, Bill Harrah sought refuge from the pressures in northern Nevada by retiring to Idaho. One suspects that his purchase of so many businesses and properties there became the excuse for frequenting his "sanctuary."

Bill had several escape valves built into his daily life in Reno, too. He acquired three auto agencies, selling Jeeps and other American Motors' products, and vehicles made by Rolls-Royce, BMW, Aston-Martin, Peugeot, Fiat, Mercedes-Benz, and Datsun. He was also the Ferrari distributor west of the Mississippi.

And then there was his true obsession: the Harrah's Automobile Collection. At the time of his death it was the largest in the world, with about fourteen hundred cars. Bill Harrah was the best-known collector, and Harrah's, arguably, owned the best automotive library and was setting the standard for car restoration. Harrah's Automobile Collection included a museum open to the public and employed 150 people. While he explicitly denied that in a crunch the collection would take precedence over the casinos, just prior to his death his real obsession became building Harrah's World—a state-of-the-art, Disneyesque museum for 350 cars, scheduled for construction on three hundred acres bordering Interstate 80 just west of Reno.

In short, for the last two decades of his life, Harrah's owned only a piece (and at times a small one) of Bill Harrah.

Harrah the Man

There was a dark side to Bill Harrah's moon. He was an overly pampered boy who grew into a self-centered and self-indulgent man. Harrah was keenly concerned about his personal appearance and his perks. Harrah noted, "Having money is fun—it gets you to the head of the line; it gets you the chauffeured limo."

Arguably, if it were not for Bill's personal foibles, Harrah's Club would have prospered far more as a company. Acquisition of the lodge on the Middle Fork of the Salmon River, which was Bill's whim but a corporate expense, cost Harrah's between $1 million and $2 million annually. The automobile collection, a pure plaything, drained Harrah's of uncounted millions and remained, until Harrah's death, essentially unaccountable within the organization. Villa Harrah, again financed by the business, sprawled over several acres of prime Lake Tahoe south-shore real estate. It had every amenity, yet only one bedroom, and Harrah was the only person to ever use it. Then there was Harrah's Air Force—two conventional and two jet aircraft with a staff of twenty-eight, clearly an extravagance for an organization with business properties in only Reno and Lake Tahoe.

In short, it is evident that over the years the lion's share of Harrah's profits went to support the boss's lifestyle. Indeed, shortly before his death Harrah pledged half his stock in the by-then publicly traded company for a $25 million line of credit at Chase Manhattan Bank. According to Dixon, the bankers thought Harrah wanted it for business purposes. However, by the time of his death he had drawn down $13 million, which he had used entirely for personal expenditures. It was in order to satisfy this debt and pay the estate taxes that Harrah's was forced to merge with Holiday Inns. There is no small amount of irony in this merger. When Harrah boasted of all of the careful planning that went into his hotel at Lake Tahoe, he stated, "Harvey built a hotel in about six months, and it was just a bum hotel. You build a hotel that fast, and it was just another hotel, just a 'Holiday Inn' type of thing."

Harrah was a person who valued machines more than people. Indeed, he tells us, "The trouble with the world and the country is people. Just cut the people out of it, and everything'd be fine. Animals are fine; it's the darn people."

There is a revelatory passage in the first paragraph of his personal narrative. He describes attending his grandfather's funeral as a nine-year-old child. He commented to the interviewer: "And the high point of the funeral [laughs], me being a car guy, was my father borrowed a Marmon automobile to transport the family, which was a much classier car than our family car. And I remember more about the Marmon than I do the funeral."

Harrah's obsession with mechanical things—planes, boats, and, above all, automobiles—was legendary and in keeping with his perfectionism. Machines either work or they don't. If they are broken, they can be fixed or discarded. Whether designing his operating manual or divorcing his latest wife, Harrah was far more mechanistic than humanistic. During one of the interviews for his oral history Harrah was asked to talk about each of his wives. At one point he had to ask his secretary for the name of one of them—an anecdote that speaks volumes.

Between marriages he drank and caroused until dawn almost nightly and was a permanent guest at either the Mapes or Riverside Hotels. Mead Dixon saw Bill as a tortured figure who, in his waning years, found a degree of personal solace and comfort in his seventh marriage. Harrah, too, described his last union as blissful. Dixon, however, also reads angst into Harrah's earlier years, which in Bill's account seems more like simple indifference and insensitivity than personal pain.

In the final analysis, Bill Harrah was a quintessential taker rather than giver. Indeed, his disinterest in his community was extraordinary. He eschewed civic clubs and charitable organizations. At one point he was pressured to join the Elks; but, he recalls, "*it was not for me at all!*" He thought it was "corney"; "I just hated it." Regarding the Chamber of Commerce, he remarked: "All that is baloney. . . . There are other people that do that." When named a Distinguished Nevadan by the University of Nevada he was peeved that he was expected to show up for future commencement ceremonies. He did approve of one organization—the Nevada Safety Council—and was active in it. Its purpose rather belied its name, since Harrah, in commenting on his participation, noted, "That was for selfish reasons; that was to keep the speed limit out of Nevada."

Conclusion

The company that Bill Harrah founded evolved from Harrah's to Harrah's Inc. to Holiday Inns to Promus Corporation to Harrah's Entertainment. Today *Harrah's* is the masthead for one of the world's largest publicly traded gaming companies. It is the stated goal of Harrah's Entertainment to have a presence in all of the emerging gaming markets in North America, as well as in selected locations abroad. At this writing (March 1996) Harrah's Entertainment had fifteen properties (including gaming operations in Auckland, New Zealand, and management contracts for Indian casinos in Arizona and Washington State). Within the gaming industry, then, Harrah's is now "McHarrah's."

It would seem to be obvious to regard Harrah's Entertainment as Bill Harrah's legacy, yet I believe that it would be erroneous to do so. What Bill Harrah regarded as *his* two top priorities in life had been sacrificed along the way. At his death, Bill's most important project was Harrah's World, the auto theme park designed to showcase what had become the world's largest automobile collection. According to Mead Dixon the project made no sense at all from a financial standpoint. It was, in essence, Harrah's monument to himself.

One of Dixon's first decisions as the new CEO of Harrah's Inc. was to cancel Harrah's World. Holiday Inns then rubbed salt in Bill's posthumous wounds by selling off many of the best cars in the auto collection. One suspects that Bill Harrah would never have lent his name to Reno's current Harrah's Auto Museum.

Bill's second priority, or rather obsession, was with quality. He never cut corners, and he relentlessly pursued a five-star ranking for Harrah's, oftentimes irrespective of cost considerations. Such a business approach was simply antithetical to the corporate culture of Holiday Inns. Perhaps inevitably, one of the subsequent CEOs of Harrah's Reno is reputed to have cut short a department head who was criticizing a policy of change by invoking Harrah's traditional standards with the comment, "Bill Harrah is dead!" Indeed.

So if we ask if Harrah passed on his torch at all, the answer might well be "Yes—but to a competitor." Steve Wynn is said to have been an early and serious admirer of Bill Harrah's approach to the business. The two men have much in common. Wynn is notorious for his high standards irrespective of costs. Some regard him to be a reckless spender. So far, however, he has certainly had the Midas touch. I suspect that were he alive today as an operator, Harrah would admire Steve Wynn more than any other gamer in the world. Bill would certainly have understood Steve's penchant for perks and toys. Like Harrah, Wynn has a fabulous house at Lake Tahoe. He also owns one of the world's most beautiful golf courses near Las Vegas. On the other hand, Harrah would likely have been appalled by *Running Scared*, Wynn's unauthorized biography. It might have confirmed his worse suspicions regarding corruption and the "Las Vegas style."

A person . . . finds it distasteful to hear his life recounted with a different interpretation from his own. —Milan Kundera[3]

Bill Harrah was a peculiar blend of strengths and weaknesses, vision and myopia. He was an extremely distant and difficult man for his intimates and close associates. In most he inspired more fear than respect. Yet his very aloofness and autocratic style was compensation for considerable insecurity. After judging him, and at times harshly, we might consider the self-evaluation with which he ended his oral history:

I'm very happy considerin', 'cause so many of the years I was very insecure, and really, I kept up a pretty good front, you know. I looked good, and my clothes were good, and my car was good, but inside I was really scared. . . . I didn't really think "I had it" and anyone [that] was successful, I admired and wondered how they did it. And I didn't think . . . really I could ever, ever get anywhere.

Whatever else one might think of William Fisk Harrah, it cannot be denied that he got somewhere. Indeed, thanks to his efforts, so did his adopted state.

Notes

1. William R. Eadington, Special Introduction, to William F. Harrah, "My Recollections of the Hotel-Casino Industry and as an Auto Collecting Enthusiast," by William F. Harrah, University of Nevada Oral History Program, 1980, vi.

2. Ben Jordan, "Interminable Harangues," *Newsletter of the University of Nevada Oral History Project* (fall 1994): 3.

3. Milan Kundera, *Immortality* (New York: Grove Weidenfeld, 1991), 60.

Hank Greenspun

Where He Stood

BY MICHAEL S. GREEN

Las Vegas always has been a bundle of contradictions. It started out as a homey railroad town disconnected from the old Nevada and grew into a resort mecca that dominates the New Nevada. Located almost literally in the middle of nowhere, it annually attracts millions to admire its entertainers, volcanoes, pirate battles, and a shopping mall presided over by talking, moving statues of ancient Romans. It is in the middle of the desert, near a manmade lake created by a dam that tamed a wild river, and increasingly full of miniature lakes at the center of major residential developments. Its hotels and casinos, varying from family-oriented vacation spots to old-fashioned gambling halls, are surrounded by a population of more than a million, many of them dependent on the resort industry for their paychecks, who attend one of the nation's largest school districts and frequent the same kinds of churches and parks to be found in any other city. This growth began with the New Deal and World War II, when expansion in federal power and national defense imported military installations and servicemen who stayed to build a politically conservative town in the state that helped create the Sagebrush Rebellion against the federal government.

If anyone can be said to have been both central to and representative of this growth, it was Hank Greenspun. He came to Las Vegas in 1946 and was involved in starting two of its major resorts, the Flamingo and the Desert Inn. He invested in a radio station, a television station, cable television, a golf course, and thousands of acres. He built the area's first major, master-planned suburb. For nearly forty years he published the *Las Vegas Sun,* a daily newspaper that made him a leading local power broker. He was one of the leaders of a small but influential local Jewish community, a booster and donor to many civic groups and activities, and was proclaimed by himself and others as a champion of the common man. In the process, he became one of the most powerful and colorful figures in Nevada's history—and one of the most controversial.

6

He fought for, and used his newspaper in, a variety of causes and crusades, prompting his supporters to celebrate him and his critics to condemn him. In a city of contradictions, a city that he did much to build, with an image that he did much to implant in the public mind, he sometimes seemed to be the most contradictory leader of all.

Understanding Herman Milton Greenspun requires an understanding of his beginnings: the Flatbush section of Brooklyn, where he was born on August 27, 1909. Greenspun described his father, Samuel Greenspun, as "a diminutive, almost saintly Talmudic scholar with an insatiable passion for learning" and no interest in material things. His mother, Anna Bella Greenspun, "dark-haired, vivacious, and often volcanic," tried her hand at such potentially profitable sidelines as bootlegging (unsuccessfully) while working hard at raising four children. From his father, Greenspun inherited the curiosity necessary to a crusading publisher and the tendency to be a soft touch. But he derived much of his personality from his mother. "She was the driving force in the family and always had been," he said, and she imbued him with her toughness and shrewdness: When a customer on his paper route refused to pay him and used anti-Semitic epithets, his mother slapped the man, who never bothered young "Hymela" (his Yiddish nickname) again. "The episode taught me a lesson I would never forget: cowards generally avoid a target that hits back." He would apply that lesson with a vengeance.

Indeed, Greenspun was a product of his environment. His family briefly lived in the black section of New Haven, Connecticut, where other children often beat him up and he met a rich pastiche of citizens on both sides of the law; but mostly they lived in Brooklyn, a rural area going urban. With its feelings of inferiority and anger toward its richer neighbor, Manhattan, Brooklyn combined a spirit of community and feistiness, for which Greenspun became known in Las Vegas. He also was part of a family with a deep sense of its Jewish identity: His paternal grandfather was a cantor in a synagogue, and his family greatly admired Theodor Herzl, the founder of the Zionist movement, and Supreme Court Justice Louis Brandeis.

Plans for Greenspun's career, and what actually happened, reveal the conflict between his desires to please his family and to make both money and a mark. "I had never really decided to become a lawyer, I had simply been told from earliest childhood that I would *be* a lawyer when I grew up," he recalled. He entered St. John's University, earned his baccalaureate, and clerked in the law office of Vito Marcantonio, a liberal Republican congressman, in preparation for passing the bar. The man influenced Greenspun's political views, but the job left him unhappy (with defending those he knew to be guilty) and bored (with paperwork). In college, Greenspun had worked for a theatrical ticket agency that nurtured his interest in the Runyonesque characters who would later populate Las Vegas and the newspapers that covered them, but he turned instead to the steel industry. He hoped to capitalize on the expanded market created by the war in Europe; but he fell short of his goal when he lost his investment in a business deal and then "received a lively little letter headed by the word 'Greetings.'"

Greenspun's four years in the army during World War II profoundly affected his future. He worked on a camp newspaper and found that "for the first time in my life, I seemed to be in my proper element." He also worked in ordnance, which gave him expertise in guns and ammunition. His chance to fight Nazis, and see vestiges of the Holocaust, enhanced his sense of his own religion. In 1944, attending Yom Kippur services in a French synagogue the German army had left standing only to store supplies, "I became aware of Jewish responsibility for the fate of all Jews." He received the Croix de Guerre, but contended that his biggest battle was winning the hand of Barbara Joan Ritchie, a Jewish colleen he met and married in Ireland in 1944. That led to another battle: He went AWOL from his hospital bed—a severe case of frostbite led to trench foot and gangrene, nearly causing the amputation of his feet—that New Year's Eve to see her. In September 1945, "two consequences of my New Year's Eve A.W.O.L. caught up with me: I received the Army's final decision . . . demanding the payment of a twenty-five-dollar fine" for violating regulations, "and Barbara gave birth" to their first child, Susan.

Discharged in December 1945, Greenspun faced a challenge awaiting many soldiers: how to return to civilian life, support a family, and relieve the boredom that was bound to follow serving in a war. Greenspun tried the law again, but by the fall of 1946 he hoped to find something different. At this point, one of his clients, Joe Smoot, asked him to become his partner in building a racetrack in Las Vegas. Greenspun decided to look at the desert town, and he liked what he saw. A ranch area that the Union Pacific and Senator William A. Clark, a Montana copper king, had turned into a railroad town in 1905, Las Vegas began taking baby steps toward boom times in 1931, when the federal government began building Hoover Dam and the state legislature made gambling legal. The combination transformed Las Vegas from a whistle-stop into a tourist stop, having quadrupled the town's population to more than 20,000 by the time Greenspun arrived late in 1946. Greenspun noticed the construction of a new hotel, the Flamingo, and checked into the four-year-old Hotel Last Frontier, a ranch-style, glorified motel. "I had driven in vile weather," he wrote, while Las Vegas seemed "a perfect paradise of majestic mountains, infinite skies, and balmy air that looked and felt like warm, breathable crystal. . . . I went for a swim in the pool, emerged, phoned

Barbara and announced jubilantly, 'Pack everything, baby, and come on out! We won't be going back.' "

At the time, new arrivals to Las Vegas could indulge in a variety of money-making opportunities, and Greenspun was no different. Described by writers Richard Donovan and Douglass Cater as "a typical hustler and as industrious a hand-pumper as any man in town," he joined two reporters, Ralph Pearl (whom he had known in law school, and who was later a *Sun* columnist) and James Fallon, to publish *Las Vegas Life,* a semimonthly entertainment maga-zine. This venture led to two changes for Greenspun: the nickname Hank, which Fallon pinned on him because he detected a resemblance to baseball star Hank Greenberg, and an advertising contract from Flamingo builder Benjamin "Bugsy" Siegel, who liked Greenspun enough to hire him as the hotel's publicist. Greenspun called it "legitimate business. . . . There were six hundred other Las Vegans, none of them mobsters, working at the hotel"—a comment that reflected a long local battle to achieve prosperity and respect-ability while resolving the conundrum of how to justify some of the town's shadier, illicit leaders. The publicity job ended when Siegel was murdered in Los Angeles one warm June evening in 1947, and Greenspun moved into other fields: opening the town's second radio station, which would become KRAM-AM 1340, and joining with "a man I soon came to love as a brother," Wilbur Clark, in his dream of building the Desert Inn. Greenspun was to have a one-third share of the motel, 15 percent of the hotel-casino under construction, and the job of publicity director.

While Greenspun seemed like a typical postwar Las Vegan-on-the-make, he found himself involved in international affairs that diverted him from his work and a growing family that now included a son, Brian. In December 1947, his cousin, Ray Selk, introduced him to Al Schwimmer. They enlisted Greenspun's help in their work for the Haganah, a defense group run by Jewish leaders seeking arms and aid for the fight to establish the new nation of Israel. Selk and Schwimmer were experienced with aircraft, but they needed someone who knew about ordnance—as Greenspun did. "I hesitated. Like other Jews, I wanted to help in the struggle for Israel. Yet my family respon-sibilities had to come first," he related; but "I had seen too much of the 'Jewish Question' to evade it."

For the next year, Greenspun was in almost constant motion, flying to New York, Hawaii, Mexico, the Dominican Republic, Guatemala, and Pan-ama, obtaining and making deals for military supplies, and leaving his wife and friends puzzled, suspicious, and often angry—until he finally admitted what he was doing, to their relief and pride. Greenspun was responsible for sending fifty-eight crates of machine guns and ammunition to Israel, and he took part in other covert operations. He was "proud to have played a small role in bringing Israel's embattled Jews 'anything that shoots,'" he wrote, "[w]hatever the consequences." They would be far-reaching. While Greenspun was away, Wilbur Clark, needing capital to complete his dream hotel, had given control over the construction to Cleveland investors led by Moe Dalitz, Sam Tucker, and Morris Kleinman, who shared a long history in bootlegging and illegal gambling as part of the Mayfield Road Gang. Greenspun's "vague instinct of ever-growing distrust" proved accurate. By the time the new partners finished shuffling the deck, they had taken over the hotel, Clark had become a figurehead, and Greenspun's 15 percent had dwindled to a 1 percent interest and a job as publicist.

Greenspun's business concerns would take a backseat to bigger problems. On September 30, 1949, he and six others were indicted for violating the Neutrality Act, among other laws, by shipping planes to Israel without a license. Four defendants were found guilty and received lenient sentences; Greenspun and two others were found not guilty. This enabled him to return to his growing family, which now included a daughter, Janie, and his job as a publicist for the Desert Inn, which was a success from its opening on April 24, 1950. But Greenspun found himself chafing under Dalitz's power, and his legal troubles were far from over. He faced a second trial, set to begin on July 6, 1950, for violating the Neutrality Act by running guns and ammunition to Israel. This time, at the request of defense attorneys who feared the effect of having to divulge the heretofore anonymous sources of his funding, Greenspun pled guilty and received a $10,000 fine. "But the conviction meant the loss of my right to vote, . . . [which] cut deeply, leaving me with the incomplete feeling of one who had just lost an arm or a leg."

Even amid his legal problems, Greenspun put himself in a position to influence people and events in ways that his one vote never could have approached and to become widely heralded—and feared—as one of the most powerful men in Nevada. From the time he had arrived in Las Vegas, Greenspun had resented the power and policies of the town's only daily newspaper, the *Evening Review-Journal*. Born as the *Clark County Review* in 1909, it ran second to the slightly older, Republican *Las Vegas Age*. It became prosperous only after veteran mining-camp newspaperman Frank Garside bought the *Review* in 1926 and imported Albert E. Cahlan from northern Nevada as his editor. Within three years, Cahlan added his younger brother John as managing editor and turned the weekly into the town's first daily. During the 1930s and 1940s, Al Cahlan wielded influence in state and local affairs as a politician (assemblyman and national Democratic committeeman), an editorial voice in behalf of a stream of public works projects and improvements, a Colorado

River commissioner, a partner in several major local investments, and an ally of Senator Pat McCarran, whose interests the Cahlans served behind the scenes and in print as they turned the paper into an organ for the powerful Democrat.

With the postwar boom in Las Vegas came major changes in local journalism. By 1947, the *Evening Review-Journal* had swallowed the weekly *Age*. In 1949, seeking new capital and the paper's expansion, Cahlan engineered the sale of Garside's interest to Donald W. Reynolds, who was building a media empire of broadcasting outlets and newspapers in small and medium-sized towns throughout the Southwest. While Reynolds improved the *Evening Review-Journal*'s physical plant, he also inadvertently created a competitor: When his typesetters joined the International Typographical Union, he refused to negotiate, and his employees left to start their own triweekly, the *Las Vegas Free Press*. And Cahlan, who had disliked the old power structure in Reno as he went on to become part of the new power structure in Las Vegas, would find another editor seeking influence.

That editor would be Greenspun. He detested both the *Review-Journal*, which he considered racist, anti-Semitic, and antiunion, and McCarran, its ally. Nor had he been pleased when Moe Dalitz, alluding to the evening daily's power and its connection to McCarran, tried to stop him from advertising the Desert Inn in the *Free Press*, whose printers were looking for a buyer. Greenspun was their man. He made the $1,000 down payment with money borrowed from Nate Mack, a longtime Las Vegas investor who was Jewish and sympathized with his efforts in behalf of Israel. Greenspun took over the union sheet on June 21, 1950, with the customary publisher's salutation, which mixed a call for journalistic competition with a promise:

> I pledge that I will always fight for progress and reform; never tolerate injustice or corruption; never lack sympathy with the underprivileged; always remain devoted to the public welfare; never be satisfied with merely printing news; always be drastically independent.
>
> I will always uphold the liberal laws of the state of Nevada, and I will remain dedicated to the people of Southern Nevada because the people are always right.

On July 1, Greenspun rechristened the newspaper the *Las Vegas Sun* and expanded it to a five-day-a-week schedule. It employed several longtime and neophyte reporters—veteran Las Vegans such as Ray Germain and Ed Oncken, former *Review-Journal* hands, and newcomer Adam Yacenda, a veteran New York and California newspaperman—who went after stories that the older daily had ignored because of its editors' connections and their belief that publishing bad news about the city would be bad for the city.

The pugnacious attitude and writing of its publisher also contributed to the *Sun*'s success. The day before Greenspun took over, Al Cahlan's editorial-page column, "From Where I Sit," lamented the deleterious effects of strikes on business. Believing this article and others to have been aimed at him, Greenspun wrote a rebuttal, "From Where I Stand." When his composing-room staff accidentally dropped the word *From,* Greenspun's own front-page column was born. For four decades, "Where I Stand" featured his "primitive, pungent, and unpredictable prose." Greenspun shared Cahlan's desire for growth and development and often consulted with his counterpart when either had a story that might create problems and unrest. But Greenspun understood that to compete, he had to be different. The result was a news-paper war that enhanced Greenspun's power and reputation, even nationally, while providing Las Vegans with a daily dose of entertainment and two vastly different versions of what was really happening in their city.

One key difference between Greenspun and Cahlan was over McCarran. "The most difficult of all pursuits is to break into a newspaper field where a monopoly exists, unless you have something so different, so outstanding, that it can succeed despite everything. I did everything wrong and it turned out right. I didn't like Pat McCarran's Nevada. . . . And I said so," Greenspun said. Conceding that he had no need or desire to parrot the *Review-Journal,* he also "saw in McCarran what my old mentor, Fiorello LaGuardia, had seen in Tammany Hall: a political machine bent on throttling all opposition, de-stroying democratic processes, dictating policy, and thriving on the pro-ceeds." He resented what he called McCarran's "crude anti-Semitic jibe" at Senator Herbert Lehman of New York—a reference to the "cloak-and-suit" crowd—when he was passing a restrictive immigration bill. While McCarran encountered opposition from other editors, none fought with the vehemence of Greenspun, who called him the "old buzzard," assailed businessmen and politicians tied to his machine, and alleged all manner of corruption, espe-cially in the gaming industry, already reeling from the probe by Senator Estes Kefauver's Special Committee to Investigate Organized Crime in Inter-state Commerce. In 1952, Greenspun supported another Nevada newcomer, Thomas Mechling, in the Democratic Senate primary against Alan Bible, McCarran's political protégé, and he turned up the heat on the senator when Mechling won the primary but lost the general election after McCarran opposed him. Senator George Malone, a Republican, won reelection.

Smarting from the attacks, McCarran struck back. On March 20, 1952, two casino owners warned Greenspun to back off. Four days later, almost every casino in Las Vegas canceled its advertising in the *Sun;* Greenspun's friend Benny Binion, who owned the Horseshoe, refused to join them, so the publisher pulled the ad to protect him. Greenspun raced to the Desert Inn and asked Dalitz what was going on. "You should know. Why did you have to attack the Old Man?" he replied, pointing out that McCarran and his machine controlled the state licensing apparatus. The *Sun* learned that a phone call from Washington to Thunderbird owner Marion Hicks had led to a meeting of the casino owners and an agreement, as one of them put it, to "bust" Greenspun. He countered by suing McCarran and about forty gaming executives, charging conspiracy and demanding $225,000. When Greenspun produced evidence of the key phone call instigating the boycott, attorneys for the gamblers agreed to a settlement of $80,500 and continued advertising in the *Sun.*

The case proved extremely important to Nevada history and politics, then and later. It ensured that Greenspun's venomous exchanges would go on with the *Review-Journal,* with Cahlan and his staff, and with reactionary syndicated columnist Westbrook Pegler, who exhumed Greenspun's employment with Siegel and accused him of receiving more than $1 million for shipping arms to Israel. Greenspun responded by attacking "the unprincipled, whiskey-sodden tramp with a typewriter," and welcomed the help of another national columnist, muckraker Drew Pearson, who was published in the *Review-Journal*—except when he was critical of McCarran. Greenspun's courtroom victory nicked McCarran's armor: Although the senator was, technically, accused of nothing in the end, he clearly had lost; and it had happened in the courtroom of one of his appointees, U.S. district judge Roger T. Foley. The result ensured that the *Sun* would keep attacking the senator, not only because the case revealed, and the settlement increased, McCarran's hatred for Greenspun (the Internal Revenue Service reviewed Greenspun's tax returns, and the Federal Bureau of Investigation produced a nasty report on him, thanks to McCarran's friend and ally, J. Edgar Hoover), but also because the advertising made the paper's survival more certain. It also meant that Greenspun had arrived on the Las Vegas scene, an unpredictable but powerful force to be reckoned with.

While Greenspun was shaking up the state, he won national renown and respect for his stand against a staunch McCarran ally, Senator Joseph McCarthy of Wisconsin. When McCarthy came to Las Vegas on October 13, 1952, to campaign for the Republican ticket, including Dwight Eisenhower and Senator Malone, he already had held the nation in thrall for more than two years with his bogus claims that Communists had overrun the federal government under Democratic rule. A Republican until he lost his right to vote, and previously a staunch Eisenhower supporter, Greenspun disagreed with McCarthy's tactics, and he issued a blistering welcome to the visitor:

> McCarthy has contributed absolutely nothing to checking the communist conspiracy in this country. He has, however, furthered this conspiracy by establishing a new pattern of recklessness and irresponsibility in American public life. He has spread suspicion and fear among the people and by these very acts has weakened our defenses against the dangers of communism. . . .
>
> Any Republican candidate who sits upon the same platform with Joe McCarthy endorses his vicious demagoguery. They condone his lies and deceit, and glory in his evil.

That night, McCarthy initiated an exchange that helped elevate Greenspun to the rank of hero among civil libertarians of the time. He called Greenspun, who was in the audience, an admitted "ex-communist"—a lie and a mistake, since he meant to say "ex-convict," and thus a slander, told without the immunity that he enjoyed on the Senate floor. Greenspun rushed the stage and rebutted the departing McCarthy, capturing the crowd. From then on, aware that a lawsuit from McCarthy would give him the opportunity to countersue, Greenspun went on the offensive. Using material that Pearson had turned up in Washington but lacked the freedom to print, Greenspun wrote a series of columns asking, "Is Senator McCarthy a Secret Communist?" and questioning McCarthy's sexual preferences: "It is common talk among homosexuals in Milwaukee . . . that Senator Joe McCarthy has often engaged in homosexual activities. The persons in Nevada who listened to McCarthy's radio talk thought he had the queerest laugh. He has. He is." Charging McCarthy with corruption and condoning Communism and Nazism, Greenspun called him "the scabrous, slimy, loathsome thing," a "scheming swashbuckler," a "sadistic pervert," and "the queer that made Milwaukee famous."

On January 8, 1954, Greenspun published a typically anti-McCarthy column, with an atypical result:

> I've never been one to make predictions but when a thing is inevitable, even I can foresee the future.
>
> Sen. Joe McCarthy has come to a violent end. Huey Long's death will be serene and peaceful compared with the demise of the sadistic bum from Wisconsin.
>
> Live by the sword and you die by the sword! Destroy people and

they in turn must destroy you! The chances are that McCarthy will eventually be laid to rest at the hands of some poor innocent slob whose reputation and life he has destroyed through his well-established smear technique. . . .

Really, I'm against Joe getting his head blown off, not because I do not believe in capital punishment or because he does not have it coming, but I would hate to see some simpleton get the chair for such a public service as getting rid of McCarthy.

As a result, the federal government, at McCarthy's behest, prosecuted Greenspun for "tending to incite murder and assassination." In 1955, a federal jury in Las Vegas acquitted him. By then, McCarthy himself was in decline, and would die in 1957, moving Greenspun to write, "No flowers, please! . . . Send the money to the rehabilitation fund for victims of McCarthy's recklessness and demagoguery."

Greenspun's attacks obviously were vituperative—but for a reason. "Sure I called him a faggot. Maybe he was," he later said. "He was as much a homosexual as the hundred homosexuals he said worked in the State Department, [the evidence of] which he never produced. It was fighting the devil with fire." The situation paralleled his battle with McCarran. Greenspun understood that he was free to attack McCarthy, and that gentlemanly remonstrances were useless. In the process, he gained a great deal of national attention, which fed his local power. And McCarran's death, in the midst of these events, left a leadership vacuum to be filled by, among others, Greenspun. He did not run a machine, but his paper had influence—muckraking and serving as a civic conscience, according to his friends, or flexing its muscle, according to his enemies.

While Greenspun had clearly helped Mechling defeat Bible in 1952, the 1954 gubernatorial election would demonstrate the extent of the publisher's potential power. Republican Charles Russell sought reelection against Vail Pittman, whom he had defeated four years before when the McCarran machine put personal enmity toward Pittman above party and aided Russell. This time, however, McCarran and the Cahlans backed the Democrat. Indeed, it was while making a speech in Hawthorne in support of party unity on September 28, 1954, that McCarran died of a heart attack.

As Democrats sought an elusive unity, Greenspun had his own problems. He had family concerns: an automobile accident that left him in a body cast, an illness to daughter Susan, and the impending birth of son Danny. Of more interest to the community and its press, was an FBI raid on Roxie's, a Las Vegas brothel, in April 1954. Clark County sheriff Glen Jones then followed suit. The *Sun* charged that Jones had let Roxie's stay open because he was receiving payoffs, and threw in for good measure a front-page photo of Jones on a bicycle, with the caption, "Sheriff Glen Jones pedaling a little on his own." In turn, Jones filed a $1 million libel suit against Greenspun, whose key witness went before the grand jury and, the publisher wrote, "developed wide lapses of memory and almost no powers of speech." Facing a courtroom and financial defeat, Greenspun and reporter Ed Reid helped conduct a sting operation. They hired private detective Pierre LaFitte to pose as hoodlum Louis Tabet, who wanted to buy some Las Vegas properties, and set him up in a Strip hotel; then Reid and a deputy district attorney hid in the closet and recorded what went on in the suite.

They heard and taped a lot. The owners of Roxie's told Tabet that Sheriff Jones had been on their payroll. Besides reaching agreements with the sheriff and County Commissioner Rodney Colton on payoffs, Tabet hired a law firm, Jones, Wiener, and Jones. The Joneses (no relation to the sheriff) were Cliff and Herb, the brothers of Florence Lee Jones, a longtime *Review-Journal* reporter married to John Cahlan. When Cliff Jones, the outgoing lieutenant governor and a partner in the Thunderbird Hotel, met the would-be buyer, he welcomed the news that Tabet planned to buy the *Sun,* bragged about his influence at the *Review-Journal,* and promised that after Pittman's election, he would control the Nevada Tax Commission, which issued gaming licenses.

When the *Sun* printed the story, the ramifications were enormous. Glen Jones dropped his suit, Cliff Jones resigned as Democratic national committeeman, Pittman's defense of his fellow Democrat cost him support and aided Russell's reelection, and the Nevada Tax Commission investigated the Thunderbird. Eventually, Cliff Jones and other gaming operators pushed a bill through the legislature to emasculate the state's power over gaming control; when Russell vetoed it, the legislature came within one vote of overriding him. The entire affair also showed Greenspun's power. What began as an attempt to gather evidence for a lawsuit mushroomed, and Greenspun reveled in the embarrassment of his competitors. However, in unhorsing several corrupt leaders, he and the *Sun* performed a public service and did much to preserve gaming enforcement. And he clearly established himself not just as a gadfly, but as a big-time player on the political scene.

In the 1950s and early 1960s, Greenspun also was publishing an interesting, entertaining, often good newspaper. His managing editor, Yacenda, was a veteran newsman. His staff was excellent, breaking many stories, and many of them went on to long and productive careers in local journalism, advertising, and politics. Bryn Armstrong spent fifteen years as executive editor; one of his city editors, Noel Greenwood, would become deputy managing editor of the *Los Angeles Times*. In 1954, Greenspun added Ruthe Deskin, his details person and organizer for more than three decades and still an important part of the *Sun* in 1997. Deskin was also longtime director of the *Sun* Youth Forum, an annual event that gathers local high school students to discuss current issues. The *Sun* also was very much a family operation, with Greenspun's siblings and brothers-in-law holding various positions.

In years to come, Greenspun's influence grew, inside and outside journalism, and his opponents would question whether he exercised that influence responsibly. Greenspun and the *Sun* reported various allegations of corruption involving George Franklin, a Las Vegas attorney who also would serve as North Las Vegas city attorney and Clark County district attorney. Franklin sued for libel and, after a series of legal maneuvers on both sides, received legal expenses and no more, due to a technicality. Greenspun also invested wisely. He helped start the city's first television station, KLAS-TV-8 in 1953, and snapped up land. He built the Paradise Valley Country Club and bought several thousand acres in Henderson. He received two loans from the Teamsters Central States Pension Fund, controlled by Jimmy Hoffa, the union boss accused of organized-crime ties and corruption whom Greenspun defended as a friend to Las Vegas and to Israel.

Greenspun also was active in state politics and policies. In the late 1950s and early 1960s, he was a powerful force for civil rights in his "Where I Stand" column and behind the scenes, working with Governor Grant Sawyer, Las Vegas mayor Oran Gragson, and local African American leaders to help desegregate the Las Vegas Strip—a move to cure a social ill and improve the business climate. In 1958, his early endorsement of Sawyer helped the Democrat beat back Russell's quest for a third term. While Greenspun hailed Sawyer's support for civil rights and tougher gaming enforcement, he grew to consider the governor too cozy with the casino operators he was supposed to be regulating, and became an ardent critic.

In 1962, on the heels of his pardon by President John F. Kennedy and restoration of his civil rights, Greenspun entered the political fray himself. Several friends appealed to him to run for governor, but he declined: "Too many newspapers have been destroyed by publishers with political ambitions. This I will never permit, for this paper means more to me than all the rewards which high office can bring." More pragmatically, he knew that Lieutenant Governor Rex Bell, a popular Republican, would challenge Sawyer. But when Bell died of a heart attack on July 4, two Republicans filed in the primary: Gragson and Greenspun. While joking "I hadn't voted for all of ten years and I liked the idea of voting for myself," he contended that Nevada needed a

governor "who would neither pussyfoot, pass the buck, nor dodge artfully."
Despite a hard-working campaign in which he targeted the governor more
than Gragson, Greenspun lost to his primary opponent, 16,538 to 9,176. Not
surprisingly, his detractors came out in force: the *Review-Journal* attacked
him unremittingly; pamphlets accused him of excessive ambition and, ironically, compared him with McCarthy; and the gaming industry strained every
nerve to defeat him. Dalitz told a reporter, "Hank Greenspun says it cost a
quarter of a million? Hah, it cost almost twice that, but we got results! Why,
we threw the money away like water." It would be Greenspun's only foray
into politics, which, he admitted, was not his "field."

Greenspun may have abandoned elective politics, but he remained a force,
even if events in the early 1960s worked against his paper. With the *Sun*
gaining on the *Review-Journal*, Reynolds forced out the Cahlans and imported as his editor Robert L. Brown, a former reporter for United Press
International who met the *Sun*'s challenge by building up the paper's staff
and circulation. Bidding an unexpectedly fond farewell to the Cahlans (later,
Al Cahlan wrote his column for the *Sun*), Greenspun focused on Reynolds,
writing, "His credo is the buck and his methods are destructive. He absorbs
competition or liquidates it. And he approaches all battles with the ferocity of
a bellowing bull and the morals of the head skull crusher in a Chicago
slaughterhouse." But Greenspun soon suffered a crushing blow himself. On
November 20, 1963, the *Sun*'s building on South Main Street burned. Although he rebuilt it with a modern publishing facility, the *Review-Journal*
had opened a large lead in advertising and circulation and never looked back.
Nonetheless, while his newspaper ran an increasingly distant second, Greenspun's personal influence only increased, because of his crusading instincts, as
friends said, or his willingness to use the *Sun* for his own purposes, as detractors contended.

The debate over Greenspun's motives increased after Howard Hughes's
arrival changed the face of Las Vegas and expanded Greenspun's bank account. When Hughes occupied two floors of the Desert Inn on Thanksgiving
weekend in 1966, he took up space that might have been more profitably
occupied by high-roller gamblers; asked to leave, Hughes instead bought the
hotel and went on a spree, buying several other resorts and adding to his
already vast land holdings. He also wanted to be able to watch movies on
television all night, prompting him to buy Channel 8 from Greenspun (who
wrapped the check, reportedly for $3.6 million, in his copy of the *Sun* and
temporarily misplaced it). In 1967, Hughes loaned Greenspun $4 million at 3
percent interest to be repaid within eight years—to make up for a deal gone

sour that led Greenspun to buy 2,500 acres southeast of Las Vegas. Hughes, who certainly had no financial worries, had wanted the loan to be interest-free. The loan was later recast to be payable at the turn of the century, and Hughes gave the *Sun* a prepaid, fifteen-year advertising contract for $500,000. Greenspun later said, "He might have *thought* he bought my editorial policy."

If so, Hughes would prove mistaken. For a while, he clearly enjoyed Greenspun's support. The publisher lobbied state gaming regulators in his behalf and welcomed Hughes into gaming. "I thought he'd be good for Las Vegas, good for Nevada," because while Greenspun refrained from excessive criticism of the town's main industry, he also welcomed any means of reducing the "suspect elements" who populated it. The 1960s had been difficult for the state's "peculiar institution": FBI chief Hoover and Attorney General Robert Kennedy had stepped up federal efforts to find out what hidden interests influenced gaming, and Nevada's already dubious image had been tarnished even more by the publication of such critical books as *The Green Felt Jungle* and *Nevada: The Great Rotten Borough*. Although Greenspun had long employed co-author Ed Reid and had criticized some of the book's subjects, the *Sun* publisher objected to the portrait painted in *The Green Felt Jungle* and appeared with Reid and others on David Suskind's *Open End* talk show to dispute it. In keeping with the state's efforts to combat bad publicity, Greenspun also confessed to sitting on the story of Hughes's arrival in Las Vegas: "I knew he was coming to Nevada. I knew that any publicity in the press might frighten him away because he left Boston for that very reason. . . . He wanted his privacy and every person is entitled to a certain amount of privacy, unless he's breaking the law, of course." His explanation might displease reporters, but it reflected his concept of his role in the community. His thinking also contributed mightily to the growth of Las Vegas and helps explain why he often refrained from criticizing the gaming industry and such contributors to it as Hoffa and the Teamsters:

> I'm not only a newsman, I'm a publisher and an editor. I have to weigh what is best for the community. That's a publisher's job. This community was small. It looked to the editor to provide a livelihood for the citizens of this community. In my judgment at the time, it was in the best interest of Nevada that he come and settle here because of his wealth and his intentions.

But in 1970, when Hughes fired Greenspun's friend Robert Maheu, until then his right-hand man, and left for Nassau, the publisher obtained about two hundred of the memoranda in which Hughes had written instructions to his subordinates. Now "I could see what kind of guy he was," and Greenspun began to assail the Hughes interests in his column. His actions also won notice outside Nevada: The Committee to Re-Elect the President, formed to run Richard Nixon's campaign in 1972 and responsible for the Watergate break-in, feared that the memos contained information about shady financial dealings between Hughes and the Nixon family (especially the president's brother, Donald) and hoped that they included dirt on Nixon's opponents. While Greenspun was on vacation in August 1972, his office was broken into, but whoever did it proved unable to crack the safe where the memos were stored. Whatever his role in Watergate—some participants believed that the connection was clear—Greenspun understood the impact of the Hughes years. He appreciated the new aura of respectability that Hughes brought to gaming and thus to Las Vegas, but he wrote: "It is a little late but I must freely accept blame for helping create [Hughes's domination]. I had prostituted my newspaper sufficiently in Hughes' interest and would have no more of it."

While feuding with the Hughes interests, Greenspun also found that time, and the community growth he had encouraged, were playing a trick on him: A new, underdog competitor appeared to accuse him of the kind of hunger for power that he had complained about in the Cahlans. Alternately with Greenspun's help and opposition, Yacenda built his own triweekly paper, the *North Las Vegas Valley Times.* Declining health forced him to sell it in 1973 to Bob Brown, who decided to expand the *Valley Times* to a daily, serving Las Vegas. Brown trained his sights on Greenspun, whom he accused of using the *Sun* as a "blackjack to advance his own personal ends" and of seeking to rule Nevada, and he briefly enjoyed advertising from Hughes's Summa Corporation. The *Sun* countered with references to a "scandal sheet" and in 1978 broke a story that accused Brown of a form of journalistic extortion: telling Robert List, then running for governor, that he would withhold a damaging story if List would support a gaming license for Frank Rosenthal, a Stardust Hotel executive with ties to organized crime. Brown denied the story. By the early 1980s, though, when another fire closed the plant and the *Times* let the *Sun* use its presses, Greenspun proved more sympathetic toward Brown, whose journalistic ability he admired enough to have tried to hire him in the 1960s, and concentrated his attacks on the *Review-Journal* and publisher Donald Reynolds.

By then, Greenspun was financially and politically secure. In the late 1970s, his American Nevada Corporation began developing some of his holdings into Green Valley, the area's first master-planned suburb; by the mid-1990s, its growth turned Henderson into Nevada's third-largest city, behind

Las Vegas and Reno. He obtained the contract for a local cable-television service, and Dimension Cable, later Prime Cable, became a multimillion-dollar company. And his crusades amply showed his muscle. The *Sun*'s exposure of wrongdoing by other candidates helped elect Mike O'Callaghan to two terms as governor, in 1970 and 1974. No one could accuse Greenspun of partisanship, since he was a Republican and O'Callaghan a Democrat. When the popular governor left office, he joined the Greenspuns and Deskin in running the paper. Although not a journalist by training, O'Callaghan provided the *Sun* with a Democratic voice and additional contacts in that party. Despite his loyalties, however, neither he nor Greenspun expressed blatantly partisan views. While the *Sun* remained far behind the *Review-Journal* and failed to show a profit, it constituted the locus of Greenspun's political power.

Events in the late 1970s and 1980s led increasingly to charges that Greenspun used his paper, not, as he said, because he was "an honest fighter who does what he thinks is best for the community," but "as a bludgeon to build and maintain power in Nevada." Friends and enemies cited his stormy relations with the federal government as a case in point. While Greenspun enjoyed good relations with Ronald Reagan, mainly because the publisher saw him as a friend of Israel, he also stepped up his opposition to federal policies and tactics toward Nevada during Reagan's administration. Part of this was because of, and manifested itself in, Nevada's role in nuclear power. In the 1950s, Greenspun had championed the Nevada Test Site and its above-ground detonations. But the more that became known about what the federal government knew of the dangers and failed to disclose, the more Greenspun questioned both the government and the industry. He crusaded against a privately owned nuclear repository near Beatty and federal efforts to locate a national, high-level waste dump at Yucca Mountain—in the latter case, contributing mightily to a cause that has long survived him.

Greenspun also resented the federal government's treatment of Nevada. He had fought for many years with the Internal Revenue Service, personally over his own taxes and journalistically over what he saw as its singling out of gaming-industry employers and employees. For years, the *Sun* offered free legal representation to anyone battling the IRS. But his biggest fight involved the FBI and, eventually, the case of U.S. district judge Harry Claiborne, accused of filing false tax returns. Greenspun believed that Joseph Yablonsky, the FBI's agent-in-charge in Las Vegas, was out to get Claiborne as part of a broader federal vendetta against Nevada. Greenspun objected to "Yobo," an FBI sting operation against several of the state's politicians, which critics considered entrapment. He also questioned federal efforts to obtain incriminating testimony against Claiborne from Joe Conforte, who owned the Mustang Ranch brothel near Reno and whose own tax debts the government forgave, although his contribution to the federal investigation proved useless. Amid stories accusing Yablonsky of misconduct that might lead to Reagan and his attorney general, William French Smith, Greenspun told one interviewer, "A federal judge is being hanged by a pimp. It's outrageous."

While Claiborne was guilty—he had, after all, filed the returns—Greenspun stood by him, emphasizing the larger constitutional issues involving the federal government. During Claiborne's trial in Reno before visiting federal judge Walter Hoffman, Greenspun, sometimes accompanied by his son Brian, was a courtroom regular. He positioned a *Sun* news rack outside the courthouse; at one point, Judge Hoffman bought up the day's copies and ordered the rack removed because he felt that the *Sun*'s pro-Claiborne coverage might influence the jury. Later, Claiborne became the first federal judge since the Civil War to be impeached by the House and convicted by the Senate for high crimes and misdemeanors while in office, and he served a brief term in federal prison. For his part, Greenspun maintained a steady drumbeat of criticism of the federal case and those behind it, saying, "Everyone is entitled to due process. Claiborne never got that. No man should be unfairly targeted." Not only did banner headlines and "Where I Stand" columns praise Claiborne's stand against the federal government and allege federal wrongdoing, but after Yablonsky retired from the FBI, he claimed that Greenspun's threats kept local businessmen from giving him a job.

Another controversy involved Las Vegas businessman Milton Schwartz. The *Sun* crusaded against the presence of potentially explosive propane gas at his taxi company's headquarters until Schwartz moved the tank, at considerable expense and after considerable public debate. Schwartz charged that Hank and Brian Greenspun complained about the tank, not because they were concerned about public safety, but because they were financial competitors: He owned a competing cable-television firm. He and other critics of the Greenspuns also pointed to a cable-television deregulation bill that the state legislature passed in 1983, claiming that this measure was aimed at Schwartz and accusing the *Sun* and its owners of threatening lawmakers who balked at voting for it. The Greenspuns dismissed the charges. Eventually, Schwartz sued the *Sun* for libel and lost.

That kind of controversy and criticism were characteristic of Greenspun and the *Sun* in the 1970s and 1980s. The publisher had indeed accumulated great power and wealth—as much, in some cases, as those he once had attacked, prompting friends and enemies alike to suggest that the combination made him more conservative and less interested in serving the public, a charge with which Greenspun heatedly disagreed. The *Sun* remained the cornerstone of Greenspun's power in Nevada, a bully pulpit important enough for him to turn down lucrative offers to sell it, including at least one from Rupert Murdoch. Yet Greenspun's newspaper clearly was in decline; it had never been a large moneymaker, and the red ink was rising rapidly. Despite Greenspun's frequent attacks on the Audit Bureau of Circulation, which he accused of toying with the numbers because Reynolds's Donrey Media Group had representation on its board, the *Review-Journal* enjoyed a large lead over the *Sun* in readership. Low salaries, including cuts, meant that the *Sun* kept some loyalists but lost many talented young reporters and editors to the *Review-Journal* or, more often, to out-of-town papers. Greenspun responded to critics that his staff's salaries were comparable to those at similarly sized papers and that "no man has ever been drowned in sweat." Family friends and longtime columnists dotted the *Sun,* and his favorite people received favorable treatment: Binion, Frank Sinatra, and, in a reversal of form, Dalitz, whose advancing age, stature in the community, and dedication to charitable causes and Israel softened Greenspun's view of him. Unlike many chain or corporate newspapers, the *Sun* remained a reflection of its publisher's dynamic personality.

Greenspun remained active and interested in the *Sun* but played a less visible part in its operations in the 1980s than he had before, mainly because the transition to another generation had begun. While Deskin remained and O'Callaghan bridged the gap, Greenspun's sons became *Sun* executives and assumed larger roles—Danny in production and technology, Brian in business and editorial—in addition to their involvement in the family's land and cable-television investments. Greenspun's sons were less involved in crusades than their father had been, and a new cadre of younger editors and writers had stepped in, bringing different standards and less of a desire for personal journalism. After many years of struggling to establish himself and his paper, Greenspun clearly had succeeded. Additionally, Greenspun was one of Nevada's most powerful figures and renowned citizens, and accordingly reaped rewards: not just financial benefits, but honorary degrees and awards and recognition from the federal government and the increasingly strong nation of Israel. Finally, Greenspun was growing older, albeit not altogether gracefully, which was as he preferred it. He remained a character as interesting and important—often more so—as those of whom he long had written, and a player, if often a cantankerous one, still relishing a good fight.

Inevitably, Greenspun's last fight proved unsuccessful and helped prompt the end to a different kind of battle. On July 22, 1989, a month shy of his eightieth birthday, he died of stomach cancer, from which he had suffered for about eighteen months. His funeral reflected the town he had helped to make. Joined by politicians and gamblers, rich and poor, Greenspun's children and O'Callaghan remembered a fighter for causes who maintained a "Magic Closet" in his office to give toys to any child who visited him. In his last months, Greenspun had been involved in negotiating a joint operating agreement (JOA), which the *Review-Journal* and the *Sun* announced shortly after his death. The Department of Justice permits JOAs between competing newspapers when one of them would otherwise be unable to survive financially—in this case, the *Sun*, which was losing as much as $3 million a year. The *Sun* retained its editorial independence, but at a price: It would shift to the declining afternoon market while the *Review-Journal* moved to the more lucrative morning; they would issue combined weekend and holiday editions; and the *Review-Journal* would be responsible for advertising and circulation, in exchange for a 10 percent interest, possibly worth $30 million, in the Greenspun family's highly profitable cable-television business. The two papers would continue to snipe at each other—some of Brian Greenspun's "Where I Stand" columns and various news stories showed that the old antagonism survived—and *Sun* reporters reveled in their ability to beat the *Review-Journal* on many local news stories. But the real war was over; as in most cities, one morning daily would dominate the market. Greenspun often had been called the last of the "personal journalists"—editors and publishers who stamped their personality on their product. And so he may have been. His publication survived him, but in a vastly different form.

That the *Sun* faced a mixed future reflected Hank Greenspun's mixed legacy. He earned countless accolades, and deservedly so, but as Greenspun cheerfully conceded, he was no saint. He maintained journalistic competition in a community that desperately needed it and created a crusading newspaper, but his crusades often sparked criticism that he was looking out for his own interests. He was, in many ways, a pioneer—builder of the Las Vegas area's first master-planned suburb, owner or co-owner of the city's first television station and first major cable-television system, participant in the creation and success of the Strip's first two plush resorts—but in providing extremely favorable coverage of Howard Hughes and attacking potential business competitors in the *Sun,* he raised doubts in the minds of many of his critics about his fairness. He challenged the political machine of Pat McCarran and triumphed over it, then became a kingmaker himself and heard directed at him charges similar to those he had directed at McCarran. Yet he won deserved national renown and respect when he questioned and assailed the witch-hunt led by Joseph McCarthy, understanding the need to fight fire with fire. And in an age of chain ownership of newspapers and of publishers interested in profits and in avoiding boat-rocking, he used the *Sun* as a forum and an agent of change. That epitomized Greenspun: From childhood through war, when his city's reputation was tarnished and when the need to desegregate Las Vegas had long since arrived, and especially when the existence of a Jewish homeland was in danger, he stood up for his beliefs, risking life, limb, and reputation.

Greenspun was a man of the past, present, and future. As a publisher, chewing an expensive cigar as he pounded out his columns on a 1950s Underwood typewriter while his reporters worked at computer terminals, he was a throwback to the earlier journalists whose personality permeated the headlines and news stories in their newspapers, in Nevada and elsewhere. Despite the criticisms he received from Las Vegans who believed the *Sun*'s reporting in the 1950s hurt the community, he did a great deal to make Las Vegas a more modern city. His support for civil rights changed the local social structure for the better, although not enough, and less than he would have liked. His stance against entrenched powers like McCarran and gaming and in favor of Hughes contributed to the rise of corporate gaming—and, indeed, to the evolution of Las Vegas into a more family-oriented resort mecca. His investments in cable television and Green Valley reflected the work of a businessman who was far shrewder than he received credit for being, but they were also visionary. His family's endowment of the Greenspun School of Communications at the University of Nevada, Las Vegas, the *Sun* Youth Forum, the *Sun* Summer Camp Fund for needy children, and the naming of the Barbara and Hank Greenspun Junior High School reflect his interest in education and preference for looking ahead rather than back, as Las Vegas, long a transient community, struggles to create a sense of community among a rapidly expanding populace of recent arrivals and often tends to exalt the future at the expense of the past.

Thus did Greenspun reflect and lead his time and place. Indeed, when Greenspun was seriously ill, Brian Greenspun took him to look at Green Valley and, as they toured the burgeoning area, asked his father whether he ever expected that kind of growth. Yes, he replied. His son recalled, "I said, 'You did not.' He said, 'I did, but I expected my great-grandchildren to be the ones to see it.'" Like the other leaders of postwar Las Vegas, he hoped to create a city out of a town, and they succeeded beyond their wildest dreams. Like his city, he could be a hustler, an opportunist, a man on the make, unswervingly loyal to friends and devastating to enemies. He used his newspaper to build his city and build himself, and both were the better for it. Whatever Hank Greenspun's faults, whatever the controversy that surrounded him, O'Callaghan's eulogy was correct: "His almost 80 years . . . made this a better world." Without him, Las Vegas and Nevada would not be what they are—and they most assuredly would have been much less interesting.

Alan Bible

The Politics of Stewardship

BY PATRICIA ANDREW

In his oral history, "Reflections of a Nevada Native Son," Alan Bible recounts that one evening in 1918 as he and his family were returning to their small ranch from a picture show in Lovelock, they spotted what they thought to be the aurora borealis lighting up the sky. When they got closer to home, they realized that the brilliance in the sky providing them enjoyment was their house burning. Tragically, there was little chance of putting out the fire: The water available from a nearby irrigation ditch was pitifully inadequate for the task.

With their home destroyed, the Bibles pulled up stakes and moved to the nearby town of Fallon. With an abundance of water, Fallon was a virtual oasis in the desert, thanks largely to the efforts of Congressman Francis Newlands. Sixteen years earlier, Newlands had secured federal funds to support water projects to turn the bleak desert surrounding Fallon into productive farming area. Although it was impossible to know at the time, Alan Bible would come to do more throughout his career as state attorney general, private attorney, and U.S. senator to bring water to the parched state of Nevada than any other person, including the highly lauded Newlands. Like Newlands, Bible realized that the sparsely populated state could, on its own, ill afford water projects of the magnitude that created Fallon. Federal involvement and financial assistance were essential.

The Bible family had come from Germany and settled in Virginia, but prior to the Civil War Alan's grandfather Harrison moved to Ohio. He then chose to join the Union army, a decision that precluded any future relationship with the family remaining in Virginia. After Harrison Bible returned to Ohio from the war, his son Jacob, Alan's father, ran away from home and joined the stream of prospectors headed west. Like other emigrants who failed to strike it rich in California, Jacob ended up in Nevada, finding employment on a ranch near Lovelock. Later, in order to earn money to buy his own ranch, he began working in the local grocery store. His gold fever

7

never waned, and although Jacob supported his family as a rancher and grocer, his son speculated that his father preferred to be out prospecting.

Jacob married Isabel Welch, a young woman of Scottish-Irish ancestry whom he met in Lovelock. Alan was told by his mother that her father had been a professor at the University of Edinburgh, Scotland, before immigrating to Nevada and settling in Unionville, a typical Nevada boom-and-bust mining town north of Lovelock. Perhaps her father's background instilled in Isabel, the only girl in a family of six children, a desire for learning, for she was well educated for the times. She attended the University of Nevada in Reno for two years prior to returning to Lovelock to teach, and later marry Jacob.

Alan Harvey Bible was born in Lovelock in 1909 and lived on the small ranch six miles outside of town until the fire destroyed the family home. He and a younger brother received most of their schooling in Fallon, where Alan first tasted the success of elected office. He was popular with his classmates and was elected president of his freshman and senior classes at Churchill County High School. Years later in his oral history, he could remember many of the names of other students and knew of their achievements. This lifelong concern for his friends and interest in their accomplishments are qualities many people remark upon when describing Alan Bible.

Like many young men with a nascent interest in politics, Bible developed an enduring love of debate. In 1926, he won the state high school oratorical contest and went on to compete, though none too successfully, in the regional championship in California. Coming in last, he took the defeat as a lesson in humility and as a challenge to work harder. In later years, he credited the skills he developed in debate—to seek out information on all sides of an issue and to argue a position forcefully—as providing a foundation for his success in the Senate.

Growing up in Fallon, Bible could not help but be influenced by results of an activist federal government. All around him were lush fields created by irrigation waters coming from the government-financed Lahontan Reservoir, completed in 1915. The area was honeycombed with canals, diversion dams, and ditches designed to carry precious water to turn desert land into productive fields. As he came to political maturity, Bible retained the belief that the federal government should plan, finance, and use science to manage natural resources for the benefit of local residents.

Disappointing his father, who wanted him to stay in Fallon and become a grocer, Bible followed instead in the footsteps of his mother and attended the University of Nevada. There he studied economics, graduating in 1930, intent on becoming an attorney. Because the university had no law school, bright young Nevadans interested in legal careers routinely found their way to Georgetown University Law School in Washington, D.C. Their choice of Georgetown was no doubt influenced considerably by a practice established by Nevada senator William Stewart and continued by subsequent senators: Promising young Nevadans were given the opportunity for employment in the Senate to help finance their legal educations.

Although there is no evidence that Bible knew Patrick McCarran before arriving in Washington, the senator offered him a job as elevator operator one day earlier than Senator Key Pittman. McCarran's assistance and subsequent influence led Bible to a lifetime commitment to the Democratic Party, and the two men enjoyed a long, mutually beneficial association. Years later, following his retirement from the Senate, Bible reflected on the association begun in his youth: "I had a very close relationship with McCarran. He was a dynamic man who had a tremendous following. He was the head man and didn't want anybody interfering. He was the boss and laid down the rules. He taught me you have to build up friends and they have to be loyal."

McCarran invited Bible to join his languishing Nevada law firm upon completion of law school in 1934. McCarran spent considerable time in Washington and had little opportunity to practice law in Nevada, so he planned to use junior lawyers, fresh from Georgetown Law School, to generate legal fees for his firm. Alan Bible was one of the first of several of young men to serve in this capacity. Within a few months after passing the bar in 1935, however, Bible left active participation in McCarran's law firm to begin fulfilling his real life's goal, a career in politics.

Responding to a suggestion by McCarran, the board of supervisors of Storey County appointed Bible to the post of district attorney to complete the unexpired term of W. Howard Gray, who had become deputy attorney general of Nevada. Three years later, Bible followed Gray once more, replacing him as deputy attorney general. With the demands of this appointment, Bible resigned from McCarran's law firm. He subsequently surprised his friends when he announced his candidacy for attorney general in 1942, an election he easily won. He served two terms before returning to private law practice in 1951. During his tenure as attorney general, Bible continued his association with the senator, becoming an integral part of the McCarran machine. He was one of McCarran's legendary "boys."

Bible gained valuable experience in each of the political offices he held. By his own account, he found the small-town politics and the legal demands in Virginia City congenial, calling this period one of the most pleasant in his career. Precluded by poor eyesight from serving in the military during the

Second World War, he enjoyed and flourished in the attorney general's office. It was a small operation, comprising only the attorney general and two deputies, so Bible became well grounded in state law. His work ranged from the nuances of taxation law to economic and social issues.

This period, from 1935 to 1951, spanned the heady days of the New Deal, the Second World War, and the postwar boom, a time of unprecedented change in Nevada and the American West. In the 1930s, the economy of the western United States was based on ranching, mining, and farming; each was deeply affected by the depression. During the Roosevelt years, however, with the passage of the Pittman Silver Purchase Act and the Taylor Grazing Act in 1934, federal economic assistance began to trickle to Nevada's ranchers and miners.

Real transformation of the West occurred when the federal government began investing large sums of money in the development of water resources. These projects not only met the needs of agriculture and growing urban areas but also created an important by-product: hydroelectric power. The pool of surplus electric power attracted government contracts and private investment once the United States entered the Second World War. For Nevada, Hoover Dam symbolized the value of federal investment in the development of water resources.

At the outset of the war, with available water and a government contract to purchase production, the enormous Basic Magnesium Plant was built in Henderson in southern Nevada. Nevada's proximity to the Pacific Ocean, good year-round flying weather, remoteness, and sparsely populated landscape attracted military investment in the form of the large Nellis Air Force Base near Las Vegas, and other bases in Fallon, Tonopah, Stead, and Hawthorne. The economic stimulus provided by these federal military posts produced a crucial impetus for the rapid expansion of the postwar Nevada economy.

By the end of the war a vast westward migration of men and women attracted by the high-paying jobs in war-related industries had taken place. The newcomers were ready to spend freely for entertainment and recreation. Nearby Californians, whose numbers had especially multiplied during the war, turned to Nevada for skiing and hiking in the Sierra Nevada and swimming, boating, and fishing at Lake Mead and Lake Tahoe. They looked as well to Nevada for yet another form of recreation, an industry independent of the traditional cyclical farming and mining industries and with great potential for economic development: gambling. Californians not interested in the outdoor Nevada flocked to the new indoor recreational centers. From his position in the attorney general's office, Bible became convinced that the state's economic development was tied on the one hand to the acquisition of federal funds for water to support anticipated growth and on the other to the careful nurturing of the rapidly growing gaming industry, especially its careful regulation and control. He played a pivotal role in this process.

The Gambling Act of 1931 assigned to Nevada's county governments the primary responsibility for licensing and collecting revenue from gambling establishments. Initially, the state did little to establish a regulatory environment, preferring local control. But it did receive 25 percent of the tax revenue, and a precedent was set: Government services in Nevada would be supported by gambling revenue. By the end of the war, with a growing population requiring additional and expanded services, legislators began reexamining the gambling-revenue split with the counties. Thus, in 1945 they established a new tax on all net gambling revenues and required gambling enterprises to be licensed by the state as well as by the county. They also made the Nevada Tax Commission responsible for licensing and taxation. Gambling had become a major economic force in the state, apparently a permanent one. Whether or not it could be effectively regulated remained to be seen.

Following the murder in Los Angeles of mobster Benjamin "Bugsy" Siegel in 1947 and the revelation of imprudent relationships between casinos and the county officials regulating them, the state of Nevada began to seek ways to control gambling enough to appear respectable while not hindering the development of an industry increasingly dominating Nevada's economy. The legislature turned to Attorney General Bible to explore its authority to increase oversight of the industry. Under the doctrine of protection of public welfare, Bible's legal opinion was far-reaching and gave the state significant and primary control over gambling and the policing of individuals applying for gaming licenses. The operation of a gambling establishment was deemed a privilege, not a right, and the state could inquire into the suitability of an applicant for a license based on his past and background. Bible's opinion provided direction to members of the tax commission, who used it to investigate allegations of misdeeds until the 1949 state legislature passed laws giving the regulators outright authority and power. Current Nevada gaming regulation has its genesis in Bible's opinions as attorney general that strongly asserted the state's right to regulate, as well as tax, the industry.

Simultaneously, Senator McCarran became concerned about protecting gambling at the federal level. He recognized that if the federal government were to tax gambling—or worse, declare it illegal—the economy of Nevada would suffer greatly. "Gaming protection," a euphemism for limiting intrusive federal investigation and regulation over the Nevada industry, become a critical element of McCarran's legislative agenda. Bible would follow McCarran's strong lead in this area when he became a senator.

While in the attorney general's office, Bible also became interested in the vagaries of water law. In his final year as deputy attorney general, he completed the research that would eventually lead to the *Arizona* v. *California* suit when Gary Mashburn, the other deputy attorney in the office who had initiated the research, was seriously injured in an automobile accident. The suit was related to the amount of water Nevada could expect to receive from the Colorado River, and it held enormous implications for Nevada's future. Bible recalled, in his oral history, spending most of his remaining time as deputy attorney on this one issue.

When Bible became attorney general in 1943, he found himself involved in yet another suit related to the Colorado River. The federal government routinely makes payments to states, in lieu of taxes, to provide the revenue they would lose when the federal government builds facilities or provides an otherwise taxable service. Nevada was receiving $300,000 annually in lieu of taxes for building the Hoover Dam on the Colorado River. In turn, the state was giving Clark County, the county in which the dam was located, 20 percent of the annual amount. The county now wanted more. Making no friends in Clark County, Bible delivered an opinion supporting the legislature's reasoning that since the state has the right to create a county, it has the power to limit or define the county's sources of revenue. In this case, Bible said, the state had the power to distribute the revenue from Hoover Dam as it wished. Fearing it would lose even the 20 percent, Clark County backed down. While Clark County lost out with this decision, Bible's later efforts as senator in behalf of the county would prove far more beneficial and more than compensate for this minor loss.

During the formative years of his political career, Bible developed expertise not only in water law but also in creating legislation to promote economic development. He also established valuable working relationships by becoming active outside the state. At the end of the war, Governor E. P. Carville and Senator McCarran aggressively promoted state involvement in postwar planning for industrial development, transportation, power generation, and recreational expansion. Their preferred method was through the organization and deliberations of western regional conferences, committees, and commissions. Bible found himself a member of many of these groups, including the Colorado River Commission, which represented Nevada's interest in the river to the Interior Department, the Nevada Interstate Cooperation Committee, the California Commission on Cooperation, and the Reclamation Advisory Committee. Bible's charge was to urge the eleven western states to increase their political power by jointly pursuing their postwar planning efforts and acquiring war plants for use by private industry. By the time he left the attorney general's office, Bible had detailed knowledge of most of the legal issues that would face Nevada and the West in the postwar period, as well as an extended network of well-placed friends and political contacts.

Departure from the attorney general's office in 1951 did not end Bible's close involvement with the state government or with water law. He continued in private law practice with Robert McDonald, the son of Reno's *Nevada State Journal* editor, Joseph F. McDonald. Although Senator McCarran sent clients on occasion, the firm's principal client was the State of Nevada. The state needed Bible's expertise, so the firm found plenty of work on issues related to water and power. Additionally, Bible was retained as Nevada's legal adviser to the Colorado River Commission.

A confident Bible entered the Democratic primary in 1952 for the United States Senate and, in a shocking upset, lost by 475 votes to political outsider and newcomer to Nevada, Thomas Mechling. The defeat was a humbling one, as had been his defeat years earlier in the high school debate contest. He concluded that he had not worked hard enough to secure the election, relying too much on his relationship with McCarran and the belief that he knew enough people through his years in state office to win. As before, he learned an invaluable lesson. Once over the humiliation, and abandoning plans to move out of state, Bible found other ways to serve the people of Nevada while he waited for another chance.

He continued to pursue the knotty issue of water policy. In August 1952, Arizona filed its long-anticipated suit against California over its share of the Colorado River. At issue were the allocations set in the Colorado River Compact of 1922, which included Nevada's annual allotment of 300,000 acre feet. Since 1922, it had become evident that because of growth and development, California was taking a greater share of the unused water that flowed through the Colorado. Arizona was concerned that the "first in right" doctrine, which historically awarded water to the first user, would soon be used by California to justify its claim to subsequent use. With the suit Arizona hoped to codify its allocation and to exclude the Gila River flow so that future development could take place in the Phoenix metropolitan area.

Nevada's position was similar to Arizona's. The state expected the Las Vegas area to grow. The city was already exhausting the water available in the underground springs and needed Colorado River water. Nevada's leaders feared that if Arizona successfully raised the allocation issue, Nevada could possibly lose its annual allotment, one that most experts considered quite generous. Recognizing that a decision by the Supreme Court could have the far-reaching effect of changing the allocations originally agreed upon, state attorney general William T. Mathews asked Bible to represent Nevada in the suit filed by Arizona. But first, Nevada had to be declared a legitimate party to the suit. By 1954, with Bible arguing for the state in *Arizona* v. *California,* the United States Supreme Court ruled that Nevada had standing and a right to intervene in the case. This was a crucial victory for both Nevada and Alan Bible. Before the case was formally decided, however, Bible moved to a different role in a different venue—as a United States senator.

On September 28, 1954, as he concluded a political speech in Hawthorne, Senator Patrick McCarran suddenly collapsed and died of a massive heart attack. Because McCarran was one of the most powerful senators in Nevada history, many people assumed a political vacuum would result. But Bible, elected to fill the remainder of McCarran's term, surprised them. In just two years he played a key role in passing legislation affecting the water supply in Nevada for decades to come. When campaigning in 1956, Bible pointed with pride to his actions that delivered 800,000 kilowatts of electricity to the rapidly growing city of Las Vegas from the Glen Canyon Dam located in northern Arizona, the completion of a feasibility study that laid the ground-work for actually bringing Nevada's Colorado River allocation to Las Vegas, and a multipurpose project to provide flood control, irrigation, and a munici-pal water-delivery system to northern Nevada. These were significant accom-plishments for a senator with junior status in Washington. But his legal experiences had prepared Bible to step into his new role without having to go through an extended apprenticeship.

When Bible went to Washington in 1954, a number of factors were operat-ing in his favor, not the least of which was his party affiliation. The Demo-cratic Party, under the leadership of Lyndon Johnson, provided Bible with entre into leadership posts in the Senate. Moreover, according to his biogra-pher, Gary Elliott, Bible's warm and friendly personality and his collegial, unassuming manner gained him many friends within the nation's "most exclusive club," and his legal and political expertise in the area of the mind-numbing complexities of water law also worked to his benefit. These factors contributed to his impressive achievements in bringing new sources of water to Nevada, thereby meeting the needs of his constituents as if he were a senator with considerable seniority and insider clout.

In the early 1950s, Nevada's residents still numbered only 160,000, the size of many small cities in other states. The state's small population, Bible's attendance at the state's only university, and his active involvement in state government for the previous fifteen years allowed Bible to effectively practice politics based on the assumption that "all politics are local." He had developed an impressively large number of friends and acquaintances over the years and confidently assumed that he knew personally what most Nevadans wanted. Moreover, he truly enjoyed serving his constituents.

Upon his arrival in the Senate, Bible became a confidant of the powerful Texan and ambitious majority leader Lyndon Johnson, who shared Bible's devotion to the idea of the federal government assuming a major role in the development of western water resources. Additionally, Johnson had his own "all politics are local" philosophy, believing that if people are helped through economic development, their political support will naturally follow. Not realizing the importance of seniority to committee assignments and hoping to follow in McCarran's footsteps, Bible naïvely asked Johnson for his predecessor's committee assignments, the powerful Appropriations Committee and the Judiciary Committee. Johnson instead placed him on the Interior and Insular Affairs Committee and the Interstate and Foreign Commerce Committee. The more seasoned Johnson probably realized these committee assignments were far more fortuitous assignments for Bible because they dealt with water, power, mining, and public land policy, the areas in which he brought an interest and expertise and where his efforts would benefit Nevada. At the same time, perhaps prevailing on Bible's natural instinct to be cooperative, Johnson also put him on the District of Columbia Committee, an assignment that was avoided by other senators because of its heavy workload and low prestige. Even the inexperienced Bible recognized it provided him with no opportunity to serve Nevadans.

During Bible's first term in congress, the Eisenhower administration, through a number of powerful western senators, proposed the Upper Colorado Storage Project. A great deal can be learned about Bible by following his actions in the development of this project and a subsequent one, the Washoe Project. The lessons he learned during these first two years would guide his actions during his twenty-year Senate career. Bible quickly earned a reputation for being a Senate workhorse with a vast storehouse of technical knowledge, and someone who favored a fair and honest approach to public policy. He also elected to stay outside the public eye, disapproving of senators who actively sought publicity with outlandish public statements or other inappropriate behavior. Bible's traits were valuable, especially in a Senate controlled by the Democrats.

Earlier, as a lawyer representing the state in *Arizona* v. *California,* Bible's goal had been to keep as many options open as possible for the development of additional water projects. Now he attempted through legislative action to do the same while the Supreme Court deliberated its decision in that important case. In this instance, legislative action that took the form of the Upper Colorado Storage Project was truly monumental. In the process of formulating and passing this legislation, Bible developed a close working relationship with Democrat Clinton P. Anderson of New Mexico. As a senator from an equally arid state, Anderson had fought the water wars for many years. As early as 1949, he had been a pivotal player in the passage of the Central Arizona Project to provide water for Phoenix. Now the Upper Colorado Storage Project proposed by the Bureau of Reclamation dwarfed it.

The bureau proposed a $1.5 billion project consisting of six dams, storage facilities, power-generation plants, flood control, and irrigation projects along with seventeen smaller developments. In the project, New Mexico, with Albuquerque as the major user, would get its share of the Colorado from the San Juan River through a diversion ditch to be built over the Continental Divide and through the Navajo Indian Reservation. Reflecting on the history of the efforts to pass the Central Arizona Project, Anderson anticipated endless litigation with the Indians and preservationists, so he set out to effect a compromise. Bible, as a hardworking junior senator with critical expertise in the arena of water law, followed his lead. In the process their attitudes toward development and resource utilization evolved to include a place for Indians as well as others who wanted to preserve natural treasures.

Perhaps for the first time, Bible also came in contact with a public figure of considerable standing who did not want to develop a natural resource. Horace M. Albright, a former director of the National Park Service and considered its founding father, was a symbol of Bible's belief in the need to hear all sides of an issue, especially if the arguments seemed well informed. Along with his predecessor, Albright, who was appointed director in 1929, had worked to form a professional ranger and manager corps free from patronage and immune from the pressures of miners, loggers, and grazers— just the type of individuals who comprised Bible's political constituency. Albright had left the Park Service in 1933 and now represented the Council of Conservationists, a group that sought to change the Upper Colorado Storage Project proposal in order to protect Rainbow Bridge Monument and to eliminate a dam at Echo Park Dam that would have destroyed Dinosaur National Monument. He believed that development was not always the highest and best use of natural resources; protecting the land for future generations was equally, if not more, important. In order to work out a compromise, Anderson and Bible had to incorporate the preservation ideas of Albright into their planning. As a result, they decided no dam or reservoir would be built within any national park or monument.

Bible thus evidenced an ability to grow, to incorporate new ideas into his policy formulation, to take a more complex perspective on land use and public policy. The fight over Dinosaur National Monument gave the preservationists a seat at the table of future negotiations. For his part in the compromise over the Upper Colorado Storage Project, Bible secured for Nevada a share in the 800,000 kilowatts coming from the Glen Canyon Dam and money to study the feasibility of pumping water from Lake Mead to Las Vegas. From this small feasibility study eventually came the Southern Nevada Project, which would transform the state.

While Bible could claim these successes with his water efforts for southern Nevadans, his accomplishments for his northern constituents were less clear. In 1955, he reintroduced legislation proposed by McCarran in 1954. Known as the Washoe Project, it was a complex reclamation and flood-control plan. Specifically, the construction of a number of reservoirs high in the Sierra Nevada would provide flood protection for Reno along the Truckee River basin, storage capacity for water in dry years, and even limited hydroelectric production. What the project attempted to resolve, without success, was an answer to the question of who possessed the rights to the water stored in the reservoirs. Competing for these rights were the growing cities of Reno and Sparks, the Paiute Indians, and the Fallon-area farmers. Because the headwaters of the Truckee River actually rose in the California Sierra Nevada, the state of California claimed an interest as well. Although legislation was written and passed that authorized reservoir construction, it left the ownership question unsettled. Nonetheless, the result of Bible's efforts appeared to be a promising first step.

Despite Bible's success in his first two years, his tenure in Washington, D.C., apparently was to be brief. His family was urging him to return to private life. Early in 1956, Bible announced he would not run again for his Senate seat. However, he had not taken into account the legendary persuasive powers of Lyndon Johnson. The Democrats held control of the Senate by the slender majority of one seat, and Johnson was determined to maintain or increase that margin. Bible's reelection, which had appeared likely, became critical to Johnson. He went into action, prevailing on Bible's sense of duty to his party, constituents, and country. Bible got the full Johnson "treatment":

"He twisted my arm so much it almost broke," the mild-mannered Bible later recalled with a smile.

Thus Bible reluctantly changed his mind and agreed to run again. His vacillation, however, caused him considerable anguish. Several of his long-time Democratic friends and colleagues, particularly Harvey Dickerson, Mahlon Brown, and Jay Sourwine, had taken him at his word and already announced their candidacy in the primary race. After he reversed himself, Bible easily received his party's nomination and campaigned forcefully in the general election, defeating the popular Republican representative Cliff Young in November. His victory assured a grateful Johnson of his position as majority leader and the Democrats their control of the Senate. His personal embarrassment aside, Bible's reversal created a debt he used to advantage with Johnson in the future.

Following his reelection, Bible parlayed his faithful work on the District of Columbia Committee into a seat on the most powerful committee in the Senate. In 1959, Bible agreed to continue as chair of the District of Columbia Committee only if Johnson would appoint him to the Appropriations Committee. With his seniority and influence growing in 1961, Bible became a member of the Subcommittee on Mining and chair of the Subcommittee on Public Lands. He later traded this chairmanship for the newly formed Subcommittee on Parks and Recreation, a position he held from 1965 to 1974.

While his efforts with the Washoe Project showed promise in 1956, the negotiations surrounding the allocation of the Truckee River's flow broke down completely when the agreements reached the federal level in 1971. The water rights spelled out in the Orr Ditch decree that had been painstakingly established and litigated for more than twenty years included a minimal allocation for the Paiute Tribe. When the original water-rights suit had been filed, the Bureau of Indian Affairs, acting for the tribe, had negotiated for enough water for the tribe's use as farmers, an occupation few ever practiced. By the 1950s, they challenged the assumptions on which the rights had been made and adjudicated. It had been federal policy to transform them into farmers, not the tribe's. They now sought a sufficient allocation to return to their traditional way of life as fishermen and to protect their endangered fish, the cui-ui. The downstream users, the Fallon farmers especially, vigorously contested the new claims. Moreover, the political atmosphere changed during the 1960s in favor of the Paiutes. A sympathetic national public opinion supported Native American claims, and so attempts to allocate the water among the users remained tied up in federal court. Although allocation of usage remained in conflict, the Stampede and Boca reservoirs to the west of Reno were finished ahead of schedule in 1970. These two reservoirs would control possible flooding, improve water supplies for the cities of Reno and Sparks, and provide recreation sites for boaters and fishermen.

With his increasing power in the Senate and the ability to deliver federal dollars for Nevada's capital-improvement projects, Bible played a critical role in the development of the city of Las Vegas. From the earliest days, the Las Vegas Land and Water Company provided water to the town. With an eye to the existing supply, the company refused to expand service beyond the city limits, effectively curtailing the town's growth. In 1954, the company sold its holdings to the newly organized Las Vegas Valley Water District, a body that supported expansion. With Las Vegas's growth no longer impeded, the wells that had adequately served the smaller town began reaching their limits by 1960. Therefore, federal, state, and local leaders began discussions to bring about delivery of the long-anticipated Colorado River allocation from Lake Mead. However, not until the 1963 Supreme Court decision on *Arizona* v. *California* gave Nevada, and specifically Las Vegas, 300,000 acre feet per annum did actual plans for development of the necessary pipeline once again go forward. Bible's influence was necessary to make it happen, and he faced daunting challenges at every juncture of the political process.

The first test of Bible's skill came at the committee level. In August 1963, Secretary of the Interior Stewart Udall was working on his counterpart to the earlier Upper Colorado Storage Project, now called the Pacific Southwest Water Plan. He included southern Nevada's water appropriation within it. The plan, however, carried the exorbitant price of a billion dollars and called for two dams within the Grand Canyon. Recalling his early experience with the Echo Canyon Dam and perceiving a negative reaction to the sheer size of the project, Bible correctly feared the Nevada appropriation was in jeopardy. As chairman of the committee holding hearings over the Interior Department's budget, he exercised his considerable negotiating talent to save Nevada's appropriation. In the course of those hearings, in return for supporting the department's annual operating budget he forced a public commitment from the secretary for a separate appropriation for Nevada. He then skillfully managed the passage of a smaller bill, and the Southern Nevada Water Project was born.

Favorable reaction to the smaller bill at the committee level ensured, Bible's next step was Congress as a whole. Nevada remained trapped between California and Arizona in the political conflict raging over water, and Bible could ill afford to offend either state until final passage of his new bill. In 1965, the Southern Nevada Water Project bill, which included funding for six pumping plants, a regulatory reservoir, a four-mile tunnel, and about thirty-one miles of pipeline from Lake Mead to existing pipeline in Las Vegas, was passed in the Senate. Throughout this delicate stage, Bible worked carefully with delegations from both states, assisting with each project until he was assured of support for his smaller measure.

An ongoing feud between Nevada's only congressman, Democrat Walter Baring, and other House Democrats and the president created yet another hurdle. Irritated House Democrats attempted to embarrass Baring, who consistently, and with considerable public attention, refused to support Johnson's Great Society legislation. To punish him they eliminated the water project from the general appropriations bill passed in the House. Bible was forced to use his influence once more, this time to restore the appropriation in the conference committee.

Finally, there remained only the president's signature to make the Southern Nevada Water Project law. Given Bible's close relationship with Johnson, presidential endorsement should have been easily achieved; but even this endeavor turned into no small task, since by then a sizable amount of the nation's resources was tied up in the Vietnam conflict. Additionally, Johnson was infuriated by Baring's lack of cooperation on legislative matters. Still Bible prevailed. Johnson invited him to dinner at the White House, and before Bible could ask for a special favor, Johnson slyly told him not to worry about his project: He had the signed legislation in his pocket. In return, Johnson now had in tow a grateful senator who would provide unstinting and unquestioning support for his Vietnam policies.

From 1965 through 1970, appropriations for planning and then construction were cut from budgets as money was siphoned off to Vietnam. Squabbles over Baring's behavior continued. Time and again Bible reconstructed and resurrected the funding for the water project. Finally, on June 2, 1971, the first phase of the project was completed. The Bureau of Reclamation turned over control of the plants and operating facilities to the Nevada Colorado River Commission, and the Las Vegas Valley Water District and southern Nevada could begin receiving the first 132,220 acre feet of the allocated water. Bible, fittingly, was honored by local Nevada officials as the "Father of the Project" in the dedication ceremony.

The second phase, begun in 1977, was completed in 1982. Finally, after sixty years of effort, the Las Vegas Valley could take delivery of its entire annual allotment of 300,000 acre feet of the Colorado River. The availability of this water triggered the incredible growth and economic expansion of Las Vegas. Practically overnight, Clark County's population skyrocketed, from 272,288 in 1970 to nearly 1 million by 1990. Alan Bible, the product of rural

Nevada, had used his considerable legislative skills to provide the essential foundation for the New Nevada.

While the Southern Nevada Project provided him with personal satisfaction, Bible was disappointed by his inability to create a national park in Nevada. From his position as chair of the Parks and Recreation Subcommittee of the Interior and Insular Affairs Committee, it would appear to have been a relatively easy task. The Wheeler Peak area in northeastern Nevada met all the National Park Service's criteria for creation of a national park. The chambers of commerce in nearby towns, the governor, and the state legislature all supported the concept. Bible saw it as another opportunity to provide an economic stimulus to an area long plagued by a dearth of economic activity. Creation of the Great Basin National Park would bring tourism dollars to an area with few other economic resources.

However, he had not counted on the resolute opposition of ranchers and miners of northeastern Nevada who adamantly opposed any program that involved the federal government. Over the years Bible had championed legislation to provide support for copper and silver prices and to minimize foreign competition for the miners and had worked to promote advantageous grazing rights for ranchers. But on the issue of creating a national park, a few miners and ranchers, using Congressman Walter Baring as their foil, successfully blocked his efforts. The skills he honed as a compromiser in the Senate, the careful study that went into identifying the boundaries, and his introduction of legislation over many years came to naught. Only long after he left office did the Great Basin National Park finally become a reality, on October 27, 1986.

As chairman of the Interior Committee's Subcommittee on Parks and Recreation, he had been at the heart of the debate on the value of public lands for wilderness and recreation in an era of critical change. Beginning with the battle over Echo Park, and exposed to the notion that wilderness was in fact vanishing, he came to favor a land-use position of balance between preservation and development of the natural environment, a position far removed from that of his eastern Nevada constituents. Although Bible was unable to create a national park in Nevada, the nation as a whole benefited greatly from his consensus building and legislative efforts. At the time of his death in 1988, an unprecedented expansion of the park system had taken place.

Through his work on the Subcommittee on Parks and Recreation, Bible helped establish eighty-six parks, historic sites, and national monuments, from the Gateway National Recreation Area along the New York–New Jersey shoreline and Cape Cod National Seashore in Massachusetts to Point Reyes National Park in California. Fellow senator Ted Stevens, however, placed one accomplishment above all the others: the Alaskan Wilderness Bill. He believed that only Bible, with his skills at compromise and reputation for fair hearings, had the ability to bring together the senators on so massive a bill. While it remains unequaled in size, it is a lasting memorial to Bible in another way. It symbolized his commitment to a balance between development and preservation.

From a Nevada perspective, Bible's greatest legacy is found in his efforts to bring water to Las Vegas. In 1965, water from the Colorado River remained little more than an allocation on paper. With a series of skillful legislative moves, Bible detached Nevada from the long-standing controversy between California and Arizona and secured enabling legislation to fund the Southern Nevada Water Project. While all Nevadans, and most westerners, yearned for a dependable, long-term water supply, Bible enabled Las Vegas to achieve that dream. His efforts established a foundation for the explosive growth of Clark County, ensuring that even the political power balance of the state tipped from north to south. By obtaining water for his arid state, Bible was instrumental in creating an engine for economic development that shows no sign of faltering as the twenty-first century draws near. This unimposing but hard-working man whose roots are found in the small northern Nevada towns of Lovelock and Fallon was a major architect of the New Nevada.

Robert Laxalt

Creating Culture in the Desert

Our earliest memory was of the sound of the typewriter, because it was there always, in the early morning hours as we woke, in the late night as we slept, in the background as we played. It had its own rhythm: a steady, continuous rap . . . then a slower rap . . . then a stalling, uneven rap . . . then silence . . . then an endless silence . . . then explosion into a flurry of sound . . . then quiet again. —Monique Urza, *The Deep Blue Memory*

BY CHERYLL GLOTFELTY

On a snowy September 24 in 1923 a Basque woman gave birth to her second son in a doctor's house in the small town of Alturas in Northern California. The woman's husband, a Basque sheepherder who spoke some English, was caught in the early snowstorm and failed to arrive on time for his son's birth. The shepherd's wife, who spoke no English, could only shake her head mutely at the doctor's questions. Thus it happened that to this day the boy's birth certificate reads "No Name Laxalt."

From this inauspicious beginning, the boy, Robert Peter Laxalt, would go on to make quite a name for himself. From 1968 to 1978, Laxalt was honorary consul for France in Nevada. In 1978 he received a Decade Award from the Nevada State Council on the Arts and, the same year, was cited by Governor Mike O'Callaghan for exemplary service to the State of Nevada. He was named Distinguished Nevada Author in 1982 by the Friends of the University of Nevada, Reno, Library, and Distinguished Nevadan in 1984 by the Board of Regents of the University of Nevada. In 1988 Robert Laxalt became the first inductee to the Hall of Fame of Nevada Writers. His twelve books include the best-selling *Sweet Promised Land,* the critically acclaimed *A Man in the Wheatfield,* and the gemlike *The Basque Hotel.* His books and hundreds of articles have won numerous national and international awards. In sum, Robert Laxalt has emerged as Nevada's preeminent author, literary spokesman for the Basques, and beloved chronicler of the "other" Nevada.

Many people believe writers to be recluses who prefer to write about the world rather than to live fully in it. Indeed, some authors do conform to this lonely garret image. Robert Laxalt, however, has been engaged just as actively in the world as he has in his study, and his list of achievements extends well beyond the titles of his books. In his youth, this literary laureate was a Golden Gloves boxer, so good that he considered turning pro. During college he worked as a news reporter and created the Capital News Service in Carson City. In 1961, he

8

founded the University of Nevada Press and directed it for more than twenty years. He helped to establish the internationally recognized Basque Studies Program at the University of Nevada, Reno. He was co-organizer of the first Western Basque Festival, progenitor of numerous similar festivals held throughout the West today. Indeed, the institutions and traditions that Laxalt helped to initiate have become vital elements of Nevada's continuing heritage.

Before considering Robert Laxalt's literary and public career, let us first reflect on his boyhood and youth, on the early forces and family stories that shaped the man. Robert's father, Dominique Laxalt, immigrated to America from the Basque country in the French Pyrenees. Not yet twenty years old and speaking no English, Dominique made his way to Nevada in 1906 to herd sheep for another man's outfit. Before many years had passed, Dominique went into the sheep business with two brothers, and in 1918 he became a partner in the Allied Land and Livestock Company, which flourished. The partners became very rich, and banks persuaded them to borrow money to expand their business even further. In 1921, flush with success, Dominique married Theresa Alpetche, also an immigrant from the Basque country, who had come to America to be with her dying brother. The next year the market went bust, the banks foreclosed, and the Allied Land and Livestock Company went broke.

With the little remaining money that they could scrape together, Theresa insisted that the fledgling family buy a small hotel in Carson City, Nevada, which they ran as a boardinghouse, primarily for Basque sheepherders and cattlemen. Robert's father eventually grew restless with this indoor life and returned to sheepherding, leaving Theresa with six children to raise and a hotel to run. This stalwart woman insisted that education come first for her children, and she urged them to learn English. She bought the boys boxing gloves so they could work out their differences. The first book that Laxalt can remember is the family's well-thumbed illustrated encyclopedia of every ranked prizefighter in the world. All four boys became good boxers, and they even boxed locally for money. Laxalt recalls the days when he was the only white kid on the Stewart Indian School Boxing Team. The Indians were so good at boxing that Robert used to look forward to weekends when he would not have to go to practice.

When the boys were not in school or in the boxing ring, they joined their father in the hills to help with the sheep. There, they enjoyed the outdoor life and Dominique's good camp cooking, but they bristled at the hard work, close calls, and frequent discomfort that the shepherd's life entailed. Laxalt recalls that it was on one of these trips that he first "discovered" Nevada.

Their father had led the boys on a scramble to the top of a windy peak in the Sierra Nevada. From that vantage point, Robert remembers,

> as far as we could see, there was nothing but open land. Range upon range of desert mountains followed one upon the other into interminable distance, each with its own hue of rose or gray or violet, until they disappeared finally into a haze. There was simply no horizon to it all. And not another town or even a house to be seen. It did not seem possible there could be that much land and so few people in the world.
>
> When we had lowered ourselves down, my father said, "Well, that's your Nevada out there."

The Carson City of Laxalt's youth was a small town of sixteen hundred people and had the distinction of being the nation's smallest capital. It seemed that everybody knew everybody else, and he remembers waving to all the familiar people as he walked down the streets. Growing up in this small town gave Laxalt a sense of security and of belonging, planting the seeds of loyalty to the state of Nevada that would grow into acts of service throughout his later life.

In such a small western town, raised in a family for which English was a second language, and spending most of his free time outdoors, how was it that Laxalt developed a taste for literature? There were perhaps two main factors at work in those early years. First, there was a schoolteacher named Grace Bordewich, to whom Laxalt later dedicated *The Basque Hotel.* When Mrs. Bordewich read poetry aloud in class, Robert became enraptured by the texture and the beauty and the expressiveness of language. Second, as a young boy, Laxalt contracted a nearly fatal case of rheumatic fever. While the other children were outside playing, Robert was confined to bed for three months. Visitors brought him library books, magazines, and newspapers, and he became permanently hooked on reading.

In 1941, Laxalt entered Santa Clara University in California, a Jesuit college for men. Nothing had prepared him for this intellectually grueling experience. Here, he was plagued with frequent headaches, which were caused by the demands of rigorous courses in philosophy and logic. In this strict institution, failing a test meant being expelled from school. To make up for the deficiencies of his small-town education, Laxalt got up at 4:30 in the morning to study, and studied again after lights-out with a flashlight under his blankets. Despite the exhaustion of these years, Laxalt found them to be one of the most rewarding experiences of his life, as new worlds of ideas and thought opened before him.

World War II interrupted Laxalt's college career. He enlisted for combat duty, but was disqualified because the doctor detected a heart murmur. Enraged, Laxalt signed up for noncombat duty and asked his superiors to send him to the worst place there was. He was trained in Washington, D.C., as a decoder and was sent by the U.S. Foreign Service to the Belgian Congo in Africa. The tropical landscape delighted him with its lush greenery and voluptuous flowers and exotic wildlife, but the racial prejudice he witnessed was harrowing, and he caught several serious diseases, including chronic malaria, yellow jaundice, amoebic dysentery, and a form of skin disease. A doctor advised the skeletal Laxalt that if he did not leave the country soon he would die, so friends helped to smuggle him to the coast and onto a Swedish freighter, which sailed through a heavy combat zone. His instructions were that if the ship went down, he was to strap the coding machine onto his body so it would sink with him.

Upon his return to the States, Laxalt had to make a decision between taking over his father's sheep business or returning to college. It was a difficult choice. Of all the sons, Robert showed the most interest in the outdoor life, and it would please his father to keep the business in the family. Yet, Santa Clara University had introduced Laxalt to the rewards of learning, and his mother wanted him to finish his degree. In this fork of life, Laxalt chose the college route, and in 1945 he entered the University of Nevada in Reno, at the time the state's only institution of higher learning, intending to train for the diplomatic service. Accordingly, he majored in English and minored in philosophy and history, earning his B.A. in 1947. In contrast to Santa Clara University, at Nevada classes seemed relatively easy, and Laxalt enjoyed an active social life. He met his future wife, Joyce Nielsen, when he accidentally knocked over her books in the Student Union cafeteria one day, and he fell in love at first sight. They married in 1949 and had three children: Bruce (born 1951), Monique (born 1953), and Kristin (born 1956).

To support himself through school, Laxalt worked for a news service in Carson City, a job that led directly into a full-time newspaper reporting job after graduation. In 1947 Laxalt started his own news bureau, the Capital News Service, which covered Nevada politics. From 1948 to 1953 he was a staff correspondent for United Press International, covering northern Nevada and writing prodigiously, sometimes as much as nine thousand words a day. His most loathsome beat was reporting on executions, which forced him to witness many gas chamber death scenes. His first big break as a reporter came when he discovered that the murder of a resort-casino owner in Tahoe Village at Lake Tahoe was connected with the Mafia. Up until Laxalt's story broke, it was thought that Mafia presence in Nevada was limited to Las Vegas. Laxalt received a telephone death threat during these years, to which he coolly replied that whomever they sent to shoot him better be a good shot because he definitely was.

Characteristically, Laxalt's ambitions were bigger than his job. He began writing magazine stories after work to supplement his income and to perfect his craft. The problem with this arrangement was that after writing for the newspaper all day, he was too tired by evening to write well. He solved the problem by getting up at 4 A.M. and writing before work. He also wrote on weekends, which meant that he had to give up sports—first playing them and then watching them on television. But his sacrifices paid off. He sold his first big story to the *Saturday Evening Post* in 1952: "What Has Wide-Open Gambling Done to Nevada?" The article weighs the pros and cons of open gambling in Nevada, where gaming was legalized in 1931.

From this first success, Laxalt went on to write more than two hundred magazine articles and short stories for periodicals, including *Atlantic, Saturday Evening Post, National Geographic, National Geographic Traveler, Vista USA, True, Mademoiselle, Cosmopolitan, Bluebook, American Weekly, Business Week, Reader's Digest,* and *Nevada Magazine.* Many of Laxalt's magazine pieces—both journalism and short stories—feature a Nevada subject or setting. The majority of these pieces are about "old" Nevada, a Nevada of ranching and mining days, a land of gunmen and desperados, ranchers and prospectors.

A large share of Laxalt's magazine pieces spring from his travels throughout the American West, Europe, and South America. Many of these informative travelogues were commissioned by *National Geographic.* Among his dozen *National Geographic* articles and book chapters, one that stands out is "The Other Nevada" (1974), in which he describes the "Nevada that few people see, where personal freedom and the chance to be an individual thrive in an uncrowded landscape." For "The Other Nevada" Laxalt was given the Golden Spur Award for Western Writing for the best nonfiction story of 1974, awarded by the Western Writers of America.

As a beginning writer, Laxalt felt the need to meet an established writer, someone who, in his words, could "provide me with the key to the magic kingdom I knew nothing about." He happened to see an article with the headline "Walter Clark Does It Again," a story occasioned by Clark's recent novel *The Track of the Cat.* Without having read any of Clark's work, the brash Laxalt telephoned Nevada's leading author Walter Van Tilburg Clark and asked Clark if he would look at one of Laxalt's short stories. When they met, Clark scanned Laxalt's story and began asking him what books he had read. Other than *Beowulf,* works by Shakespeare, *War and Peace,* and some poetry,

Laxalt had read little of literary value. Clark took out a slip of paper and began writing down the titles of some books that he believed would help Laxalt in his writing. This list of seventeen books is reprinted in Laxalt's foreword to the new edition of Clark's *The City of Trembling Leaves;* it includes works by authors such as Joseph Conrad, D. H. Lawrence, Stephen Crane, Ivan Turgenev, Fyodor Dostoyevsky, William Faulkner, Ole Rölvaag, and Willa Cather. Thus began a rewarding friendship that was to last nearly twenty years, until Clark's death in 1971. Although their western settings and subjects are similar, Clark's expansive style bears little resemblance to Laxalt's lean one, but Robert Laxalt learned from Walter Clark about the life of a writer.

Laxalt would one day compile his own list of recommended reading, consisting of many of Clark's suggestions as well as books by authors such as Jack London, Gustave Flaubert, Mark Twain, James Thurber, Thornton Wilder, John Steinbeck, and Ernest Hemingway. Indeed, critics frequently compare Laxalt's writing to that of the latter two, citing Steinbeck for his ability to write beautifully about the grubbiest elements of society and Hemingway for his spare style. Laxalt's books have received uniformly favorable reviews in newspapers and magazines across the country, including the *New York Times* and the *Boston Globe.* They have won numerous awards and earned international recognition, having been translated into several languages and published in England, France, Germany, Spain, and South America. Through his writing, Laxalt has put Nevada on the literary map.

Several signature themes emerge in Laxalt's writing. Much of his work juxtaposes old and new ways or describes a clash between the Old World and the new, the Old Nevada and the New Nevada. Because he believes that there is value in the old ways that are rapidly passing away, his writing is often tinged with nostalgia, and a strong impulse behind his work is to preserve these fading traditions for future generations. Laxalt's books are peopled with Basque characters—European Basques in the Basque country of France and Spain, immigrant Basques in America, and the American-born children of Basque Americans. Still another predominant theme in Laxalt's work is the American West, particularly Nevada. His landscape descriptions evoke the stark beauty of this often maligned high-desert land. Against this austere canvas, the characters that most ignite Laxalt's imagination are the people who live on the land—the sheepherders, the ranchers. His books honor pioneers like his parents, whose endurance, hard work, and enterprise created unheard-of opportunities for their children.

As a newspaperman, Laxalt developed a column for the *Nevada State Journal,* entitled "The Tales Old Timers Tell." Laxalt's first book, *The Violent Land:*

Tales the Old Timers Tell (1953), is based on these columns. The stories are set in small northern Nevada towns and places such as Virginia City, Aurora, Carson City, and Paradise Valley. As its title suggests, violence is the common thread uniting this collection, and the reader, cowering safely behind the pages of the book, witnesses saloon fights, Indian battles, narrow-eyed killers, swaggering gunmen, unscrupulous horse traders, grisly miners, and hot-headed soldiers. The stories resemble western dime novels in their shoot-'em-up plots and colloquial dialogue.

During what might be called Laxalt's apprenticeship years, he wrote many short stories about Nevada of the early 1950s. Some of these were published, but many were rejected by popular magazines because of their serious bent or unmarketable backgrounds. One such story, "The Snake Pen," was rejected with a note that warned, "Snakes are practically automatically out." These early experiments in writing fiction were buried in Laxalt's files for forty years until Thomas Radko, then director of the University of Nevada Press, asked him to submit them to the press for consideration. In 1994 sixteen of these stories finally saw the light of day in *A Lean Year and Other Stories*. Drawing upon Laxalt's multifarious experiences in Nevada, the cast of characters includes both reformed and crooked gamblers, Paiute Indians, ranchers and sheepherders, inept hunters, high school graduates from immigrant families, Mafia bosses, murderers, and snake handlers. In *A Lean Year* one may glimpse a Nevada of earlier days and observe the young Laxalt experimenting with language and form.

The turning point in Laxalt's career as an author is marked by the composition of *Sweet Promised Land* (1957). Until that book, he had been tinkering; with that book, he got serious. *Sweet Promised Land* is nonfiction, narrated in the first person by Laxalt. It tells of his father's visit to the Basque country of France, forty-seven years after he had left it. The book is based on a trip that Robert and his father took in 1953. For years Dominique had been saying that he wanted to visit his homeland, but nothing ever came of it. Finally, upon receiving news that one of his sisters had a stroke, the family decided that it was time for Dominique, himself an old man, to go back home, and Robert's mother appointed him to be his father's companion to ensure the safety of his journey and to see that he returned to America.

This trip was the first time that Laxalt had seen the Basque country, met his Basque relatives, and gotten to know his father. He had planned to take enough notes to write an article when he returned, but an editor recommended that he write a book instead. For a year he struggled unsuccessfully to write the book. A colleague had suggested that he write an epic of the West, but that suggestion seemed to lead to a writer's block. Finally, making one last attempt to write, Laxalt rolled a blank piece of paper into his old Royal typewriter and watched as his hands typed out the sentence, "My father was a sheepherder, and his home was the hills." From that first sentence the rest of the book flowed.

Although Laxalt rejected the idea of writing an epic, *Sweet Promised Land* does have epic qualities. The life of the humble Basque emigrant, Dominique Laxalt, who came to America as a young man to seek his fortune and was cast out into the desolate sagebrush hills under the blazing sun by himself with only a dog for companionship, responsible for a band of sheep in all extremes of weather, this life and this man take on heroic dimensions and assume a representative quality, standing for the immigrant experience in America. As Laxalt writes,

> He was the adventurer who had braved the unknown land across the sea and found his fortune. He was the rebel who had broken the bonds of their own longings and fought the battle and come home victorious. He was the youth who had gone out into the world in beggar's garb and come back in shining armor.

Many immigrants in the New World coped with the challenges of living in a foreign country by promising themselves that they would stay only long enough to earn enough money to return home and live comfortably. Dominique had likewise sustained himself with this dream, but he had never gone back. By the end of his stay in the Basque country he is anxious to return to America, at last admitting to himself that he has become an American, that the open land of Nevada has an undeniable hold on him. Robert Laxalt reflects,

> The irony of it was that our mothers and fathers were truer Americans than we, because they had forsaken home and family, and gone into the unknown of a new land with only courage and the hands that God gave them, and had given us in our turn the right to be born American.
>
>   And in a little while, even our sons would forget, and the old country people would be only a dimming memory, . . . and the melting would be done.

Sweet Promised Land keeps the memory of these Old Country people alive, granting them their rightful place in the pages of American history.

Upon publication of *Sweet Promised Land* Laxalt suddenly found himself a celebrity. The book was an instant success. It was the first selection of the National Book Society of England and an alternate selection of the Literary

Guild in the United States and was published in translation in France and Germany. Uncomfortable with all the attention, Laxalt declined his publisher's offer of a national book-promotion tour, turned down interviews, and seriously contemplated leaving the country until the fuss died down. He had learned how to write, but he had yet to learn how to live with the consequences of his success.

As William A. Douglass's excellent foreword to the 1986 edition of *Sweet Promised Land* explains, the significance of this book to American Basques and to Nevada was profound. Conditioned by years of discrimination, Basques had learned to keep a low profile and to assert their ethnicity only in the privacy of their homes. Sheepherding, the principal occupation of Basques in America, was resented by cattle ranchers and was reviled by the majority of Americans as dirty and uncouth. Laxalt's book caused Americans to regard Basques as a people of integrity, endurance, and pioneering spirit, and it helped Basques to be openly proud of their ethnic identity. For Nevada, the book had a similarly ennobling effect. With gambling, Mafia presence, easy divorce, and prostitution, Nevada was widely known as the Sin State, the place to go to do what you could not do elsewhere. *Sweet Promised Land* described the "other" Nevada, where the air is clear, where rural values survive, and where parents raise healthy children.

In 1960 and 1961 Laxalt and his family spent a year in the Basque country of France, where Laxalt was a Fulbright Research Fellow and a consultant to the Library of Congress on Basque culture. He had been working for two years on a new novel about a Basque shepherd, and planned to finish it abroad. Unfortunately, when he and his family stopped to enjoy a local festival, their car was burglarized, and a suitcase containing Laxalt's manuscript was stolen and never recovered. In vain, he attempted to re-create the novel. Out of his misery and despair was born a book of misery and despair, *A Man in the Wheatfield* (1964).

Set in an unnamed western town just after the Second World War, this story tells what happens when an American named Smale Calder moves into a small village of Italians. Calder likes rattlesnakes and he keeps them as pets. The townspeople, suspicious of outsiders, do not approve of his hobby. The priest in particular thinks that Calder is the devil in human form. Every Sunday, Calder climbs into the snake pit and lets the snakes climb all over him. Eventually the townspeople gather to watch the weekly spectacle, thus undermining the authority of the priest, who has been preaching against Calder. One night a little boy sneaks into the pen and is killed by the snakes. The townspeople retaliate by pouring gasoline into the pen and burning the snakes, but not before Calder is fatally bitten. The priest suddenly realizes that Calder was not the devil after all, but that the evil lurked inside himself.

This parable of good and evil stands out in Laxalt's canon as unusually intense in emotion and imagery, heavily symbolic, and more prone toward allegory than realism. It is Laxalt's most critically acclaimed book, a runner-up for the Harpers Prize Novel contest for American fiction of 1964 and named by the American Library Association of Washington, D.C., as one of six notable books of American fiction for 1964. Others were Hemingway's posthumous *A Moveable Feast* and Saul Bellow's *Herzog*.

Laxalt remembers *A Man in the Wheatfield* as the most difficult book he ever wrote, because it deals with material at once painful and close to his heart, namely, the presence of evil in the world. Throughout his life, having been raised Catholic during a time when the church preached a doctrine of fear, Laxalt had been plagued by periodic dreams of a figure, "monstrous and black upon black," who was looking for him. These disturbing dreams appear in the novel as those of the priest. In the most vivid of these haunting apparitions, the priest as a young seminary student imagines that he sees a shining wheat field. As he gazes out upon the beauty of the scene, he detects a figure approaching in the field, a man dressed in black. Their gazes meet, striking terror into the young man's heart. Once Laxalt wrote *A Man in the Wheatfield,* he never had the dream again.

After the painful ordeal of working his way through *A Man in the Wheatfield,* it must have been a relief for Laxalt to accept an offer to write a history of Nevada for the Coward-McCann States of the Nation series. Although intended for young readers, Laxalt's *Nevada* (1970) is entirely suitable for adults. Written in consultation with Dr. Wilbur S. Shepperson, chair of the history department at the University of Nevada, Reno, this illustrated volume makes an outstanding introduction to the history of Nevada, especially charming for its accessible style and its inclusion of anecdotes. A generous sprinkling of Nevada stories introduce readers to the state legends, such as the lavish parties and tragic ending of Comstock giants Sandy and Eilley Bowers, and the fabled mule of Jim Butler who wandered away and led his owner into a fantastic new gold discovery in Tonopah. When Laxalt wrote *Nevada,* his brother Paul was governor of the state. The book ends by quoting from Paul's inaugural address: "Most of our history lies before us. What we do now will serve not only the present, but our children and their children in generations to come. At the very least, let us give them a tradition to meet their challenges." Robert Laxalt's history of Nevada does just that.

A second foray into Nevada's past, *Nevada: A Bicentennial History* (1977), became one of the best-selling books in the States and Nation series sponsored by the National Endowment for the Humanities. The book opens with the memory of a day when World War II catapulted Laxalt to Africa. A friend sent him a letter, in whose pages was tucked a sprig of sagebrush. The smell of that little sprig unleashed a flood of memories, and upon his return to the United States, Laxalt never again took Nevada for granted. He writes,

> Always when I return, one of the first things I must do is go out into the sagebrush until its chemistry works in me and I know I am home again. But now, older, I find myself reflecting whimsically on how very much like the sagebrush the people are, at least in the hinterland that makes up the most of Nevada, setting down roots and thriving in unlikely places, hardy and resilient, stubborn and independent, restrained by environment and yet able to grow free.

As this passage illustrates, *Nevada: A Bicentennial History* is not a laborious chronicling of events but rather "a summing up—interpretive, sensitive, thoughtful, individual, even personal—of what seems significant about [the] state's history."

While managing to cover the major historical developments, economic chapters, and important figures of Nevada's past and present, Laxalt maintains a lively narrative style, interspersing his chapters with many quotations recorded from the ordinary speech of everyday Nevadans. Thus, the book has a vernacular quality, and the reader gets the impression that he or she is *hearing* the voices of Nevada. In addition to providing facts, then, this history effectively conveys the *feel* of the state.

When Laxalt accompanied his father to the Basque country in 1953, it awakened in him a desire to learn more about the Basque people and countryside. Accordingly, from 1960 to 1961 and again from 1965 to 1966, he and his family lived in the Basque country, talking with the people, attending festivals and church services, visiting pubs and graveyards, and exploring the coast and mountains. These experiences resulted in several articles for *National Geographic* and three books about the Basques and their land.

The Basque homeland extends from the seacoasts of the Bay of Biscay and runs along the ridgeline of the Pyrenees mountains, which separate France and Spain, although the Basque people are neither French nor Spanish in origin. Their origin, in fact, remains a mystery. The Basque language is unrelated to the Indo-European languages spoken throughout the rest of

Europe, and their blood type is unique. It is thought that they are an ancient people, whose isolation may reach back as far as Cro-Magnon times. Throughout their history, the Basques have resisted all invaders and have stubbornly refused to assimilate into the larger European mainstream.

Laxalt's three Basque books reveal the stories and the traditions of this ancient race. *In a Hundred Graves: A Basque Portrait* (1972) consists of forty-five vignettes, capturing the essence of life in a Basque village. These impressionistic sketches seem elemental in the same way that fairy tales and legends do, possessing a timeless and mythic quality. The book is not a continuous narrative, but is rather like an album of verbal snapshots, some of which are lyrical enough to be prose poems. The book was selected in 1976 by the American Library Association as one of the outstanding books published in the western United States during the previous five years.

A Cup of Tea in Pamplona (1985) was similarly well received. It was nominated for the Pulitzer Prize in fiction, and it led to Laxalt's being awarded one of Spain's most prestigious literary honors, the Tambor de Oro (Golden Drum). This engaging novella tells the story of Basque smugglers along the Spanish-French border, tracing the fate of one smuggler named Nikolas, a poor man who is given the opportunity by his boss, Gregorio, to take over a prosperous smuggling business. Nikolas is torn because accepting Gregorio's offer will cause him to rise above his allotted station in life, thus incurring the icy disapproval of the villagers. This story explores the institution of smuggling, showing that it, too, follows a code of conduct and that there is an unspoken understanding between the smugglers and the border guards, almost as if they are players in a never-ending game.

In *A Time We Knew: Images of Yesterday in the Basque Homeland* (1990), Laxalt collaborates with photographer William Albert Allard to produce a handsome, large-format book that chronicles the passing of a European peasant society from the old way of life into the age of tractors and mechanization. Laxalt's eloquent chapters revisit territory and events depicted in his *National Geographic* articles and earlier books, including descriptions of Basque troubadours, of fishermen heading out to sea, of market day, of a dove hunt with nets, of Sunday mass where men sit in the upper gallery, and of an old village deserted by its young people. As in some of Laxalt's Nevada writings, a note of nostalgia creates a wistful mood:

> How sad it would be to see the oxen go. To trade the warm barn smell
> of an animal for the unlovely smell of oil. To trade a hand-hewn yoke of
> polished wood for a steering wheel. To trade the nuzzling touch of a
> great soft nose for cold, unloving metal. To trade a friend for a machine.

But I knew even then that that was progress. And one would be fool-
ish to argue against it, because he would not have reason on his side.

In the composition phase, the Basque-family trilogy started out as one long
novel. When the project began to seem unwieldy, Laxalt showed the manuscript to a friend, who proposed that he break it up into three related books.
The resulting trilogy is based on the experiences of the Laxalt family, but
being fiction, the scenes are selective and suggestive rather than rigorously
factual or exactingly chronological. Family names are changed, so that Laxalt's father, Dominique, is renamed Petya, his mother, Theresa, appears as
Maitia, Robert goes by the name Pete, and his older brother Paul becomes
Leon. Nevertheless, the trilogy reveals the personal stories and internal dy-
namics of the Laxalt family, and as such, it breaks the Basque code of family
privacy. This trilogy, then, is as American as it is Basque.

The first book in the trilogy, *The Basque Hotel* (1989) follows the life of the
boy Pete as he grows up in Carson City in the 1930s. Laxalt does a remarkable
job of conveying the flavor of Carson City at a particular moment in time and
of showing how broad historical events, such as the Great Depression, felt to
an individual living through them. The narrator, Pete, recalls how Okies got
into bar fights with locals and how the townspeople scrambled when word
went around that Prohibition officers were in town. Because the story is told
from the young Pete's perspective, an effect of dramatic irony is achieved, in
which there is more meaning to certain incidents than the narrator himself is
aware of. This slender rites-of-passage story is one of Laxalt's best works. Each
of its short, poignant chapters can stand on its own as a jewel; taken together,
they form a masterpiece. *The Basque Hotel* was nominated for a Pulitzer Prize
and was chosen by the New York Public Library in 1991 to be on the Books for
the Teen Age list.

"I could never have written it when Mama was alive," Laxalt once said
of *Child of the Holy Ghost* (1992). This second book in the Basque-family trilogy imaginatively chronicles the life of Pete's mother as she grew up in
the Basque country. It is revealed that she is an illegitimate child—a "child
of the holy ghost"—the product of her pretty mother's love for a French
officer, who returned to marry her but was banished forever at gunpoint by
her strict father. The book contrasts the Old World with its rigid customs
and strict parental authority and the New World with its permissiveness and
individualism. Of all Laxalt's work, *Child of the Holy Ghost* is most sensitive to the experience of women. In Laxalt's other books, women figure
as mothers, wives, and seductresses, but they remain in the background
while men take center stage. This book, however, with great sympathy and

understanding, enters into the minds and hearts of women, focusing on their stories.

The final book of the trilogy, *The Governor's Mansion* (1994), is likewise exceptional in Laxalt's canon, but for a different reason. It is both the longest and the most contemporary of all his works. Robert's brother Paul (named Leon in the book) is the protagonist of this gripping saga, which charts the ups and downs of his political campaigns and career as governor of Nevada and as a United States senator. Gone is the note of nostalgia found in the other works. Rather, this action-packed page-turner reads like a political intrigue, as narrator Pete reveals the backroom strategizing and behind-the-scenes machinations that typify American politics. With a cast of characters in the hundreds, *The Governor's Mansion* mixes real names, such as Howard Hughes and J. Edgar Hoover, with invented names for otherwise identifiable Nevada political figures, such as Grant Sawyer, Rex Bell, and Howard Cannon. Buffs of Nevada politics will enjoy figuring out who is who. For readers less well acquainted with the political scene, this book may be disillusioning as noble sentiments and high ideals evaporate in the dog-eat-dog atmosphere of a campaign.

This book is a fitting conclusion to the Basque-family trilogy, since the campaign is a family effort. Leon's brothers, two of whom were Democrats, both become Republicans in order to help with the campaign. The family house in Carson City becomes an informal election headquarters and is wired with extra phone lines to receive the fast-breaking election returns. With Leon's visibility, the privacy of this immigrant family is forever shattered. From Dominique's humble beginning as a Basque sheepherder and within his lifetime, the Laxalts have become prominent Americans.

While a review of Laxalt's literary achievements may give the impression that he must have become a full-time writer, he has in fact always held other jobs, some of them noteworthy in their own right. His career at the University of Nevada, Reno, has left a wealth of accomplishments and institutions that continue to play a central role in Nevada's cultural life.

In 1954, Laxalt quit the newspaper business in order to work for the University of Nevada, Reno, as director of news and publications, a position he held until 1967. In this capacity, Laxalt was responsible for all university publications, including the university catalog, alumni magazine, and news releases. The job entailed producing nearly as much copy as had the United Press International job, but it offered him greater stability and—in light of the death threat—considerably more safety.

By 1960, Laxalt began conceiving of a new enterprise for the university.

The University of Nevada had been established in 1864, but nearly one hundred years later, it still had no press. Most of the nation's better universities were affiliated with presses, and if Nevada intended to strive for excellence, it needed to follow suit. In order to found the university press, Laxalt presented a proposal to the new university president, Charles Armstrong, who was solidly in favor of the idea. Laxalt then persuaded the board of regents that it was time to establish a press. He argued that Nevada's history was not being recorded and that valuable sources of information were dying and disappearing. In 1961 the Nevada legislature approved the idea and gave the press a small initial grant.

As founding director of the press, Laxalt sought the counsel of well-established university presses, hoping to avoid most of the pitfalls that had sunk fledgling presses elsewhere. One piece of advice that was repeated from all quarters was "don't get too big too fast." Accordingly, in its early years, UNP limited its publications to one or two books per year, attempting mainly to fill up the holes in Nevada history. However, in 1970, under Laxalt's directorship, the press undertook a bold new venture by launching its Basque Book series, devoted to the study of Basque culture, history, and politics in America and Europe. The immediate success of its first book, Rodney Gallop's *A Book of the Basques,* convinced the press that it had made a good move. This popular series continues to be the only one of its kind in the country and enjoys international recognition. Laxalt donated the royalties from *In a Hundred Graves* to the series.

Another ambitious series initiated by Laxalt was launched in 1980 with an unprecedentedly large grant of $550,000 from the Max C. Fleishmann Foundation. The Max C. Fleishmann Series in Great Basin Natural History publishes works dealing with the flora, fauna, and natural resources of the region. To date, books in this series have covered geology, biogeography, birds, fish, trees, and shrubs. Each book is authored by a leading authority in the field and is written so that it can be both easily understood by lay readers and satisfying to scholars.

The four original goals of the University of Nevada Press continue to guide the press today: to disseminate knowledge, to preserve Nevada's heritage, to stimulate scholarship, and to enhance the university's academic reputation. From its small beginning, UNP has met these goals admirably, having published approximately 250 books and won numerous awards. Laxalt retired as director of the press in 1983, but he continues to demonstrate his loyalty, publishing his recent fiction with UNP rather than with a more lucrative trade publisher.

Laxalt still leads an active university life. In 1983 he was named a Reynolds

Distinguished Visiting Professor in the university's Donald W. Reynolds School of Journalism. In 1986 he was named Edward W. Scripps II Visiting Professor in Journalism, and in 1988 became the first occupant of the Distinguished Nevada Author chair at the university. The courses he has taught range from "Feature Writing for Magazines" to "Literary Journalism," which studies the work of writers such as Stephen Crane, Jack London, John Steinbeck, Ernest Hemingway, Katherine Anne Porter, and Alexander Solzhenitsyn, all of whom began their careers in journalism. His most recent course consists of a tutorial for a small group of handpicked aspiring writers, in which each student will produce a novella. Thus, not only has Laxalt left a legacy of his own writing, but in dedicating his time to teaching, he is helping cultivate the next generation of Nevada writers.

If it were not for Robert Laxalt, it is doubtful that one would see red, white, and green bumper stickers on Nevada cars and trucks, proclaiming "PROUD TO BE BASQUE." Laxalt has worked hard to stimulate Basque pride and to preserve the Basque heritage in Nevada and throughout the American West. In 1957 *Sweet Promised Land* generated a flood of letters from immigrants throughout the West, thanking Laxalt for telling their story. He became the literary spokesman for Basques in America. So when John Ascuaga, himself a Basque, and the entrepreneurial owner of the Nugget hotel-casino in Sparks, Nevada, wanted to host the first Western Basque Festival, he approached Laxalt for help. Laxalt and state senator Peter Echeverria became the two principal organizers of the festival, which was held at the Nugget on June 6 and 7, 1959. The initial mailing list used to announce the event was compiled from all the letters Laxalt had received in response to *Sweet Promised Land.*

The first Western Basque Festival mushroomed into a huge event, attended by more than five thousand people, including ambassadors from France and Spain. The planning committee, headed by Laxalt and Echeverria, essentially had to invent the festival program from scratch, since there had been no such festival in America before. There were speeches, a memorial service, a sheepdog exhibition, a Basque card game, contests of skill and strength, a tug-of-war between sheepmen and cattlemen, singing, dancing, and plenty of traditionally hearty Basque food. This festival became the inspiration and prototype for the numerous Basque festivals held throughout the West today. Thanks largely to these lively events, the Basque role in American history is recognized, and Basque culture is celebrated in the United States.

Still another contribution Laxalt made to preserving the Basque heritage in Nevada was to help establish the Basque Studies Program at the University of Nevada, Reno. In the 1960s, a group of outside consultants advised the university to initiate a Basque Studies Program, recognizing that Reno is the geographical center of the Basque peoples of the American West and that the university aspired to develop specific centers of excellence. Laxalt agreed to facilitate this effort by making contacts with leading scholars in the Basque country during his one-year stay there in 1965 and 1966. He met with the aging Basque scholar Philippe Veyrin and arranged to have the university acquire his extensive library. Veyrin's books formed the core of what would become the largest library of Basque materials in the Western Hemisphere, a magnet for Basque researchers all over the world. Laxalt also met with a young anthropologist, Reno-born William A. Douglass, who was hired to direct the new Basque Studies Program and who later served as editor of UNP's Basque Book series.

In 1988, a committee was discussing the idea of erecting a national monument to the Basque sheepherder of the American West. As a member of the American Monument Committee, Laxalt journeyed to the Basque country with Reno newspaperman Warren Lerude to help raise funds for the project. Accompanied by Basque sculptor Nestor Basterretxea, they met with officials, businessmen, and cultural leaders. Laxalt declared that the monument would stand as a symbol of the Basque presence in the history of the United States, and he warned, "In not too long a time, that presence would be swallowed up in the melting pot that is America." The visit was a success, and today one may view the tall copper sculpture in a county park in Reno, where the striking monument stands on a sagebrush-dotted hillside where shepherds once tended their flocks.

Robert Laxalt's advice to young writers is that they should take their work very seriously. But, he characteristically continues, they should not take *themselves* too seriously. In this spirit of humility, Nevada's distinguished author plans to hang his "No Name Laxalt" birth certificate in his office to bring him down to earth when his opinion of himself gets too lofty. Laxalt's modesty is as deep-seated as his Basque roots. As he explains, in Basque culture one does not praise someone's baby for being beautiful or clever, because that praise could bring the baby bad luck. When I interviewed Laxalt and asked him to identify his three or four major contributions to Nevada's heritage, he declined to answer, insisting that an answer would be too self-serving. Speaking for Laxalt, then, and hoping not to bring him bad luck, I would suggest that his major contributions are cultural and they have to do with giving Nevadans a tradition to meet their challenges.

Certainly, Laxalt's most celebrated achievement has been his writing. The many awards he has received affirm that his literary talent has been widely recognized and appreciated. Through his writing, Laxalt has shown Americans the "other" Nevada, a rural Nevada, an immigrant Nevada, a family-oriented Nevada. His books and his community service have created a Basque heritage in the American West. Supplementing his writing, Laxalt's public career has benefited the state immeasurably. As a hard-hitting reporter, hard-working university news and publications director, visionary founding director of the University of Nevada Press, and distinguished professor of journalism, Laxalt has left a trail of thriving institutions and eager new writers.

And at age seventy-three, Laxalt continues to make his mark. He recently completed a term on the National Council on Humanities; he is still teaching; and he is working on two more books. Happily, the final chapter of his life story remains to be written.

Grant Sawyer

A Liberal Governor for a Conservative State

BY JEROME E. EDWARDS

Grant Sawyer, governor of Nevada from 1959 through 1966, is an anomaly among Nevada officeholders. Certainly the most liberal Nevada governor of his era, he was generally successful in winning office in a decidedly conservative state. He served as governor during a time of transition and unprecedented growth, and he succeeded in redefining issues for the state's rapidly changing population. In the words of Richard Bryan, another Nevada governor and a U.S. senator, "He was the first modern Nevada governor."

Sawyer was born in Twin Falls, Idaho, on December 14, 1918, the son of two osteopathic physicians, Harry William and Bula Belle Sawyer. He was the youngest of three boys. His parents, both individuals of fiery temperament and mismatched from the beginning, divorced when Grant was three. For most of the year, he lived with his mother and brothers near Twin Falls; he spent summers with his father, who settled in Fallon, Nevada. His mother later married a farmer, but this marriage also dissolved.

His early years were not easy. Growing up on a forty-acre farm near Twin Falls, he had to work hard. "Farm life was pretty bleak," he later said, "and I didn't care for it at all." The family grew most of its food on the farm, but there was hardly cash to pay for luxuries.

However disparate in temperament his mother and father were, both wanted young Grant and his brothers to work hard and to achieve something in life. They also shared a love of politics, and young Grant was both ambitious and politically oriented. His mother was a lifelong Democrat with a social conscience. In later years he credited his social sensitivity to her influence. "Mother felt that everyone should have a fair shake and an equal opportunity, no matter who they were or what their circumstances." His father became a Democratic Party wheelhorse in Fallon, with ambitions to become governor. The highest political office he obtained was to represent Churchill County in the Nevada State Senate from 1935 to

1939. His parents' passion for politics was shared by Grant. "If there is a political gene, I carry it."

In high school his primary interests were speech and theater. His mother saw to it that he received elocution lessons, and he placed fourth in a national oratorical contest. He appeared in virtually every school play performed. He learned how to tap-dance, and he appeared at Grange meetings and around the county. Grant pushed himself forward: "I was pretty breezy with every-body." He was president of his junior high class. Yet, among fellow students, his cocksure attitude did not make him popular, and he was scorned as a country boy, "a poor farm kid," a rube compared to the sophisticated Twin Falls town students. When he attempted to join a fraternity upon entering high school, he was rejected. This "was really a blow to my ego and one that I will ever regret." Ruminating about it more than sixty years later, Sawyer said: "I was deeply wounded and when I have gone to class reunions and seen men who were in a fraternity and wouldn't invite me to join. . . . More than anything in the world I have always wanted people to accept and trust me, . . . [b]ut I was rejected in high school." In his junior year he was accepted into a fraternity, but it was the earlier rejection that gnawed in his memory. Later he admitted that he had tried to move too fast and, by so doing, created resent-ment. "I learned that I couldn't live in an isolated world and be so cocksure that what I was doing was the great thing."

Despite his poverty there was never any question of his going to college. For two years he attended Linfield College, a small Baptist school in McMinnville, Oregon. A scholarship student and ever the compulsive joiner and office seeker, he was elected president of his freshman class and was on the student council as the representative of the sophomore class. At the end of his second year, he was asked to leave, since he had run afoul of the school's puritanical, restrictive atmosphere.

Grant had no choice but to transfer to the University of Nevada, located in Reno, because of his father's residency in the state. Nevada, with its freer atmosphere, provided a much happier experience for Sawyer than had Lin-field. The only university in a state of 110,000 residents, it had approximately 1,000 students. Sawyer could indulge in his love of acting ("I was in all the plays") and remained the indefatigable joiner, active in fraternity life, presi-dent of Alpha Tau Omega in his senior year, and a member of Coffin and Keys, an elitist secret society. The university attracted students from all over the state and was an educational training ground for future state leadership. Sawyer later remembered, "There was a lot to be said for going to college in Nevada if you were going to live in the state, because your classmates would be important to you the rest of your life." He developed many close relationships, particularly in his fraternity, that would be useful to him as he later made his way in political life. He graduated in the class of 1941. Germany was astride Western Europe and the Far East was standing on the brink of war.

After college he decided to go to law school, and, like many ambitious young men, decided to attend under the patronage of Nevada's powerful senator Patrick A. McCarran, then highly placed on the Senate Judiciary Committee. Since Nevada was by far the nation's least-populated state, it had no law school. What more natural then, than to attend in the Washington, D.C., area with the support of a Nevada senator? Many young Nevadans, ambitious to become lawyers or politicians (or both) went the same route. Grant's father and Senator McCarran had once been close friends, but by 1941 they were not speaking to each other. However, keeping a previous promise, Senator McCarran took Grant under his wing, and in the fall of 1941, Sawyer started law school at George Washington University. He worked for McCarran as a Capitol Hill security officer, which meant that he worked at night and could sit and study for eight hours. He attended law school for only one year before entering the army in 1942.

Sawyer spent four years serving his country in the military. He went through officer candidate school and graduated as a second lieutenant. Although he never saw combat, he spent a year in the Philippines before the war ended. He also served in Korea for a year. He later declared that the four years he spent in the military were the most valuable years of his life. The army taught him how to handle people and forced him to deal with people of diverse backgrounds. It widened his experience. He came out "much more mature, a great deal more understanding of the other person's point of view." Like millions of other G.I.s, he was in a hurry when he was released from the service: "We felt we had lost time." But Sawyer seemed to have more focus; he wanted to finish his education and get along with a law career.

Senator McCarran, now the chair of the United States Judiciary Committee, took him back again in his office, and with the senator's help and the assistance of the G.I. Bill of Rights, Sawyer transferred to Georgetown University Law School. He soon married Bette, whom he had met in Reno. He now worked in McCarran's office on veterans' problems, helping Nevada constituents who came to McCarran for help. Although Senator McCarran had a well-deserved reputation in the Senate and among fellow politicians of being difficult to work with, he treated the assistants in his office with great kindness and respect, and those Nevadans who went through law school under his patronage developed a deep affection and loyalty to him. "What the hell," said one. "McCarran took me off the street when my belly had wrinkles on it. He fed me and clothed me, and put me through law school and helped me get started in practice. What kind of jerk would I be to turn on him now." As for Sawyer: "We all looked upon him as the Holy Ghost: we thought anything he did was just terrific." Ideologically the senator was increasingly out of sympathy with the dominant Truman wing of the party, but Sawyer never questioned his policies, "not even in private." He was very proud then and later to be a "McCarran boy" (as they were popularly called in Nevada), and from the experience he learned the value of loyalty in politics. "He was my mentor, and I will never be apologetic for any association with him," said Sawyer. McCarran's political organization in Nevada was a personal one. He did many things for his constituents and for his "boys," and he asked only one thing in return: undeviating loyalty. He got it from Sawyer.

McCarran's boys were expected to enter politics and to do good for the senator. Since Sawyer had never actually lived in Nevada except as a student at its university for two years, he was not tied to any particular community. So after traveling around some of the cow counties, he and his wife decided to live in Elko. The personable, able young Sawyer now determined to make up for lost time, and his being a McCarran protégé and a veteran carried him far. In 1950 he ran for district attorney of Elko County, overwhelmingly defeating the incumbent, Leo Puccinelli. He also became a hard party worker, chairing the 1952 Nevada State Democratic Convention. In 1954 he was chairman of the Elko County Democratic Central Committee, and then was elected to the state central committee. In 1956, he was a delegate to the Democratic National Convention and served on its resolutions committee. In 1956 he ran for a seat on the University of Nevada Board of Regents with the idea of removing the university's dictatorial president, Minard W. Stout. He ran well, for an unknown, but was narrowly defeated. Quite fortuitously, the size of the board was expanded after the election and Governor Charles Russell appointed him to it anyway. Sawyer had the pleasure of serving on the Board of Regents just long enough to fire Stout, then resigning to seek higher office.

That higher office was the governorship. In most states, a bid to its highest office by a political unknown—not yet forty years old, with a record of having been elected only to one county office—would have been an act of extreme folly. It worked for Sawyer in Nevada for a number of reasons.

First, the path to advancement within the Democratic Party had been opened up by the death of Senator Patrick McCarran in September 1954. By hanging on so long, McCarran had kept the lid on advancement for many promising individuals. His influence in the Democratic Party had been personal, not ideological, and with his death the cement of his machine dissolved. What was left remained under the control of "old boys" such as Norman Biltz and Errett L. Cord, conservative, bipartisan, establishment businessmen; but they preferred to work behind the scenes and had no electoral following. During the 1950s, Democrats such as Alan Bible and Howard Cannon were to be elected to the United States Senate from Nevada, and opportunity opened up for the likes of the increasingly liberal Grant Sawyer.

Then too, Nevada was changing at an exceptionally rapid pace. Although its number of residents was still tiny, Nevada was experiencing the fastest rate of population growth in the nation. Newcomers were swelling Nevada's population from 110,247 in 1940 to 160,083 in 1950 and 285,278 in 1960. The reasons for this astonishing growth were twofold: legalized gambling, which was catching the imagination of tourists; and vastly increased government and military spending within the state. For the newcomers, the old politicians and the old attitudes did not mean much. Ranching and mining no longer controlled everything, except in sentimental attachment (and legislative apportionment). A new chief city, Las Vegas, was expecting its special interests to be carried out and its needs to be fulfilled. For the cow counties and the old establishment leaders, gambling was an afterthought, something that had been relegalized in 1931 almost in a fit of absentmindedness, something that could be regulated in time if need be—and for the most part, they denied any need. Wealthy individuals who had come into Nevada in the 1930s and 1940s, individuals such as Cord and Max Fleischmann, had great but unseen influence. They had fled high taxation elsewhere, and what they wanted from Nevada was a very conservative, very low tax structure. They were not interested in attacking the problems resulting from growth, and if the problems were to be attacked, the price was not to be paid by the wealthy.

The old, conservative, establishment coalitions still ran the legislature. Particularly in the state senate, where each county had one senator, the cow counties, with their no-growth, ranching and mining temperaments, held tight control. Despite Nevada's electorate being basically Democratic, the state senate was controlled by Republicans in every session from 1941 through 1965. Even the Nevada State Assembly, apportioned ostensibly by population, was not truly representative, since every county, no matter how tiny, was constitutionally ensured at least one assemblyman, Thus in 1960, when Clark County (which includes Las Vegas) had 44.6 percent of Nevada's population, it held only 32.4 percent of the seats in the assembly and 5.9 percent of the seats in the senate. By contrast, the four smallest counties (Storey, Esmeralda, Eureka, and Lander) combined had 1.2 percent of the state's population but 10.8 percent of assembly seats and 23.5 percent of senate seats. This unrepresentative legislature was to be a constant impediment to the young, dynamic, but inexperienced governor.

Sawyer's march to the governorship was surprisingly easy. He had an engaging campaigning style and came across as youthful, earnest, and idealistic. And he was, after all, a veteran, and an old McCarran boy. He was pro-labor, supported further gaming control, and stated "Nevada's not for sale"—a not-too-oblique allusion to the wealthy E. L. Cord's influence in the state. Nevada was still small enough for him to meet most of the voters, and he seemed a fresh, vital influence. He handily won the Democratic primary against establishment candidate Harvey Dickerson and maverick George Franklin. In the general election, he was adequately financed by casino money out of the Strip (in the form of cash) and defeated, by a large margin, incumbent Republican governor Charles Russell, who was attempting an unprecedented third term. Sawyer's 1958 win reflected victories by Democrats throughout the nation and the American West, including the election of Democrat Howard Cannon to the United States Senate from Nevada.

But governing would not to be so easy. Although Sawyer might have seemed the harbinger of a new Nevada, there were many entrenched individuals in the legislature and the bureaucracy who thought he had come too far too fast, that he was too articulate and cocky and had not properly earned his spurs. Some thought he was too slick. He needed to be knocked down a bit. And he was dreadfully inexperienced. As he later said, "I immediately discovered that my margin of victory had very little to do at all with my influence, particularly in the legislature." His first years in office were "a terrible ordeal." He floundered, not being particularly knowledgeable about state government or about the people with whom he had to work. The legislature and the bureaucrats were not impressed by the size of his victory or his stated need for new policies. "I found that some situations," he later admitted ruefully, "would probably have gone better had I stayed out of debate." The governor of Nevada does not have particularly strong powers to begin with, and Sawyer was to feel buffeted by one crisis after another, and by an increasingly rejuvenated Republican Party.

By the time Sawyer became governor, the gambling "industry" was by a considerable margin the state's largest employer. It had become indispensable for Nevada's prosperity; its removal would have brought economic collapse. It was catching on with the American tourist. Gambling gross revenues had soared from $21 million in 1946 to $74 million in 1953 and $145 million in 1958. The state had become hostage to its continual growth. By the time of Sawyer's accession to office in 1959, revelations from Senator Estes Kefauver's special committee investigation of organized crime had given it a tarnished, and well-deserved, reputation as being mob-ridden. As the Kefauver Committee had intoned in 1951, "As a case history of legalized gambling, Nevada speaks eloquently in the negative." Most Nevadans wore blinders to the fact that there was any problem with mob infiltration into the state; the smug general attitude was that the Kefauver hearings had been sensationalized and that if there indeed were a problem, honest Nevada citizens in due course would take care of it. Indeed, many of the people who were accused of mob connections had become model pillars of the Las Vegas community. Yet there was the obvious problem that if the "sensationalist" charges were in fact true, the federal government might swoop in and destroy Nevada's special institution. So in 1955, the state took the first hesitant step to regulate (and therefore save) its chief industry, creating a state Gaming Control Board under the state Tax Commission, with sole licensing power. People who already held licenses, however, were "grandfathered" in without any inconvenient investigations.

In January 1959, in Sawyer's first state-of-the-state message, the governor recommended a new independent state Gaming Commission with licensing powers, a recommendation that passed the legislature by an overwhelming margin. He was careful to appoint new members to both the new commission and the old board who were not involved with the gambling industry and therefore presumably more disinterested. Also important was the creation of a Black Book (officially, the List of Excluded Persons) by the Sawyer administration upon the advice of commission chairman Ray Abbaticchio. The Black Book was a brief list of individuals with lengthy police records who were to be forbidden from entering a hotel-casino. Names were entered in the book without stated cause or right of appeal. The list was published under Sawyer's public imprint, although privately he thought it of doubtful constitutionality. "I didn't see how we could put somebody's name on a list and say, 'You can't go into a public accommodation.' But they thought differently, and because I was in favor of doing anything within the law to keep those people out of Nevada, I authorized them to go ahead." John Marshall, an individual with a lengthy police record, brought suit against the Black Book in federal court, which upheld its constitutionality. The most important, and flagrant, flouting of the rules of the Black Book occurred in 1963, when singer Frank Sinatra entertained Chicago boss Sam Giancana (listed in the Black Book) at his hotel, the Cal Neva, located on the north shore of Lake Tahoe. Sinatra, who subsequently became quite abrasive toward Gaming Commission secretary Ed Olsen when called to account on the matter, lost his Nevada license, with the support of Governor Sawyer.

Sawyer's chief problem with gambling regulation stemmed from his increasingly difficult relationship with the Kennedy administration, which thought the state was acting too slowly and ineffectually in staving off Mafia infiltration. Sawyer, who was the only prominent state Democrat to have backed John F. Kennedy in 1960 for the Democratic presidential nomination, might not have expected such pressure from this source; but the president's brother, U.S. attorney general Robert F. Kennedy, had become obsessed with the ties of the Teamsters union with organized crime and how the Teamsters Central States Pension Fund had showered money into the construction of major hotel-casinos on the Las Vegas Strip. From the standpoint of state authorities, this meant the indispensable infusion of money into a capital-starved industry at a time no bank would dream of lending money to such a suspect enterprise. To Robert Kennedy it meant a sinister alliance between organized crime and Nevada gambling. In the words of sociologist Jerome H. Skolnick, "Kennedy was planning to clean out what he called the 'bank of America's organized crime,' and failing that, 'he would press Congress to close down gambling.'"

In summer of 1961, Sawyer learned that the Department of Justice had asked state attorney general Roger Foley to deputize sixty-five federal agents to raid every major casino in Las Vegas and Reno. Sawyer immediately flew to Washington, D.C., to see Robert Kennedy and try to thwart the secret plan.

> The day after Roger told me, we got on a plane and went to Washington and I made an appointment to see the attorney general. To my recollection it was on a weekend, because when I was shown into [*sic*] see Bobby Kennedy I found him dressed for a game of tennis or something. I asked if he was planning to raid Nevada; and, if so, why? We had a heated discussion, to say the least, and there was no give or compromise on his part at all. He looked at Nevada, as many people then did, as a den of iniquity. . . . [E]verybody who lived in or came to Nevada was corrupt, including me, and to clean the state up he was ready to assign a substantial force of agents to raid it.
>
> . . . It was that attitude that Bobby Kennedy projected: "You are a bunch of peasants out there; you're all sort of sleazy. We here in the East, who know all, are going to come out there and set you right, whether you like it or not." As a personal matter I was particularly offended, because I got the impression that Bobby looked upon me as someone who had just stepped out from behind a crap table; and he seemed to imply that I was connected with the mob, which really burned me up. I remember pounding the table and just feeling that I was making no progress with him at all.

Sawyer went to the president, who called off the raid; but the federal government kept intact a system of illegal wiretaps. Sawyer was offended by Washington's tactics and never forgave either Robert Kennedy or J. Edgar Hoover. Even as governor, he denounced Hoover's "Nazi tactics." He was the first major public official to call for Hoover's resignation. In later years he stated that Hoover was "contemptuous of the Constitution, and . . . relentless in his abuse of federal power." Neither Hoover nor Robert Kennedy ever provided the state with any useful information it could act upon, although much of the illegally obtained material on mobsterism in Nevada was leaked to newsman Sandy Smith of the *Chicago Sun-Times,* with devastating consequences for Nevada's image. In truth, neither state nor national government trusted each other, and they wasted much energy throwing salvos at each other.

Sawyer's record on the regulation of gambling was decidedly mixed. He cemented the state's regulatory structure in a fashion that earned respect elsewhere. The Frank Sinatra and John Marshall incidents demonstrated that Nevada meant business. On the other hand, mob influence remained pervasive in Las Vegas throughout Sawyer's tenure. The governor was correct when he later asserted that during his gubernatorial service the state never licensed anyone who later turned out to be a member of organized crime. But the problem was the state's (and Sawyer's) refusal to go after individuals who already had a license; the worst offenders were those who had been grandfathered in from a more permissive period. The policy was always aimed at preventing new infusions of mob infestation rather than rooting out the old—or as Sawyer put it weakly, "There wasn't really anything I could do about those who were already here and licensed before I was elected except watch them carefully." Too drastic an uprooting of the gang element in Nevada gambling would have led to a collapse of the industry, for who could have replaced the existing ownership? Sawyer was always concerned, and defensive, about Nevada's image, and the consequences of a vigorous clampdown on mobster elements would have been too deleterious to the image: Nevada would have had to admit it had a serious problem.

So the state and the federal government refused to speak to each other during Sawyer's tenure, and the vast majority of the evidence regarding Mafia infiltration on the Strip was obtained, not by the Nevada authorities, but by enterprising "sensationalist" reporters and by the federal government using illegal tactics. Not until Howard Hughes arrived in Las Vegas in November 1966 was useful progress made. Hughes bought out much of the mob and provided a much brighter "image" to Nevada's peculiar industry. The switch to corporate-owned gaming after 1969 also pushed Nevada into different directions and provided viable alternative financing opportunities for capital construction. In the end, the market forces of capitalism, more than state regulation, destroyed the mob in Nevada, and Sawyer was involved with none of it.

The crowning glory of Sawyer's record as governor was his intense and heartfelt commitment to civil rights. Far more than any other Nevada politician, Sawyer's name is identified with this issue. His record is unique among Nevada politicians. When he became governor in 1959, Nevada's primary industry was entirely segregated. Major casinos and hotels forbade black dealers, much less black customers. Only a few small clubs, such as the New China club in Reno or the Mardi Gras in Las Vegas, both under minority ownership, attempted integration. If popular black entertainers like Sammy Davis Jr. or Nat "King" Cole entertained (they did bring in big bucks from the white customers), they had to sleep off the premises; nor could they eat in hotel restaurants or gamble in the club. This discrimination was woven into the whole culture of the gambling industry. Casino owners claimed that white customers would desert them if their hotel-casinos were open to blacks. It was an exaggeration to call Nevada the "Mississippi of the West" as some did, but the canard certainly holds true with the state's chief industry. Until 1959 state authorities were quite complacent about the situation.

Sawyer had not made civil rights an issue in his 1958 campaign ("It would have been political suicide."). But from the beginning of his administration he provided moral vision and political leadership to end this deplorable state of affairs. It was an issue of his own choosing. No previous Nevada politician had ever made civil rights a major (or minor) issue. In his inaugural address Sawyer stated:

> In a democracy, there should be no gaps between principles and practices when the civil rights of a man are involved. A community conscience may be apprized by the way it is concerned with those rights and privileges which are guaranteed by law to each individual regardless of his membership in any racial or ethnic group: the right to employment, to education, to housing, to the use of public accommodations, to health and welfare services and facilities, and the right to live in peace and dignity without discrimination, segregation or distinction based on race, religion, color, ancestry, national origin or place of birth.

The spirit was genuine, but the brave words were impossible to implement immediately. Sawyer found the old mind-set extremely difficult to break through. There was the Nevada state legislature, neanderthal in its attitude on social issues, particularly the regressively apportioned state senate. Initially Sawyer had difficulty finding any legislator to introduce *any* civil rights legislation; eventually Maude Frazier introduced AB 122, which outlawed discrimination in *public* employment. Sawyer signed such a bill in March 1960. This of course did not address the deeper issue of discrimination in private business, particularly in gambling. In 1961 the legislature set up a Civil Rights Commission but purposely gave it no authority or adequate funding.

The legislature was hopeless, so Sawyer was forced to act on his own. He attempted moral suasion. When the owner of the El Capitan Motel in Hawthorne refused to allow an African diplomat, on his way to the Winter Olympics in Squaw Valley, to register as a guest, the governor got on the phone to successfully persuade him to change his mind. Sawyer also used veiled threats. Since the governor does have considerable powers over gaming, he called a meeting of some of the major casino owners in the state to announce that "so far as the regulation and enforcement of gaming were concerned the policy of the state was that there would not be discrimination in either public accommodation or hiring." He threatened hearings on licensing for those casinos that flouted this policy. Although Attorney General Harvey Dickerson intoned (probably accurately) that the governor had no authority to do this, Sawyer did it anyway. The governor received valuable support in this policy from demonstrations and lobbying organized by the NAACP. In 1964, the issue was settled anyway with the passage of the United States Civil Rights Act. But Sawyer had gone out of his way to exercise the full moral authority of his office to accelerate the desegregation and stop the discrimination in the state's leading industry. His rhetoric was unprecedented for Nevada politicians of this era, and eventually it was implemented by federal muscle.

Grant Sawyer was a leader in increasing funding for education. During Sawyer's tenure as governor, enrollment in the two state universities increased by 116 percent, and many new faculty were hired. Nevada Southern University in Las Vegas, which had just opened its doors in 1955, grew rapidly—but not at the expense of the University of Nevada, which by 1966 had some 5,000 students. Average daily attendance at public schools in the state soared from 53,000 in 1958–1959 to 98,000 in 1965–1966.

He was a believer in growth for his state, and to obtain that growth Nevada needed water. The Southern Nevada Water Project, achieved in 1965, had his strongest support, although it was Senator Alan Bible who helped push it through Congress. This enactment gave Las Vegas necessary water until the year 2000. Sawyer envisioned eventually bringing Columbia River water to Nevada. "The Columbia River dumps millions of acre feet of water into the Pacific every year while Nevada and California are starving for water." At the same time, the governor was proud of his efforts to protect Lake Tahoe and supported a national park there, a proposal that went nowhere. More successful was his support for the creation of Great Basin National Park, centered at

Wheeler Peak. Sawyer resented that the United States government controlled so much Nevada land (87 percent), but he also looked to federal largess to underwrite the state's expansion.

At times Sawyer's liberalism hurt him politically in conservative Nevada. His support of an early-prisoner-release bill in 1965 contributed to his defeat the following year. It worried him that Nevada was incarcerating more people per capita than any other state, and was sensitive to the social conditions that put people into prisons. Sawyer wanted to get out of the cycle of putting more and more individuals into prison and then building more and more prisons.

Increasingly, Sawyer was interested in civil liberties and Bill of Rights protections. In later words that could have been spoken by few other politicians, and which referred to his feelings during his governorship, he declared, "Even in those days I was more concerned about the real enemy within— police state tactics, the power of the FBI, the American people being disenfranchised by their own government—than I was about communists. Senator Joe McCarthy's witch hunts, and J. Edgar Hoover, and the secret government that was controlling our lives were what truly troubled me."

Perhaps the most fundamental change to Nevada's governance during Sawyer's tenure had nothing to do with him, but it made the state government far more responsive to the issues raised by growth. In 1962 the United States Supreme Court declared, in *Baker* v. *Carr,* that the apportionment of state legislatures, a matter traditionally left up to the states, could be reviewed by federal courts. In 1964, in *Reynolds* v. *Sims,* the high court got specific: It ordered all states to apportion both houses of their legislatures by population. Sawyer waffled on the issue, contending it was a purely legislative matter. "My attitude was simply, what difference does it make? This is now the law of the land, and there is nothing we can do about it." Infuriated cow-county legislators lost their tight grip on the state legislature, and after 1970, a majority of legislators would come from just one county, Clark. Gambling interests rather than ranching and mining were to run the state, and with the growth produced by gambling, the new generation of legislators would generally be more responsive to the problems raised by that growth. At least they were more representative of what the state was about.

Grant Sawyer handily won reelection in 1962 against Mayor Oran Gragson of Las Vegas. His only political option in 1966 was to run for a third term: the two U.S. senators, both Democrats, were entrenched, and Sawyer, always the good party loyalist, would not have dreamed of challenging them anyway. But by 1966 Sawyer faced bitter divisions in his own party, and he had two serious challengers. One was Ted Marshall, the district attorney of Clark County, who charged that the governor was soft on crime. The other was

Reno attorney Charles Springer, who made serious allegations that Sawyer had accepted $100,000 from gamblers in 1962. He defeated both opponents with 70 percent of the vote; but the division hurt him grievously, and he faced a far more formidable opponent in the general election, Lieutenant Governor Paul Laxalt. Laxalt, a man whom Sawyer neither liked nor respected, had come within forty-eight votes of defeating Senator Howard Cannon in 1964. A chief issue in the 1966 campaign was Sawyer's assertion of J. Edgar Hoover's "Nazi tactics" in the state, an issue that Sawyer could not have hoped to make a winning one. Sawyer was also vulnerable on the "soft on crime" charge leveled against him. Near the campaign's end, Laxalt sent a letter to Hoover, apologizing for the governor's language and behavior. Hoover then wrote to Hank Greenspun, publisher of the *Las Vegas Sun,* in words immediately published, that organized crime had infiltrated Nevada gambling and that Sawyer did not deserve reelection. By this time, Sawyer's number had come up. He lost, not too narrowly, the victim of an unusually acrimonious campaign.

With that defeat, the starch went out of him. His political ambition, which had defined his life, no longer remained. Circumstances were against him: Senators Bible and Cannon held the two U.S. Senate seats, and Sawyer, increasingly disillusioned by the Vietnam War, had no desire for an appointment from the Johnson administration. His years as governor had revealed a surprisingly thin skin, and his wife, Bette, and daughter, Gail, detested public life. He also found his lack of accomplishment as governor to be exceptionally frustrating. The last campaign had been nastily fought. "I was physically, emotionally, and mentally exhausted, when the 1966 campaign was over," he later confessed. "I had not the slightest desire ever to rerun that particular movie." He certainly should have taken comfort in the fact that although his governorship had not been particularly fruitful from the standpoint of practical accomplishments, except in the important area of civil rights, he had provided real moral leadership and direction for repositioning the state for its future. And he had demonstrated the utmost political courage in his political stances, a principled courage that certainly contributed to his defeat but that would earn him the greatest respect and devotion from a new generation of political participants.

He was not through with politics, either. He remained the consummate political insider and confidant of leading Democrats for more than a quarter of a century after his defeat. He had a great capacity for friendship and was held in affectionate regard by a new generation of politicians who sought his advice. He also became one of the most important (and well remunerated) attorneys in the state, and Lionel Sawyer & Collins, launched in February 1967, became Nevada's largest and most prestigious law firm, with offices in

Las Vegas and Reno. As always he was a participant in numerous organizations, the choice of which demonstrates his interests. He was active as Democratic National Committeeman from Nevada from 1968 to 1988, served on the national advisory council of the American Civil Liberties Union, was a longtime member of the NAACP, participated on the UNLV Foundation Board, and was on the board of directors of the National Judicial College. He fought hard against the establishment of a nuclear-waste dump at Yucca Mountain. Sawyer remained active in political life until he suffered a crippling stroke in July 1993, which forced him to curtail his public activities. He died of complications from the stroke on February 19, 1996, at the age of seventy-seven.

Molly Flagg Knudtsen

Rancher, Environmentalist, Educator

by Don D. Fowler

Molly Flagg arrived in Nevada in 1941. She came, as many women did in the 1930s and 1940s, to obtain a divorce. In doing so, she reached the end of her first life, and began a second in Nevada. Her accomplishments in her new life made her a very well-known and highly respected citizen of Nevada. She became a prominent cattle rancher and purebred stock breeder, served with distinction for two decades as a University of Nevada regent during a time of explosive growth and transition to the University of Nevada System (now the University and Community College System of Nevada), was actively sought after as a citizen adviser to a wide range of federal, state, and local groups, became an accomplished amateur historian and archaeologist, and continued to write short stories and poetry.

After her arrival in 1941, Molly spent the required six weeks' residency at a ranch owned by Francesca Blackmer, a relative of her stepfather's. Like Molly, Francesca was from a socially prominent eastern background and, like Molly, had earlier come to Nevada to obtain a divorce. She had married Bev Blackmer and remained to open a "divorce ranch," the River Ranch along the Truckee River, east of Reno. Molly spent her time helping to train the Blackmers' thoroughbred racehorses. She had ridden all her life, and in 1932 had earned a coveted diploma in equitation from the Royal Institute of the Horse in London, the training school for the British cavalry. To prepare for the examinations, she had studied with Major Faudel-Phillips, one of the great horsemanship teachers of the time. Now, her involvement with horses was the entré to her second life.

First Life

Thyrza "Molly" Benson Flagg was born in New York City on September 13, 1915, to Thyrza Hoe Benson and Montague Flagg. Molly was named for her mother but was known (by

10

her own choice) as Molly from her early childhood. Her maternal great-grandfather, Robert Hoe III, had presided over the great R. Hoe & Company, manufacturers of high-speed newspaper printing presses. The development of those presses in the nineteenth century brought the Hoe family great wealth and social prominence in the interlocking circles of Americans intermarried with British aristocracy who moved between East Coast America, England, and France.

Robert Hoe III was a great collector of rare books, an obsession that began at age eleven. He later expanded his collecting to include manuscripts and incunabula. He was greatly interested in the arts and was a founder of the Metropolitan Museum in New York. Hoe died in 1909, and in 1911 his 141,000-volume library was sold at three great auctions. Major buyers included Henry Huntington, busily forming his own library in San Marino, California; Peter A. B. Widener, benefactor of the Harvard University Library; J. Pierpont Morgan, who had competed with Hoe for rare books for years; and Henry Folger, founder of the Folger Shakespeare Library in Washington, D.C. Molly's mother, also a collector, bought some of her grandfather's books as well. Molly's own lifelong love of books thus had an almost genetic family basis.

Molly's father, Montague Flagg, an architect trained at the Massachusetts Institute of Technology, was an eighth-generation descendant of Thomas Flegg, who had come to Massachusetts Colony with the first Puritans in 1637. Generations of Flaggs made their fortunes in shipping, ships' chandlery, and perhaps the slave trade, centering on Newport, Rhode Island, and Nantucket, Massachusetts. Later Flaggs were prominent artists—society painters—and architects. Ernest Flagg, Montague's uncle, designed the Corcoran Gallery in Washington, D.C., and the Singer Tower (for a time the tallest skyscraper in New York, and the only one with a mansard roof), among other prominent commissions. Montague Flagg was best known for designing the Banker's Trust building in New York, another early skyscraper.

The Flagg family moved between a townhouse in New York and Brookville, their house on Long Island, where horses were kept. After World War I ended, trips resumed to Paris and the South of France. Molly's mother had her clothes made in Paris. When she was in New York, Molly attended Miss Chapin's School, as did most young ladies of her circle. Molly and the other young ladies took dancing lessons at the Colony Club and riding lessons in a "large, dank indoor arena" near Central Park, overseen by a series of long-suffering governesses and grooms.

Montague Flagg served as an officer in the U.S. Navy during World War I. Following the war, he and Thyrza became estranged and were divorced in

1922. He died in 1925, when Molly was ten. In 1927, Molly's mother married Harold Fowler, whom she had known for some years. Molly, who had idolized her father, deeply resented the marriage. She was packed off for a time to London, where she unhappily attended Miss Spalding's School. In 1928, she was sent to Foxcroft School in Middleburg, Virginia, spending summers and vacations with the Fowlers in New Jersey, on Long Island, or in Europe. Foxcroft was, and remains, a remarkable institution for educating young girls. It had been founded in 1915 by Charlotte L. Noland, who had very strong views about the outcome of the "recent unpleasantness," otherwise known as the Civil War, and equally strong views about the education of young women during her forty-year tenure as head mistress of the school. In addition to schoolwork, riding and sports were stressed. There also was a constant theme of social responsibility and public service that went well beyond the lip-service ideals of noblesse oblige; the tradition continues in the 1990s.

Molly wanted to be a writer. She read voraciously—as she has all her life—and wrote poetry, essays, and a first (unpublished) novel, while winning all the school athletic prizes and simultaneously failing English, which outraged her mother. A later novel ("as I recall, something about incest") was accepted by Scribner's on condition of some rewriting. A well-known editor, Maxwell Perkins, was assigned to help, but Molly did not complete the rewrite. Molly graduated from Foxcroft in 1931, but returned in 1932 for a stint of the community service Miss Charlotte deemed necessary for finishing a proper education.

Harold Fowler was handsome, witty, and socially prominent, a great horseman (he rode twice in the British Grand National—the most demanding steeplechase race in the world), and a hero of World War I. While he was all these things, there was also his "secret work," for which many of his activities were "covers." In 1906, Fowler had been asked by President Theodore Roosevelt to become involved in "secret service" matters for the United States. He agreed, and remained, until his death in 1957, a secret agent. Neither Molly nor her mother ever knew much about what he did; he would simply be gone for extended periods. A wealthy family moving through American and European social circles and making world tours was seemingly an excellent cover for his other activities.[1]

In the fall of 1933, Molly made her formal debut in New York, and the following spring was presented at the Court of Saint James, in London. She enrolled in King's College, University of London, in the fall of 1934, and shared a mews apartment with Countess Helen Spinolla. Molly formally studied the minor metaphysical Elizabethan poets, and informally, the art of serious partying. Between terms, she either joined her family in London,

France, or the States, or toured on the Continent. A July 1935 *New York Herald Tribune* photograph shows her "on the way to the beach" at Southampton, on Long Island. Not shown, but apparently near, were a variety of eager swains. In 1937 she became engaged to Robert Pinkerton Gibb. Very soon thereafter she had her first major horse accident. She recovered sufficiently to marry Gibb in the fall of 1937. But the accident had crushed a kidney, which was only later determined, and there were periodic bouts of serious illness. To recover, Molly spent most of 1938 and 1939 at Cannes, staying with family friends, the Herman Rogers family, who were also friends of Wallace Simpson. After Edward VIII abdicated the throne and married Mrs. Simpson, the couple, as the Duke and Duchess of Windsor, moved to a house near the Rogers's. Molly spent various evenings at the Rogers's table discussing horticulture and silvaculture with the duke, and as little as possible with the duchess.

SECOND LIFE

By mid-1939, Molly had recovered sufficiently to return to the United States. Before coming to Nevada for her divorce, she continued riding and trained greyhounds for coursing in New Jersey. In 1941 she devoted her requisite six weeks of Nevada residence to helping train Francesca Blackmer's horses. Prior to World War II, thoroughbred racing was a prominent activity in Nevada, as well as at the big tracks in California: Santa Anita, Bay Meadows, and others. During this time, Molly met Richard "Dick" Magee, who had a string of thoroughbreds and the Grass Valley Ranch in central Nevada.

Grass Valley is a long valley, typical of many in the Great Basin. It is high desert country par excellence: Its floor, at six-thousand-feet elevation, and foothills are covered with shadscale and sage; further up is the zone of piñon and juniper, then mountain mahogany, with tall pines beyond. East of Austin on U.S. Highway 50, there is a small "Grass Valley" sign marking a gravel road headed north. Twenty miles of dusty travel on the road brings one to the headquarters of the Grass Valley Ranch, surrounded by lush hayfields. Beyond the headquarters is a large dry lake bed, Lake Gilbert, named for the famous nineteenth-century government geologist Grove Karl Gilbert. Looming benevolently over the valley on the west is Mount Callaghan. As Molly described it:

> On a still day in January you can hear the mountain talking to itself.
> Rumbling. Grumbling. The sound comes from deep in its huge body.
> Mount Callaghan is an old mountain. It mourns aloud, like an old

man, for the days of its youth, when rocks danced in the sky and the world was a wonder of fire and ice. All that has come after is only erosion. Time has left the mountain bald, stoop-shouldered, dying down eternity. The glacial snows have melted, leaving great scars along its flanks. The warm waters have receded until only the fossilized starfish remain.

Down the scars, the canyons of its flanks, comes water to the verdant meadows that give Grass Valley its name. Farther north are the remains of the town and mill of Cortez, at one time said to be the third-largest silver mine in the world. Still farther north is a canyon that opens into Crescent Valley, with its several major ranches and the settlement of Beowawe, originally a railroad stop. There are several other ranches in Grass Valley, but its central focus has been, for more than 120 years, the Grass Valley Ranch.

Grass Valley Ranch was pieced together, beginning in the 1870s, by John Spencer, who had made a fortune in various Nevada mining ventures. Spencer assembled the ranch the same way others acquired their ranches in the nineteenth-century West: Homestead the areas with springs and creeks, and have ranch hands take up other such places and prove them up, then sell them to the rancher. Ultimately, the Grass Valley Ranch came to be a very large operation, one of the largest deeded ranches in central Nevada.

John Spencer died in 1893. His two sons quarreled with that vexatious bitterness unique to strongheaded siblings. They did agree that one would buy out the other, but neither would sell his share. Finally, in 1904, they put the ranch up for sale at a public auction held on the steps of the Lander County Courthouse in Austin. It was assumed that one of the sons, backed by the mother, would outbid the other. But when the bidding was over, the ranch belonged to Walter Magee, of San Francisco.

Walter Magee, son of Thomas A. Magee, founder of a wealthy and venerable San Francisco real estate firm, had three years previously married Flora Dean. Flora's mother was Eva Wenban, daughter of Simeon Wenban, owner of the Cortez silver mine in Grass Valley. Eva had married Joe Dean, who had come to Nevada in the 1860s and built up vast holdings in Crescent and Pine Valleys, centered on the Dean Ranch. He owned large herds of cattle and ran six thousand head of branded horses in the mountains around Crescent Valley. He employed Indian and white buckaroos, and Indian women worked as domestics on the ranches, as they did throughout much of Nevada. Joe Dean was murdered in the 1880s in an altercation with a sheepman. His widow remained at the ranch with her two small daughters, Flora and Ethel, and was assisted in its operation by managers.

The Dean girls were raised in San Francisco, and spent their summers in Crescent Valley, learning to ride and rope and help work the cattle. In San Francisco, the girls were known for their beauty, elegance, and wit. After graduating from a finishing school in the city, they attended Vassar. Flora Dean married Walter Magee in 1901. Having purchased Grass Valley Ranch, the couple and their year-old son, Richard, moved there in 1904. Indian ranch hands and domestics came from the Dean Ranch to help. But matters were not idyllic; Walter Magee drank heavily. One night an angry Flora confronted her inebriated husband. In the ensuing argument, Magee shot and killed Flora's dog at her feet. The next day, Flora and the Indian retainers packed up Richard and her belongings in wagons and traveled the forty miles back to the Dean Ranch. Flora and Walter were divorced. Walter apparently never touched another drop of liquor. In 1908, Grass Valley Ranch was sold to the Lander County Livestock Company, one of the many interests of famed Nevada entrepreneur George Wingfield Sr. In 1917, Wingfield sold the ranch to John Savals, a Basque sheepman. His widow sold it in 1931 to George Watts.

After Flora Dean divorced Walter Magee, she married Walter Hobart. Richard Magee grew up partly on the Dean Ranch, but much of his youth was spent in eastern boarding schools, overseen by his aunt Ethel and her husband, Frederick Hussey, of Pittsburgh. Richard went on to Princeton, graduating in 1928. He then returned to Nevada to manage the Dean Ranch. In the next few years, both Flora and Ethel were widowed, and Walter Magee died, leaving his money to Richard. The heavily mortgaged Dean Ranch was lost in 1934 in the Depression. That year, Richard (by then known to all as Dick) bought Grass Valley Ranch from the hapless Watts for $35,000. Flora and Ethel moved to Grass Valley with him, but spent their winters at Ethel's home in San Mateo, California.

During the 1920s, the University of Nevada College of Agriculture had developed a herd of registered purebred Hereford cattle, under the guidance of F. W. "Prof." Wilson (the father of the late Tom Wilson, well-known Reno advertising executive and the grandfather of Thomas "Spike" Wilson, attorney and former state senator). The depression forced the university to sell off the herd, and Dick Magee began buying registered cattle from it in 1931. Because he held these as personal property, they were not lost with the Dean Ranch. In 1934, he moved his cattle to Grass Valley, where they became the foundation of the registered herd from the ranch that was finally sold by Molly in 1993 and 1994. Dick, like many Nevada ranchers before World War II, also bred and raised thoroughbred horses. Some were raced; others, the studs, were bred to range mares, and the "green broken" offspring sold to the U.S. Cavalry Remount—a practice that ended only in 1943, when the army reluctantly decided that jeeps, tanks, and half-tracks had, indeed, replaced horses and mules.

RANCHER, HISTORIAN, STOCKBREEDER, ARCHAEOLOGIST

It was mutual interest in horses that first brought Dick Magee and Molly Flagg together. Molly was quite taken by the "very attractive" six-foot-four rancher, some twelve years her senior. They continued to meet at various racetracks and fairs. In mid-1942, Molly was driving from Omaha, Nebraska, to Seattle. She stopped at Grass Valley to see Dick. "Somehow or other" they decided to get married. A justice of the peace in Fallon performed the ceremony in July 1942. Their only child, William "Bill" Magee, was born in June 1943, in Reno. Molly then moved to Grass Valley and began her second life in earnest, that of a rancher, far removed from the places and people she had known previously.

Molly Magee was entranced by Grass Valley and its inhabitants, human and otherwise, by its history, and by the land itself. But learning the ins and outs of ranch life was difficult, especially for someone who knew very little about cooking.

> The cook had departed in the middle of the night. I was left with twenty-eight men to feed. Boiling water was a challenge; I viewed the cadaver of a cow with terror. I asked Dick, "What do I do with it?" The words, spoken fifty-some years ago, still resound in my ears: "Cut it up and cook it," he said, and walked away.

In time, she became a fair ranch cook, but loathed it all the while.

When the U.S. Army quit buying remount horses in 1943, Dick Magee's focus turned increasingly to the racehorses. The range horses were "chickened," that is, sold for chicken food and dog food. Gradually, Molly learned about the cattle, the purebred herd kept to produce range bulls for sale. Ultimately, she came to know a great deal, not only about the "working," that is, the care and feeding of range cattle in the high desert, and the genetics of cattle and the elaborate bureaucracies dedicated to ensuring that all registered cattle are "purebred," but, of central importance, about bovine psychology. Her monograph, *Cow Sense,* published by the University of Nevada Press in 1977, is an exquisite distillation of her acute observations of cow behavior over (by then) nearly thirty-five years.

With the advent of the Bureau of Land Management in 1946 and its mandated enforcement of the Taylor Grazing Act of 1934, the Magees were forced to develop a commercial cattle herd—that is, cattle raised and sold for meat. They did so by culling from the purebred herd. Until the end of World War II, all haying on the ranch was done with draft horses, and the hay loose-stacked. After the war, the ranch was "mechanized" with the addition of a cantankerous hay bailer, a "cream puff" International stock truck (still running in 1995 when the ranch was sold), a Jeep, and an airplane. For Grass Valley, as for many large ranches far from supply points, hospitals, and other necessities, the airplane was indispensable.

During the 1940s and 1950s, Molly became increasingly interested in local history, in the venerable buildings from Austin's heyday, and in the archaeology of Grass Valley. She led a campaign to re-roof the Episcopal church in Austin, which had fallen on hard times. She later purchased and preserved Stokes Castle, a stone tower on the edge of Austin, overlooking the Reese River Valley. During the height of the Austin mining boom, the tower had been built by the Stokeses, cousins of Molly's, who controlled a number of Austin mines. The tower reminded the Stokeses of one in a painting of the Roman Campagna in Italy, which hung in the family library in New York. She published numerous historic essays and poems in the famed *Reese River Reveille*, of Austin, but also in *Vogue* and *Family Circle*. A favorite theme was Uncle Dave Buel, early on the scene in the mining rush to Reese River in the 1860s. As Molly described him, he was straight out of the Sazerac Lying Club, a famed Austin institution in its glory days.

As Molly rode over the ranch and in the surrounding mountains, she found many archaeological sites, ranging in age from those abandoned by Indian people in 1917, when the ranch changed hands, to those many thousands of years old around Lake Gilbert. She collected and documented artifacts, described and mapped the sites, and sought advice from archaeologists at the Smithsonian Institution about how to proceed. In due time, she published some of her findings in *American Antiquity*, the leading American archaeological journal. Her concern with archaeology in Grass Valley and elsewhere in Nevada led her to become a trustee of the Nevada State Museum and, as a University of Nevada regent from 1962 to 1966, to take the lead in establishing the Department of Anthropology on the Reno campus.

In 1953, the "Big House," built by John Spencer in the 1880s, burned. The house, its furnishings, much tack and gear, and most of the things of Dick's and Molly's lives, including her 3,000-volume library, were lost. Molly saved only some Winslow Homer watercolors and a set of the famous colored engravings of Plains Indians by the nineteenth-century artist Karl Bodmer. Dick became increasingly involved in horse racing in California in the 1950s and 1960s. In 1968, he moved himself and the horses to a ranch in California, and

Molly bought Grass Valley ranch and its cattle from him. Molly and Dick's interests had diverged, and they were divorced in 1969. Dick Magee died in 1983.

Molly set out systematically to expand the ranch and improve and increase both the purebred and the commercial herds. Dick Magee had owned Grass Valley Ranch and portions of the adjacent Skull Creek and Cowboy Rest Ranches. As they became available, Molly added the remainder of Cowboy Rest, as well as the Callaghan, Lake, and Willow Creek Ranches, and leased the Indian Ranch, giving her complete control of the south part of Grass Valley. Her purebred bulls brought top prices at auctions throughout the West, as did the steers from the commercial herd. She continued to actively work the cattle on a daily basis. Once she owned the ranch, she saw to it that there was always a hired cook—no more cutting up cow cadavers and catering to hay hands and buckaroos. As at most ranches, this meant a long succession of idiosyncratic cooks, as repeat visitors to the ranch came to know.

In 1969 Molly married Bill Knudtsen, rancher and horse trader par excellence. Bill, who "never met a machine he didn't like," mechanized the ranch, especially the irrigation and haying operations, and nursed the two finicky diesel engines that drove the electric generators, the power source for the ranch. In the late 1980s, other aspects of the late twentieth century came finally to Grass Valley. The single-wire, multiple-party telephone line, strung over scrawny poles attached to fence posts for twenty miles, was replaced by electronic repeaters placed on adjacent mountaintops by Nevada Bell. And one day, Molly returned from working the cattle to find a television satellite dish had sprouted in the yard, to "keep the cook entertained," according to Bill.

THE BOARD OF REGENTS

In 1960 Molly ran for and was elected to the University of Nevada Board of Regents, something no woman had ever done, although some women had served by appointment. Over the years, as she moved around the state, she had become increasingly "concerned that the young people from the rural areas were not getting the kind of education that was going to help them in later life or help the state." At first she contemplated running for the Lander County School Board, but concluded she could make little difference in such a position. She thought a seat on the Board of Regents might provide her a more effective role.

The University of Nevada and its Board of Regents were created in the State Constitution of 1864. The constitution's framers saw to it that the university would meet the requirements of the Morrill Act of 1862, wherein Congress made public lands in each state available for sale, the proceeds to be used to establish state universities focusing on agriculture, mechanical arts (engineering), home economics, and military training, as well as traditional academic subjects. The State University of Nevada was first situated in Elko in 1874, but moved to Reno in 1886. Initially, regents were appointed by the legislature, but an 1888 law provided for their popular election, and a 1917 law made their election nonpartisan and established ten-year terms. In 1957, in the aftermath of five years of turmoil centering on complex issues of academic freedom and responsibility, administrative prerogatives, and faculty-administration "chains of command," the legislature increased the number of regents from five to nine and fixed the term at four years.

The late 1950s also marked the beginning of sustained growth by the university, which had remained in a near steady state for several decades. The student body reached 1,000 for the first time in 1922–1923 academic year and was less than 1,300 in 1952–1953. But rapid change and growth were under way. Courses were first offered in Las Vegas in 1951, and a Nevada Southern Regional Division was created in 1954. Maude Frazier was key to making the southern branch a reality. The National Science Foundation in 1950, followed by other federal "research and development" channels, and the National Defense Education Act of 1958 became conduits for the infusion of federal funding into university research and to support the upgrading of university infrastructures. The creation of the Desert Research Institute on the Reno campus of the university in 1959 was one response to these initiatives. At the same time, Nevada began a sustained period of growth that continues into the 1990s. All these factors—university reorganization and expansion of research, increasing enrollments, and a branch campus in Las Vegas—were major agenda items for the University of Nevada in 1960, when Molly Magee decided to run for a seat on the Board of Regents.

By 1960, Molly knew and had befriended many people throughout the state. She went to Reno to consult her old friends, Fran and Newt Crumley. Newton Crumley's father had owned the Commercial Hotel in Elko; Newt had founded the Ranch Inn there and later owned the Holiday Hotel in Reno, which had been built by Norman Biltz. Crumley was one of the state's most respected citizens—and he was on the Board of Regents. Molly sought him out at his home in Reno.

> He greeted me warmly and was delighted to see me, and I was delighted to see him. I said, "Newt, I've been thinking of possibly running for the Board of Regents; how would you feel about it?" And this awful change came over him, and he drew himself up, looked down his nose at me, and said, "The Board of Regents couldn't operate with a woman." And

somehow that struck me as terribly funny. . . . I said, "What are you boys doing on the Board of Regents that you can't have a woman on the Board?" And this absolutely enraged him. I felt there was a chill in the air, so I got in my car and drove away. But the more I thought about it, the more I thought perhaps they needed a woman on the Board.

Molly next consulted Wally Warren, a prominent lobbyist and political strategist. Warren thought she would have a very slim chance. He asked, "What will you use for a slogan?" And Molly replied, off the top of her head, "I'm going to run as Molly Magee for District Three." District Three, under the expansion of the board in 1957, included the cow counties. When Warren asked what her principles and platform were, Molly replied that she really did not know much about the university, but she would learn. In the meantime, whenever she gave a speech, she would say she thought a woman should be on the board.

So anyhow we started off, and I very quickly learned that no one cared really about what I thought the university should be. The main thing they were interested in was that I was married to Dick Magee, who was from one of the founding families of the state, so I really was part of the state, that I had been on a ranch for twenty years, and that I could ride a horse. So going with the tide, I invested in a horse trailer . . . hooked it up to the Lincoln . . . and rode the colors in the county fairs. I campaigned all over the state, including in Reno and Las Vegas, although my district was the rural counties.

Molly ran a very personal, fair-to-fair, ranch-to-ranch, and door-to-door campaign. She discovered many rural Nevadans with strong ties to European home countries, and since she had visited a number of those countries in her first life, she found much empathy with many people. She won by a landslide. "When the election came around, I gathered up the most appalling number of votes," and began her first term.

But she still had to face the hostility of eight male regents. "The hostility was such that you could cut it with a knife, really . . . but I made friends with them eventually." Since she admittedly knew very little about tax-supported state universities, she sought guidance from then-President Charles Armstrong and Vice-President Ken Young. Young gave her a long reading list of works on university governance. She devoured them and scores of others. They remain in her library, well thumbed, well read, and well understood.

Molly recalls with fondness her first few years on the board. Among the first actions in which she gladly participated was the establishment of the University of Nevada Press in 1961. In 1962 and 1963 she and Wendell Mordy, director of the Desert Research Institute, led a successful initiative to form a Department of Anthropology on the Reno campus, where it has flourished ever since.

Once Molly was accepted by her fellow regents, matters generally went well. Those with whom she worked most closely over the years were Fred Anderson, Archie Grant, Proctor Hug Jr., and Louis Lombardi. In 1964, Juanita White was elected to the board from Las Vegas. White, who held a Ph.D. in chemistry, became Molly's frequent ally, although both were very much their own persons.

By about 1965, as Nevada's population continued to boom and the southern branch continued to grow, there was increasing competition for resources between regents representing Reno and Las Vegas and related problems of dealing with many students not properly prepared for university work. After one especially acrimonious meeting, in 1964 or 1965, Molly and Juanita White were walking across the Reno quad. Molly recalls that

> Juanita said, "You know, it's getting unmanageable; this thing is just flying apart." And ever the rancher and having handled a lot of cows, I said, "You know, Juanita, when you're going down the road with two cows, you cannot keep them together, but if you've got three cows, two of them will stay together. You put the one cow in with the two cows, and then you can manage them. What we need is an institution of higher learning to fit in with the two universities. . . . What we need are some community colleges, and they can take up the slack on the unqualified students who come to the universities, [receive appropriate training], and then go on to the universities or acquire the kind of education they need at that level." Juanita said, "That's a good idea." Whether my rather rustic simile about the cows impressed itself on her or not I don't know. . . . [But] when we went back to the meeting we began talking about community colleges . . . and were favorably received.

Some of Molly's constituents in Elko had begun discussing a junior college in 1962. By 1966, encouraged by discussions among the regents and prodded by rural-area voters, Paul Laxalt included a community college "experiment" in his gubernatorial campaign platform. In 1968, a community college system was created, initially through a grant from Howard Hughes, the reclusive then-resident of Nevada. Governor Laxalt arranged the grant. By 1970, branch campuses were established in Elko, Carson City, and Clark County, and plans for others were in the works, further increasing competition for resources. There were strains between the Reno and Las Vegas campuses and between the campuses and the Desert Research Institute. In 1968, tensions came to a head, and Wendell Mordy, who had founded the Desert Research Institute in 1959, was fired. Molly, who was a close friend of Mordy and his wife, Brooke, was delegated by the board to inform him that he had been terminated. She regards it as the low point of her years on the board. The result was creation of the University of Nevada System, with an overall chancellor, and the several campuses—Reno, Las Vegas, the Desert Research Institute, and the community colleges—headed by presidents.

In 1968, Molly successfully ran for a third term. But in 1972, after the "one man, one vote" Supreme Court decision of 1965 and the legislative redistricting of the state in 1971, Molly had no district to represent, since the population of the rural counties warranted only one regent. In the redistricting, regents' terms were increased to six years and staggered. Molly's term ended in 1972, but the other regent position, held by Mel Steninger, of Elko, terminated in 1974; hence she was out. The following year, in recognition of her great contributions, Molly was awarded an honorary doctorate in anthropology by the University of Nevada, Reno, and asked to give the commencement address. Steninger did not run again in 1974, but Molly did, winning in a close election. Since no Reno or Las Vegas radio stations could be received at the Grass Valley Ranch, and there was no television until 1987, Molly learned of her reelection only when her opponent telephoned, over the single-line wire, to concede and congratulate her. In her final term, which ended in 1981, she served, as she had previously, as vice-chair of the board.

Molly played a key role in all the complex, difficult, sometimes acrimonious decisions made by the Board of Regents during the twenty years of explosive growth of the university system of Nevada. In the university centennial volume of 1974, historian James Hulse called Molly "one of the most articulate and best informed persons to function as a regent in recent years." It is still a true statement; all the knowledge from those well-thumbed books on university administration, coupled with wit, integrity, humor, and a people sense equal to her "cow sense," served Molly well.

During her regent years Molly continued to expand and develop the Grass Valley Ranch. Her acquisition of adjacent ranches allowed an expansion of the cattle herds and the hay operation to feed them through the long winters. Molly and Bill Knudtsen had a general division of labor: Molly ran the cattle, and Bill tended the (now highly mechanized) irrigation and haying operations and saw to the care and feeding of the many other machines required to operate a large ranch. Bill also generally handled the hiring and firing of hay hands and cooks—a continuing near-soap-operatic saga, as he drolly recounted it to visitors to the ranch.

Molly continued to be active in public service, as an adviser to the University of Nevada College of Agriculture and through service on Bureau of Land Management advisory boards. Her love of the land translated into a practical and careful program of environmental protection, about which she spoke eloquently in numerous public forums. The more radical, often untutored, but usually fervid environmentalists, who saw ranching as de facto degradation of the land, learned much from Molly about caring for the land, when they took time to listen. Those with a more reasoned and mature approach to environmental protection usually found hers to be a calm voice seeking long-term workable solutions to complex problems. Molly continued to write with intense interest about archaeology, anthropology, history, historic preservation, literature, poetry, and ranch life. She viewed politics at all levels as a source of simultaneous amazement and déjà vu, and with a sense that Shakespeare's Puck was correct.

In 1987, Molly was chasing a calf across a field at the ranch. Her horse stepped in a badger hole, threw her off, cartwheeled, and landed atop her, nearly splitting her liver. Two visitors happened to be at the ranch, saw the accident, and got help—but it was eight hours before she finally arrived at a Reno hospital. She later thought it would have been a good way to die. Her horse got up, shook himself, and stayed by her, as did her faithful cow dog, and it was a beautiful day in Grass Valley, where she had lived a full and rich second life for forty-five years, far in time, distance, and perception from the New York and Europe of her first life. But there was yet more to come.

Molly's recovery was long and arduous; she slowly knitted physically, keeping her characteristic toughness of mind and wit through the ordeal. Major horse accidents fifty years apart seemingly set the stages for new lives. The first ultimately led her to Nevada. After the second accident, Molly remained in Reno, managing the ranch from afar with Bill Knudtsen's assistance. From 1993 to 1994, she sold the cattle; both the registered and commercial herds were well known and were quickly purchased for good prices. In 1995, she sold Grass Valley Ranch to the Inchauspe family, longtime neighbors across Mount Callaghan.

Molly's third life includes, as always, reading, writing, research, and public service. In early 1996, she was deep in research for a biography of Joe Dean, whose murder in Grass Valley in the 1880s changed the lives of his wife and his descendants and, possibly in some ways, her own. She continues her interest in the university, especially the College of Agriculture and the Department of Anthropology on the Reno campus, and in environmental issues, becoming an adviser to the Ecology, Evolution, and Conservation Biology Program, established at the university in the early 1990s. Despite major vision problems, which she partly willed into abeyance, she reads voraciously, watches television news, and is as wryly amused as ever by the antics of the current crop of politicians, bureaucrats, and selected university administrators.

In 1994, the University of Nevada, Reno, named Molly a Distinguished Nevadan, the ultimate accolade it bestows on those whose exemplary lives and actions for the public good have brought recognition to themselves and honor to the state. She was an eminently qualified candidate. A popular song of the late 1960s, "My Way," speaks of meeting challenges and going on to new lives. To those privileged to know her, Molly Flagg Knudtsen has always done it her way, with enormous courage and energy, tempered by élan, grace, humor, and wit. Nevada would have been much poorer without her.

Notes

1. Prior to World War I, Fowler was private secretary to the United States ambassador to England, Walter Page Hines. As a young and debonair diplomatic attaché moving through the great country houses of England, he was in an optimal position to learn much of strategic interest to the United States. At the outbreak of World War I, Fowler found his way to the Royal Flying Corps (later the Royal Air Force), flew numerous missions against the Germans, and was seriously wounded at least twice. In 1917 he transferred to the American Air Corps as a squadron commander. On a bet, he flew a small airplane under the Arc de Triomphe in Paris the day following the Armistice. Somerset Maugham, himself a British agent in World War I and longtime friend, late wrote that Fowler was "a character out of our times. . . . Like one of those great adventurers of the reign of Elizabeth I. If he had been alive then he would have been a buddy of Drake and Raleigh. . . . He had, of course, the courage of the devil." After the war, Fowler alternated between banking and his "secret work," until he married Thyrza Benson Flagg in 1927.

In 1934, Fowler became deputy commissioner of police in New York City, when Fiorello LaGuardia became mayor, and served for two years. In World War II he participated in the Allied invasions of North Africa and Normandy, and was seriously injured in a plane crash in North Africa. He died at age seventy-one in 1957. In her memoir of him, Molly's mother wrote, "He had been decorated by America, Britain, Italy, Russia, Belgium and Romania. What had he done for all those countries?" Neither she, nor Molly, ever really knew. One 1932 trip using the family as "cover" for covert activities was an extended tour of the Orient—India, Ceylon, Java, Bali, Singapore, Sumatra. But in Thailand, Fowler received word that he would "have to go to China." Molly and her mother returned to Paris via KLM Fokker trimotor mail planes, sitting on the cargo and flying on during the day. Some weeks later, Fowler turned up in Paris, having come by way of China, the Trans-Siberian Railway, and Moscow, where he conferred with Joseph Stalin over matters unknown.

Paul Laxalt

Man of Political Independence

BY RICHARD L. SPEES

Paul Dominique Laxalt was a politician who was not consumed by politics. He kept his feet on the ground, never lost his sense of humor, and was unafraid to admit or accept his own limitations. He accomplished his goals by keeping his agenda limited and sharply focused. He walked away from positions of power on three occasions. His low-key style distressed many of his supporters, who constantly pushed him to run one more race or to use his accumulated power more aggressively. By heeding his own inner voice, however, Paul Laxalt's political legacy was significant.

Laxalt's parents, Dominique and Theresa, were born in the French Basque country and emigrated to the United States around the turn of the century. By the time Paul was born on August 2, 1922, the family had settled in Carson City, Nevada, located on the eastern edge of the Sierra Nevada. Dominique was a sheepherder who spent months at a time away from his family tending to his flocks in the mountains. Theresa ran a small boardinghouse in town. She was a trained cook who had studied at the Cordon Bleu in Paris. Seated at her boardinghouse table were many political leaders of Nevada, particularly during the months when the legislature was in session.

There is a great divergence of opinion among Laxalt watchers as to which parent had the dominant influence on the future governor and United States senator. The eldest of six children, Paul Laxalt became fiercely independent as an adult, often refusing to be swayed by party or personal pressures. He had a love of the outdoors and frequently retreated from Washington to a weekend home in the Virginia Shenandoah Mountains; if the time were available, he departed for the family retreat near Lake Tahoe to "clear his head." These fiercely independent traits he inherited from his father. Throughout his career Laxalt also demonstrated analytical strength and a clear thought process in arriving at major decisions. He listened to his mind, not his ego. In this regard, his mother was the driving influence. She kept order and propriety in the

11

Laxalt home while supervising a boardinghouse and caring for six children, despite the long absences of her husband.

According to Laxalt, "Both Dominique and Theresa were strict—even authoritarian by today's standards." On another occasion, describing his mother, Laxalt wrote, "In raising us, she ran a 'tight ship,' even oppressive by some modern day standards. When she made a family decision, that was it. No appeal. No due process." In discussing his college years, Laxalt tells of his desire to attend the University of Nevada in Reno, but he was given no option by his mother other than Santa Clara University. She insisted that he have a disciplined Jesuit educational experience, despite the additional costs of a private school.

These images are tempered by others. According to Laxalt, "Papa and Mama Laxalt instilled in their children a strong respect for hard work and a profound sense of commitment to their country. They sacrificed continually so that their children could enjoy more comfortable lives." Laxalt's childhood friends describe the Laxalt house as a magnet for children. On most afternoons, groups of children would start and finish their playtime under Theresa's protective view.

Laxalt's college education was interrupted by World War II. He served as an army medical corpsman in the South Pacific, and following his discharge resumed his studies at Denver University, where he earned his bachelor of arts and law degrees. Upon returning to Nevada, he began to practice law, and in 1946 he married Jackie Ross, daughter of a prominent Carson City attorney. After building a successful law practice, Laxalt followed his instincts and entered local politics in 1954, winning election as district attorney for Ormsby County.

Partisan politics was never a dominant influence in the Laxalt boyhood home, and he had no strong allegiance to either party when he began his political career. He credits his father-in-law, John R. Ross, a Republican activist, with his decision to become a Republican. In the 1950s, Nevada Democrats enjoyed a hefty edge in voter registration, but on election day many factors frequently contributed to Republican victories. The Democrats regularly engaged in intraparty bloodlettings, often in the form of embittered primary contests, that would facilitate a Republican triumph in November. In other races, given the small number of voters, a dedicated Republican candidate could overcome Democratic registration advantages by working very hard, especially by knocking on doors and making an appearance at every public event possible. The power of personal politics was indeed an important ingredient of Nevada politics, and despite their minority status, hard-working Republicans often won statewide elections.

In 1962, Laxalt was approached by state Republican Party leaders to run for lieutenant governor. The sitting lieutenant governor, Rex Bell, was already positioned to run for governor against the Democratic incumbent, Grant Sawyer. A former western movie star during the silent-screen era, Bell was an attractive candidate, well known and popular and having won statewide races. He was recognized for his flamboyant western attire, complete with boots and ten-gallon hat. His résumé even included a role as the former husband of silent-screen star Clara Bow. Although the governor and lieutenant governor are elected separately, Bell wanted to present a leadership team to the electorate even before the primary elections. Because Bell lived in Las Vegas, Laxalt was viewed as someone who could provide geographical ballast.

According to members of the Laxalt political family, the race was to feature the charismatic cowboy while Laxalt would help secure the Republican base in northern Nevada. At the time, Laxalt had no name recognition in southern Nevada, especially Las Vegas and Clark County. He was a prominent Carson City attorney, but still a young man with only rudimentary political skills. He looked upon the race as an opportunity to gain exposure outside of northern Nevada and to learn the intricacies of running a statewide campaign.

The landscape of Nevada history is littered with seldom-remembered lieutenant governors, men who held the office for a term or two and then faded into political oblivion. Had Laxalt remained in the shadow of Rex Bell, he might have followed in this well-established tradition. But fate intervened on July 4, when the fifty-eight-year-old Bell suffered a fatal heart attack after attending a Republican picnic in Las Vegas that afternoon. Republican leaders urged Laxalt to step up to run for governor in the upcoming September primary, but he declined despite considerable pressure to accept the top spot.

Had this attractive but inexperienced politician made the race, it would have made for good political theater. In fact, his novelist brother, Robert, used the situation to write an episode in *The Governor's Mansion* (1994). In this fictional account the inexperienced candidate for lieutenant governor bravely accepts the challenge and wins a narrow upset victory over a strong Democratic incumbent. But in real life the novelist's brother carefully analyzed the situation and opted to remain a candidate for the lesser position, reasoning that he had little chance to defeat the popular first-term incumbent Grant Sawyer. Laxalt deeply disappointed some party leaders by his decision, who then saw their party ripped apart by an embittered primary campaign in which Las Vegas mayor and businessman Oran Gragson soundly trounced the trenchantly outspoken *Las Vegas Sun* editor Hank Greenspun. But Laxalt's political logic was sound. He later recalled that he "had no appetite" for the governor's race. Translated, he recognized that he stood little chance of winning against the popular Sawyer, but that he stood an excellent chance of gaining statewide exposure while running for lieutenant governor against Berkeley Bunker, a relatively weak Democratic opponent.

Without the cover of a prearranged ticket, however, Laxalt had to run his own campaign. Supported by a big family and many friends, he worked tirelessly. He found campaigning to be an exhilarating experience, and the humor and enthusiasm he brought to the race came through in his upbeat message. He experimented with television, albeit clumsily, becoming one of the first Nevada politicians to use the medium in a statewide election. He bought inexpensive blocks of weekday time during late mornings on Las Vegas stations, appearing live to converse with whomever might stumble across his extended commercial. According to Laxalt, one day he rushed through his prepared text and was left with several minutes of open airtime. After several moments of embarrassed silence, he started talking extemporaneously to the camera, eventually pulling out his wallet, and showing pictures of and talking about his children. The story of this curious event quickly spread throughout the state. While it is unlikely that many viewers actually saw the wallet episode, over the years the size of the audience swelled perceptibly with Laxalt's ascending political career. One of Laxalt's other television spots featured a miner with his back turned to the screen while he panned for gold. When he turned toward the camera, the viewer could see emblazoned on the bottom of his pan "Laxalt for Lt. Governor." Another memorable advertisement featured a bootblack with a shoe-shine rag carrying the same message. These primitive advertisements were refreshingly original compared to the standard political commercials of that time. Corny, yes, but their simplistic message stuck in the viewers mind, elevating Laxalt's visibility.

Laxalt built a grassroots organization in every county, and for two months he toured small towns, as well as making frequent appearances in the two population centers. He outworked and outorganized his opponent, winning decisively even though incumbent Grant Sawyer easily swamped Gragson, whose campaign could never recover from the brutal primary contest with Greenspun.

By all accounts, Laxalt maintained a low profile in his first year as lieutenant governor. In 1964, however, he succumbed to the entreaties of state Republican leaders and challenged incumbent Howard Cannon for a seat in the United States Senate. It proved to be a surprisingly close race, and for a time, polls and pundits indicated that Laxalt might squeak out a narrow victory over the much better known Las Vegas resident. Cannon and Laxalt dueled against the backdrop of the curious presidential race between President Lyndon Johnson and "Mr. Conservative," Arizona senator Barry Goldwater. Late in the campaign, Goldwater was scheduled to make a campaign stop in Las Vegas. Any close association with Goldwater was perceived as unwise in a state that polls indicated was strongly in Johnson's camp, and Laxalt's advisers pleaded with him to avoid any public meeting. Laxalt, however, refused to embarrass his party's presidential nominee, despite the risks involved. His opponents were quick to exploit his highly visible appearance with Goldwater, but Laxalt always adhered to the concept of loyalty, and he appeared on stage with Goldwater while some other Republicans ducked the event. In this instance Laxalt's steadfastness might have cost him the election. "I would rather have lost than have abandoned Barry," he recalls.

Laxalt did lose, but in the closest and most contentious election in modern Nevada political history. He and many of his friends believe that in the final analysis the loss was due, not to the Goldwater meeting or even Johnson's overwhelming victory, but to blatant election fraud. The facts are relatively simple, but their meaning much less so. Laxalt lost the statewide election by just forty-eight votes. During the evening hours of election night, Republican poll watchers were denied entry into the Clark County Courthouse in Las Vegas, where the votes were being counted. No one from the Cannon campaign ever admitted to vote fraud, and there was never any prosecution for election law violations. And although a recount confirmed a Cannon victory, many Republicans remained convinced that fraud had definitely occurred.

Two theories regarding possible fraud quickly surfaced. One was that voting machines from precincts located in the African American sections of Clark County, where the Republican Party was weakest and precinct watchers rare, were tampered with. Some precincts showed not a single vote for Laxalt. Another theory was that a sizable collection of absentee ballots, presumed to be predominately Republican, were destroyed. In 1965, Republican Party workers encountered several registered Republicans who were not recorded as voting in the 1964 election but who affirmed that they had voted by absentee ballot. Whether election fraud actually occurred or not, it quickly became established among many Nevadans that Laxalt had been victimized.

He capitalized upon that sentiment in 1966. As early as July of 1965, Laxalt had decided to run for governor. Many observers believed that Grant Sawyer would step down after two terms, although at this juncture there existed no constitutional barrier to continued service. In fact, Sawyer had effectively raised the third-term issue eight years earlier when he defeated two-term incumbent Charles Russell. Now it was Sawyer who suffered from the same issue. Laxalt effectively portrayed himself as a fresh, young Republican, the unfortunate victim of election chicanery who was now taking on an aging Democratic political machine and an entrenched governor who had the temerity to flaunt the unwritten two-term rule. From the very first, private polls indicated that Laxalt was ahead of Sawyer, but he never let up, campaigning relentlessly until election eve.

There were several reasons for his victory. He clearly benefited from a backlash against the Democratic Party that was the result of the often-repeated (but unproven) charges of voter fraud that had allegedly cost him a Senate seat. The third-term issue apparently worked to Sawyer's disadvantage. Equally important was Laxalt's ability to attract the statewide Mormon vote, something he had not been able to do in his two previous races, when he had run against Mormon candidates. In Nevada, political operatives had long understood that the substantial Mormon population voted more in a bloc than did any other religious or ethnic group. As a Roman Catholic professing strong moral and family values, Laxalt won the admiration of the Mormon community in 1962 and 1964, but he had not succeeded in attracting their votes. In this campaign, however, he targeted this important bloc, even inviting the Mormon governor of Michigan, George Romney, to Nevada for a political reception, where he made a strong public endorsement.

Laxalt identified education as the major issue and thereby garnered the support of teachers and the growing number of voters concerned about the overburdened public school system that had never caught up with the enormous spurt of postwar population growth. He also benefited from endorsing the establishment of a community college system, a popular program that touched upon the needs of thousands of Nevadans who were unable to attend the traditional state university system, and many employers who desperately needed trained workers to assume jobs requiring technical expertise but not necessarily a baccalaureate degree.

Most important, Laxalt promised to make peace between the United States Department of Justice and the State of Nevada. Ever since the highly publicized hearings into organized crime conducted by Senator Estes Kefauver in 1950, the feud between Nevada and the Justice Department about the relationship of Nevada's primary economic enterprise to organized crime had festered. Attorney General Robert Kennedy had become virtually obsessed with allegations regarding the power of organized crime in the Nevada casino industry. Kennedy was convinced that the State of Nevada's regulation of the gaming industry was ineffectual at best, perhaps influenced or even controlled by the forces of organized crime. Kennedy perceived rapidly growing Las Vegas as the base for organized-crime activities and was especially impressed by charges that massive skimming and money-laundering operations were being routinely conducted, perhaps even with the connivance of Nevada gaming officials. Encouraged by J. Edgar Hoover, Kennedy launched a number of law enforcement initiatives in the early 1960s against the gaming industry, including stationing FBI agents in all major Nevada casinos.

Grant Sawyer was embarrassed and angered by this development, especially since it was being mounted by the national leadership of his own party. The youthful governor steadfastly and adamantly defended his state's major industry as well as the effectiveness of his gaming-control operations, vigorously denying Kennedy's charges. The confrontation took on front-page importance within the state. At one point, Sawyer even flew to Washington to reason with President John Kennedy, urging him to call off his determined brother, arguing that the Justice Department's efforts could greatly damage the Democratic Party in Nevada. For a time Sawyer's efforts seemed successful, as Robert Kennedy abandoned a dramatic plan to unleash a series of highly publicized raids upon all major Nevada casinos. But by late 1962 the attorney general was once more back on the trail of Nevada gambling interests as the FBI launched a new series of investigations.

In 1963, the FBI initiated a large number of illegal wiretaps, installing listening devices in the homes and offices of a number of prominent Nevadans, especially casino operators the FBI believed were engaged in illegal activities. The existence of these illegal telephone taps became public knowledge during a 1966 federal court case. Because the taps were illegally obtained, the damning evidence they provided was useless in prosecuting those engaged in skimming activities. Nonetheless, they also offered clear-cut evidence that the Justice Department crusade was onto something tangible. Skimming and money laundering were occurring, big time, in Nevada's casinos.

These dramatic revelations proved to be a major public relations disaster for the beleaguered gambling industry. They also constituted an enormous embarrassment for Sawyer. It was patently evident not only that his contentions about an overzealous Justice Department were ill founded but also that he had failed to protect Nevada's largest industry from corrupting influences. Many Nevadans came to believe that Sawyer's confrontational approach was ill advised and that peace had to be made somehow with the power brokers in Washington, D.C.

Laxalt proposed a different approach. He promised to have a personal meeting with J. Edgar Hoover to make peace. (By this time Robert Kennedy was no longer attorney general, thus removing one individual apparently conducting a personal vendetta.) The proposal proved politically successful for two reasons. First, Laxalt clearly established his commitment to attacking any corrupt aspects of the Nevada gaming industry: "We have to erase the image that we are in bed with hoodlums," he affirmed. Second, he gained support from those gambling executives who believed that Sawyer's war with the FBI had been counterproductive and had only intensified federal suspicions and surveillance. As a result, Laxalt's campaign coffers received a substantial boost from casino contributions. Thus when Paul Laxalt took the oath of office in January 1967, the question of how to regulate and protect the state's basic industry was something that its new governor had to confront.

Laxalt's style as governor, and later as senator, was to focus on a limited agenda but to make certain that each item was successfully concluded. A quick study, he was capable of grasping a wide range of issues, but he never felt the need to impose his views on everything that crossed his desk. Throughout his career, he was criticized by those who thought he should have tried to accomplish more in each office he held, and it is clear that he did not exhaust his political reservoir by pushing a comprehensive agenda. Instead, he was content to focus on a few major priorities.

In part his style was dictated by the fact that he easily became bored by administrative details. Thus he focused on "the big picture" and left day-to-day routine to subordinates. Much like his friend Ronald Reagan, Laxalt was an effective delegator, trusting his subordinates to accomplish their tasks with a minimum of supervision. Conversely, he became annoyed when he thought a staff member was dragging him into unnecessary administrative detail. "Can't you make them understand what I want?" he would plaintively ask. Ignoring outside criticism of his governing habits, Laxalt stuck with the style with which he was comfortable, refusing to listen to advisers or even ambitious staff who argued for a more aggressive approach.

Even before he was inaugurated, Laxalt recognized that his growing state was placing new and major burdens upon government that would require additional revenue. Although he had emerged from the election campaign as a champion of increased educational programs, including a new community college system, he had not been forced to deal with the means of financing his agenda. He thus found himself, an unshakable fiscal conservative, faced with the need to increase taxes, never a pleasant task for a Nevada politician.

To make a tax hike palatable, Laxalt decided in 1967 to spread the increase as broadly as possible. Several previous efforts to raise the sales tax had failed, and so Laxalt proposed simultaneously increasing the gross gaming-revenue tax by 24.8 percent and the state sales tax by 50 percent (from two to three cents). By combining the two and spreading the burden, Laxalt hoped to prevent a tax revolt. He also instructed his staff to design a proposal that would accomplish all of his goals with one increase. He feared that if the increase were approached in several increments, the opposition could become fully mobilized.

By proposing an increase in gaming taxes, Laxalt generated substantial public support, thereby making his proposal to increase the sales tax more acceptable. "When the gaming tax was proposed," he ruefully commented during an oral history session, "my gaming friends went wild," threatening the entire tax plan. Gaming lobbyists flooded the legislative halls in Carson City, but Laxalt was waiting. Before he announced the increases, Laxalt had cultivated the leadership of both parties, particularly Senators Carl Dodge (a Republican) and Jim Gibson (a Democrat). Members of his own party provided the most strenuous opposition, but he skillfully defused Republican opposition by using his personal charm in small meetings in which he preached the gospel of party loyalty and responsible governance. He would call in a few Republican members for a private, informal meeting, quietly reminding them that they all were "family." He encouraged them to speak freely inside the room, but only if they agreed to a unified party position before they departed. He listened carefully to all comments, sometimes making minor adjustments to his plan to appease touchy legislators, and then sent them off to do good after obtaining their professions of support. Ultimately Laxalt forged a strong bipartisan coalition to pass a tax package that included a 3 percent sales tax and a 20 percent increase in the state gaming-revenue tax, thereby making possible major improvements in the state's educational systems. Four years later, when he left office, he left a large budget surplus, a hallmark of his administration.

With revenue in place, Laxalt pursued his campaign promise of creating a community college system. He believed that the technical programs of the community colleges were vital to the state's economic growth. Laxalt was surprised, however, at the opposition to community colleges mounted by the friends and alumni of the University of Nevada. At the time, the Reno campus dominated higher education in the state and benefited from having many alumni as members of the legislature. The university leadership perceived the creation of a community college system as a threat to their budgets, to their autonomy, and to their continued domination of higher education in Nevada.

Laxalt knew that the time had come for establishing a community college system, and he had the endorsement of a blue-ribbon citizens' Advisory Commission on Higher Education. But the depth of emotions he encountered stunned the governor. He later recalled, "Facing the opposition of the UNR community, even I got shaky. The legislation almost failed."

The opposition, however, was not prepared to take on both the governor and multimillionaire Howard Hughes. Nor was it prepared to deny the legitimate educational needs of the isolated, but growing, north-central community of Elko. This mining and ranching hub had operated a small two-year college for years but could no longer sustain it financially without state assistance. Fund-raising attempts had failed, and the future of the school looked bleak. But Hughes stepped in and made a large donation to sustain the school's operations for a year. If Elko was to have its own community college, then other communities were not to be denied, and the opposition buckled. After Laxalt formally handed over Hughes's check at a highly publicized dinner in Elko, enabling legislation sped through the legislature.

Laxalt's interest in higher education served well the overall interests of the existing university system. New tax revenues were used to enhance the programs in both Reno and Las Vegas. He funded construction of major buildings on the Las Vegas campus. In 1969, the Board of Regents renamed the two schools the University of Nevada, Reno, and the University of Nevada, Las Vegas, thereby helping to establish the separate identity of the southern institution. Finally, Laxalt successfully requested authority from the legislature to create a medical school, which was located in Reno. Through these efforts, Laxalt strengthened higher education throughout the state.

The centerpiece of Laxalt's governorship, however, was his handling of the explosive issue of gambling regulation. On a political level, he had to deliver on campaign promises; but he also recognized that the economic future of Nevada rested on his ability to establish the gambling industry as beyond reproach. This meant ensuring the integrity of the industry not only to Nevadans but also to the federal government, which was poised to take dramatic action in the form of new taxes and federal regulations.

Before Laxalt took office, much of the financing for the construction of new casinos came from the Teamsters Pension Fund, and many of the owners and operators of casinos had connections to organized crime. FBI wiretaps, however illegally obtained, had nonetheless produced irrefutable evidence of massive losses of tax revenues through skimming and money-laundering schemes. When Frank Costello was murdered in a mob hit on the streets of New York City in 1957, police found in his pocket detailed reports of gaming revenues at the Tropicana Hotel.

Not only was Nevada's premier industry the recipient of notoriously bad national press, it was also the target of a determined Department of Justice. Beyond this, however, was the undeniable truth that the industry was stagnating, suffering from a lack of adequate investment capital. Legitimate investors shied away from Nevada's unique industry because of its unsavory reputation and its less-than-open financial base.

Laxalt had campaigned for governor on a promise to clean up the industry. In this endeavor he was the recipient of incredibly good luck. In late 1966, during the interval between Laxalt's election and inauguration, Howard Hughes arrived secretly in Las Vegas and moved into the top-floor suites of the Desert Inn. He had recently sold his interest in Trans World Airlines for more than $584 million, and he needed to reinvest that enormous chunk of cash to avoid heavy federal taxes. In March 1967, having tired of resisting pressure to give up the Desert Inn suites to make room for high-roller guests, he simply bought the entire hotel and casino for $13 million. Although his purchase has become the stuff of legend, it is doubtful that this astute entrepreneur made such a major decision on a whim. He was quite familiar with Las Vegas, having visited it a number of times during the 1950s, and his subsequent purchases of many Las Vegas properties suggest that his decision to buy the Desert Inn was part of a carefully considered plan.

The principal owner of the Desert Inn was Moe Dalitz, a man with a background in illegal gambling before coming to Nevada. Replacing Dalitz with Hughes, Laxalt understood, would help improve the national reputation of the industry, and he readily agreed to help Hughes obtain the necessary approvals from the Gaming Control Board.

Many people at the time and since believed that Laxalt permitted Hughes to avoid the rules in getting his regulatory approvals. For example, Hughes did not make a personal appearance before the Gaming Control Board. It is not correct to say that rules were broken, however. Laxalt did help expedite the process, but proper procedures were followed. Personal appearances before the board were required only if the board had questions about the integrity of the applicant or concerns about the source of investment funds. At the time, Hughes was widely respected and the source of his funds was well known; further, his reputation for eccentricity had not yet become common knowledge. Although Laxalt never met Hughes, the two men talked on the telephone several times.

Four months after his dramatic purchase of the Desert Inn, Hughes purchased the Sands Hotel for $14.6 million, and then proceeded to acquire the Castaways and the Frontier. While some law enforcement agencies were concerned about potential antitrust implications, the overwhelming public reaction was positive. "Mr. Hughes' involvement here has absolutely done us wonders," Governor Laxalt told the press. "I just returned from a trip to the East where I spoke to some industrialists in midtown Manhattan, and their questions no longer are concerned with the Mafia, the skimming, the under-world. . . . People come here now feeling they can come here in respectable, safe circumstances." Hughes added a much needed luster to the casino image both within and outside of Nevada.

Laxalt had moved swiftly to take advantage of a unique situation, thereby helping create a new aura surrounding Nevada's casinos. At the same time, Laxalt used the Hughes saga as an example to help pass corporate gaming legislation. He correctly perceived that the involvement of publicly regulated, major corporations would provide a much improved national image over that of Teamster-financed properties. But to accomplish this goal the state's gam-ing laws had to be amended. While existing law permitted ownership of casinos by corporations, it also required that each stockholder be individually licensed. This restriction obviously precluded large, publicly traded firms from investing in Nevada casino properties. Some corporations attempted to get around the law by purchasing casino properties that they, in turn, leased to a small, independent partnership that secured the gaming license and operated the casino. Laxalt sought legislation to remove the restrictions and to permit full-scale corporate involvement, with only the key employees requiring licenses.

The main support for the initiative came from members of the legislature who had attempted to pass similar legislation in earlier sessions. Governor Sawyer, who feared that corporations would effectively shield ownership by organized crime, adamantly opposed corporate gaming. He had been instru-mental in killing corporate gaming bills in both the 1963 and 1965 legislative sessions.

When the corporate gaming bills began to move during Laxalt's term, Sawyer used the issue to attack his successor. He was joined by several north-ern Nevada casino owners, especially the powerful Bill Harrah, who feared that their family-owned and -operated enterprises could not compete with large corporations. Neither Barron Hilton, nor Howard Hughes, both of whom favored the idea, got involved in the fight. The main industry propo-nent was Kirk Kerkorian, who wanted to substitute corporate investors for large bank loans. In 1969 Laxalt used the Kerkorian facts and the Hughes example to work with the legislature to enact the Corporate Gaming Act.

During this time, Laxalt also pushed for improved regulation and over-sight of gambling by the Gaming Control Board. He had become convinced by advocates of improved regulation that the board needed additional flex-ibility in carrying out its mandate. The only sanction available under its existing policies was denial or suspension of a gaming license. Because such drastic action would close a gaming property, board members were reluctant to take an action that could throw hundreds of casino workers out of a job. Further, any attempt to suspend a license was met with vigorous and time-consuming legal maneuvering that tended to dull the board's authority to act decisively. The result was that the board developed a reputation both within the gambling industry and among the Nevada public for tolerating a certain level of noncompliance. Laxalt convinced the Gaming Control Board to add hefty fines to its sanctions, giving it a powerful new tool in creating greater compliance. The result was more effective enforcement as well as a much-improved image of the industry.

By all accounts, the influence of organized crime in the gaming industry began to decrease during the Laxalt governorship. New and legitimate sources of investment from corporate America now began to examine the profit potentials in Nevada. Thus Laxalt helped establish a new political and regulatory environment for Nevada's primary industry, setting the stage for a sustained period of growth that would occur in the last two decades of the twentieth century. His ability to work cooperatively with federal law enforcement agencies brought to an end a period of acrimony that had endangered the casino industry; the diminished interest in Nevada on the part of the Justice Department contributed to a more favorable public image, and that in turn contributed to Nevada's prosperity and growth.

Laxalt's independent, and sometimes unpredictable, streak led to a surprising result. Although he was only partially successful, Laxalt attempted to curtail development at Lake Tahoe. He was, of course, intimately familiar with Lake Tahoe. His father had herded sheep in the mountains overlooking the lake for decades and had a base camp at Marlette Lake, a man-made lake two thousand feet above the eastern shore of Lake Tahoe, a property still owned by the Laxalt family. As a youth he had spent many summers in these mountains with his father. Paul Laxalt had essentially grown up in the Sierra Nevada; they were a part of his very fiber, and their value transcended any monetary worth anyone might put upon them.

Truly one of the world's most beautiful sites, the Lake Tahoe Basin attracted year-round visitors who came for recreational and vacation opportunities that included skiing, swimming, hiking, and boating. As the years passed more and more vacation homes were built on both the California and the Nevada sides. Then came the inevitable casinos on the Nevada side. Traffic became snarled and water quality deteriorated, even as developers in both states rushed to build more properties, primarily on the California side.

As a conservative Republican, Laxalt was a strong supporter of private property rights and limited government regulation. Many developers assumed when he was elected governor that growth would go unchecked at Lake Tahoe. But Laxalt was concerned about the quality of life at the lake. He met with a number of scientists who warned him that if development in the region was not controlled, the pristine, brilliantly blue lake would turn grey from pollution. Not only would this disastrous prospect destroy the beauty of the lake, but it would also jeopardize the primary water supply for the city of Reno. For years the environmental community had targeted Lake Tahoe for preservation. A number of attempts had been made to stop or slow development at the lake, but all had been defeated by local communities that surrounded the lake.

A comprehensive plan involving the two states was obviously needed. Laxalt contacted California governor Ronald Reagan, whom he had first met during the 1964 Goldwater campaign. They soon discovered that they shared the same political outlook. Out of the complex negotiations they initiated over the future of the Lake Tahoe Basin was forged a strong personal and professional relationship that greatly affected Laxalt's political future. These two conservative Republican governors, both elected in 1966, representing the largest and smallest of populations in the United States, agreed that preservation of the Tahoe Basin demanded unique approaches that would not necessarily please many of their conservative constituents. Although generally opposed by gambling interests, they found considerable support from wealthy property owners around the lake, who feared long-term environmental degradation would reduce property values and make their surroundings less enjoyable. Lengthy and complex negotiations eventually produced the Tahoe Regional Planning Agency (TRPA) in 1968, which was passed by both the California and Nevada legislatures and ratified by the United Sates Congress.

Originally, the TRPA was to be a planning agency; implementation of specific policies was left to the local governments. Laxalt was bitterly attacked by environmentalists, who wanted strong enforcement powers vested at TRPA. He was also attacked by some landowners who were unable to develop or sell their property. Over time, the TRPA survived many embittered battles and established itself as a major force in the struggle to balance private and public interests in such sensitive matters as taxation, the right of development of privately owned property, and water rights of two states. Although strong differences of opinion are held regarding the TRPA, most observers agree that it was at least a partial success.

Laxalt could not claim similar success from his efforts to diversify the Nevada economy. By the time he assumed office, Nevada had already bet its economic future upon the continued success of gaming. Ever since the 1950s Nevada leaders had talked about the importance of diversification, but precious little was ventured. Without much fanfare, Laxalt set out to rectify the situation, traveling extensively in an effort to visit with corporate leaders in an effort to lure nongaming businesses to Nevada. He assumed that the traditional Nevada litany of low taxes and a friendly regulatory environment would be met with a positive response. Much to his surprise and frustration, the reaction was just the opposite. He was shocked to learn that low taxes and a business-friendly atmosphere were of little importance to corporate executives who did not want to be associated with the powerful image of Nevada as a gambling den infested with mobsters. Further, the image, lingering from the 1930s, of Nevada as a place to obtain quickie divorces and where prostitution remained legal did not add to the luster of the Silver State. "We didn't get the time of day," he later recalled. Nevada's unsavory reputation was "an impossible package" to overcome.

Laxalt undertook economic diversification without adequate professional guidance. Only too late did he recognize that he was a rank amateur in the sophisticated field of economic development. "I didn't know how to market. I was inept." But he did at least make the effort, and in so doing established a modest foundation for much more successful diversification endeavors in the future.

Nothing in politics is a sure thing, but Governor Laxalt's reelection in 1970 seemed very secure. He had a legacy of accomplishment that included a budget surplus, corporate gaming, a community college system, a new medical school at the University of Nevada, Reno, much improved relations with the federal government, the decline of mob influence in the gaming industry, and environmental protection for Lake Tahoe. He was personally popular and headed a revitalized state Republican Party. It was widely assumed that he would run—and win in a cakewalk—in 1970.

But Laxalt made a shocking decision that dumbfounded nearly everyone. Rejecting the counsel and plaintive appeals of his advisers and supporters, Laxalt decided to walk away. When asked why, Laxalt explains, "I had a gut full of politics." Governing a state, of course, is politics writ large, and so why his sudden disdain for the political arena? Like his father, Laxalt valued his solitude and privacy. As governor, he was constantly under media and public scrutiny. Every decision had many political ramifications. It was a twenty-four-hour-a-day job from which there was no relief. Perhaps most important, his marriage was deteriorating, and he felt increasingly distant from his children. As the conflicting demands of politics and family pushed in on him, he decided that he needed more time and space—freedom. A man of independence, he simply returned to private life.

Discovering that four years out of political office "cleared my head," Laxalt found himself eager to reenter political life. Much had happened during those four years. Despite the best efforts of Laxalt and his wife, their marriage ended in divorce in 1972. During this period he returned to private law practice and, with members of his family and friends, built the Ormsby House, the largest hotel-casino in Carson City. Although he enjoyed success in his law practice, he found it essentially uninteresting. Further, the Ormsby House encountered severe financial problems because of a lack of adequate capital and an inability to carry the debt load, and it was sold. Laxalt decided to return to the political world when a promising opportunity presented itself in the form of the retirement of the popular United States senator, Democrat Alan Bible.

After easily winning the September primary, Laxalt faced Lieutenant Governor Harry Reid in a hotly contested senatorial race. Laxalt entered the fall campaign with a substantial lead in the polls, but disaster struck when President Gerald Ford stunned the nation by pardoning former president Richard Nixon on September 8. Republicans everywhere were running in the dread shadow of Watergate, and the extremely unpopular pardon cost them dearly. Within a month, Ford's approval rating fell from 71 percent to 49 percent, and the prospects of Republican candidates everywhere plummeted also. By early October, Laxalt's own polling figures reported the gloomy fact that he had fallen 25 points in the polls and now was a distinct underdog. At this juncture, with victory staring him in the face, Harry Reid made a major tactical blunder. Apparently believing that embarrassing questions would arise over the financing of the Ormsby House, Reid released his tax information to the press and challenged Laxalt to do the same for himself and all of his family. Laxalt refused to release the data; and when Reid sought to take advantage with pointed questions about the ethics of the Laxalt family's finances, Laxalt angrily responded by pointing out that one of the persons Reid was smearing was Laxalt's sister, Suzanne Laxalt, a Catholic nun. Overnight, the issue of integrity backfired on Reid, who found himself making clarifications and giving explanations. With the race narrowed, Laxalt strongly endorsed the Nevada Right-to-Work law, an issue that Reid, enjoying the support of organized labor, attempted to finesse, but with little success. In 1964 Laxalt had lost a United States Senate seat by 48 votes; ten years later he won by a margin almost as tiny, just 624 votes out of 450,000 cast.

But in November of 1974, in the wake of Nixon's resignation in August and his pardon a month later, any Republican who emerged victorious had won a major triumph.

Laxalt's ability to accomplish much in the United States Senate was sharply limited during the first four years of his first term. Republicans were in the minority in both houses of Congress, and Republican Senate leadership was clearly in the hands of moderates or liberals, such as Clifford Case, Charles Percy, Edward Brooke, and Mark Hatfield. The conservative Laxalt found himself a minority within a minority. When Laxalt in the summer of 1975 endorsed the effort of his friend Ronald Reagan to unseat President Ford, he was cut off from the White House and from his party's national establishment. However, his political isolation was made bearable when he married Carol Wilson in January of 1976.

President Ford had already put out the word that he was running for reelection in 1976 and had started lining up party endorsements when Reagan entered the race. Laxalt's belief that the party needed to project a more distinctly conservative message in the presidential election, coupled with his personal friendship with Reagan, made the decision an easy one. Once again, Laxalt followed his private principles and judgment against taking the safe course of action. With Laxalt's help, Reagan came close to wresting the nomination away from Ford at the Republican convention in Kansas City. After the convention, Laxalt worked tirelessly for Ford in the general election. This helped heal the breach within the Republican establishment, caused by Reagan's insurgent movement and the part it was said to have played in Ford's loss to Jimmy Carter in November.

With the former Georgia governor in the White House, Laxalt's political stock slowly began to rise again. He found himself emerging as a leading conservative critic of the new administration. Several of these political spats revolved around minor items, but a major issue emerged in late 1977, when the Panama Canal Treaties were placed before the Senate for ratification. Negotiations over the future of the Panama Canal had been under way for several years when Carter assumed the presidency. The mere fact that the Ford administration supported transferring the canal to the Panamanians had prompted shrill criticism from conservatives. Reagan had used the issue in his abortive 1976 campaign for the Republican nomination. Once Carter became president, the treaties were completed quickly and prepared for Senate ratification. The issues quickly divided the Senate Republicans. Minority Leader Howard Baker of Tennessee immediately announced his support and moderate Republicans fell into line.

Outside conservative groups were outraged by Baker's cooperation with the administration. They formed a delegation and visited a number of senators, asking each to lead the opposition. Several politely refused. They approached Laxalt, who agreed to undertake the task. Foreign policy had not been an area in which Laxalt had evidenced much interest, and he admitted he had only limited knowledge of the treaties. He instinctively objected to the loss of any strategic military asset and was offended by the argument that the United States had taken the Canal Zone illegally during the Theodore Roosevelt administration and that the time had arrived to correct an egregious wrong. Laxalt believed that both the Carter administration and Howard Baker underestimated popular opposition to the treaty. He clearly saw the canal as an issue ripe for conservative Republican exploitation. "Within the Senate itself, various elements of the Republican Party have come together in opposition to the Carter Treaties," Laxalt wrote in a letter to potential conservative donors in November 1977. "In short, these Treaties have served as a great unifying factor among Republicans and will help elect new Republicans to the 96th Congress." What the letter failed to say was that Laxalt expected most of the benefits to flow to conservative Republicans. It was part of a long-term strategy for conservatives to take control of the Republican Party.

The opposition coalition that he helped establish did not break neatly along party lines, as Laxalt wrote in his fund-raising letter, but rather tended to follow the traditional lines of the bipartisan conservative coalition that had existed in Congress since the late 1930s. Conservative Republicans and southern Democrats, especially those who were strongly committed to national defense, rallied against the treaties. The Carter administration launched a major public relations effort of its own, and Laxalt and Reagan countered with the formation of the Committee to Save the Canal. They soon referred to their organization as the Panama Truth Squad, a name that appealed to their constituency and outraged treaty supporters. They even used Reagan's 1976 campaign mailing list to raise funds. (A request from Laxalt to Republican National Committee chairman Bill Brock for party funds was denied.) The Panama Truth Squad conducted a number of activities to highlight perceived flaws in the treaties. The centerpiece was a media blitz that included an airplane full of prominent opponents who traveled to seven major cities in five days to rally public opposition. Laxalt argued that "any treaty which turns over operational control of a hemispheric 'choke point' like the Panama Canal must be rejected. . . . We hope to arouse the public to tell the Senate clearly and convincingly that it will not stand still for ratification of any document which gives up control of the canal."

By the time the debate began in the U.S. Senate, opposition to the treaties had become widespread. Letters and phone calls flooded Senate offices. The debate in the Senate dragged on for weeks as both sides tried to sway a few undecided senators. Laxalt was on the Senate floor for hours every day, monitoring the debate and answering charges and questions posed by proponents. His visibility, both within the Senate and as a public figure, rose immeasurably as it became evident that the vote would be very close. The day of the decisive vote began with Laxalt believing he would win, apparently having secured the minimum thirty-four votes necessary to prevent ratification. Ironically, it was the last-minute switch away from the opposition by Nevada's Senator Howard Cannon that secured the minimum sixty-seven votes necessary for ratification.

The Panama Canal issue thrust Laxalt into the Senate spotlight, and he emerged as one of its leading conservative Republican spokesmen. He found himself much in demand as the 1978 congressional elections approached, and he campaigned vigorously for Republican candidates throughout the country. Upon returning to the Senate after one such trip, he was chided by a colleague for missing a vote in a Labor Committee markup. He firmly but cheerfully explained that he was doing far more to advance the Republican agenda by electing more Republican Senators than "by losing a vote in the Labor Committee 18–4 rather than 18–5." His own efforts helped elect a number of new Republicans that year; three additional Republicans entered the Senate in 1979, raising the minority's number to forty-one.

Nonetheless, the Democrats still firmly controlled both the White House and the Congress. There was little opportunity to fashion policy, and Laxalt gave up trying. Instead, he focused on issues that could be used in the 1980 presidential election. He introduced the Family Protection Act, a bill that strung together a number of conservative social policies, including elimination of the higher tax liability for married couples. He encouraged the Sagebrush Rebellion, an effort by westerners to gain control of the vast federal landholdings in their states. And he continued to travel to rally the Republicans for the 1980 election.

Despite his often sharp partisan attacks, Laxalt remained a favorite among his Senate colleagues of both parties. Every year the *Washingtonian* asked senators to pick their most popular members; in most years, Laxalt was among the top vote-getters. Laxalt had the ability to disagree with individuals on policy issues while refraining from making personal attacks. When several Democratic senators were defeated in the 1978 election, he refused to gloat, offering them sincere best wishes instead. While their respective staffs looked on with horror, he was often seen trading jokes and stories with Senator Edward M. Kennedy at judiciary committee meetings.

In 1980 Laxalt ran for reelection. Personally popular in his home state, there was little doubt of his reelection. The Democrats nominated a former state senator from Reno, Mary Gojack. Her name recognition was limited, her fund-raising ability poor, and she was marked with the kiss of death for a Nevada politician: She carried the label of a bona fide liberal. Although virtually assured of victory, Laxalt did not take the race for granted and mounted a vigorous statewide campaign. He and his advisers agree that the 1980 race was the least enjoyable of all his campaigns. With the result never in doubt, he had to force himself to go through the motions. Perhaps he was tiring once again of the ceaseless pressures of political life. He was also disturbed by the frequently strident tone of his opponent, but he did not respond in kind. It was not his style; it also was not necessary.

His frustrations, however, stemmed largely from the fact that he was not able to participate actively in Ronald Reagan's presidential campaign. For the previous two years Laxalt had worked on behalf of Reagan's candidacy, serving as a member of the inner circle of advisers. For a time he was seriously considered for the vice presidential slot, his name surfacing prior to the Republican convention as one of six persons under serious consideration. Although naturally intrigued by the prospect, Laxalt initially thought his chances of selection were small. He could easily list his liabilities: He came from a small state with only three electoral votes; he came from the same western region as Reagan; he was philosophically aligned closely to Reagan; and the reputation and image of Nevada remained a liability.

Laxalt remained on the short list right down to Reagan's selection of George Bush. All things being equal, Laxalt probably was Reagan's first choice for a running mate, but the election was expected to be very close. As a result, traditional wisdom prevailed, and Bush, Reagan's major opponent in the early primaries and possessor of an extensive political résumé, was chosen over Laxalt for good strategic reasons. Laxalt was initially disappointed but understood the political realities that determined Reagan's decision. He quickly forgot the hurt and enthusiastically supported his party's ticket in the general election.

The election was extremely gratifying to Laxalt. Not only was he reelected to the Senate by one of the widest margins in Nevada history, but his close friend was headed for the White House. And for extra measure, the Republicans would control the Senate for the first time since 1954. As the new president's best friend in the Senate, and because of his visibility from the Panama Canal fight, many conservatives urged Laxalt to challenge Howard Baker for the position of majority leader. But once again Laxalt's independent streak guided him elsewhere. He correctly understood that he was not suited for the scheduling details and parliamentary fights required of the majority leader, and he announced his support for Baker, effectively foreclosing serious opposition to Baker. In return, Baker saw that Laxalt was included in all leadership meetings with the president. In 1983, Laxalt became the general chairman of the Republican Party, a position much better suited to his talents and temperament.

Laxalt refused to overplay his powerful new hand. This was a break with long-standing tradition. Nevada was traditionally represented by colorful senators who constantly and publicly did all they could to "bring home the bacon" for the state. But public commotion often hid lack of ability to get much done. In other cases, such as with Senators Newlands, McCarran, and Cannon, the public pronouncements were matched by significant accomplishments. Laxalt, however, shunned public displays of power. He continued to keep his legislative agenda tightly focused and, unlike many of his Nevada senatorial predecessors, did not exert special pressure on the White House staff or take advantage of his personal relationship with the president. His patronage requests were modest, and he continued to play by traditional rules on key issues. Yet despite this low-key approach, he accomplished his primary goals.

The most dramatic example of this was his quiet determination to prevent the gargantuan MX missile deployment system from being located in Nevada. In 1979, President Carter had announced his decision to proceed with full-scale development of a new large, intercontinental ballistic missile (ICBM), the MX, which could hold ten nuclear warheads. He also announced that the missiles would use a "racetrack" basing mode and be located in Nevada and Utah.

At the time, it was widely believed that the Soviet Union would soon have the capability to destroy 90 percent of the American ICBM force because the accuracy of the Soviet missiles was improving dramatically. Military planners suggested that the danger to the American missile force would be substantially reduced if the ICBM were made mobile. Several such basing modes were considered, but after years of study, President Carter chose to base the MX on a "racetrack," a series of widely dispersed silos connected by specially designed roadways. Under his plan, each missile would be located on a closed-loop track that connected 23 shelters; the missile would be moved between the shelters so the Soviets would never know which one of the shelters contained the live missile and which shelters were empty. It would be impossible to overwhelm this system with enough Soviet missiles to knock out the American deterrent force. Carter proposed building and basing 200 MX missiles, which would require the construction of 200 racetracks and 4,600 shelters.

The potential impact upon Nevada would have been enormous. If built as proposed, the system would have required 50,000 construction workers, the development of a deployment area of 30,000 square miles of desert land, and the allocation of 121 billion gallons of precious water for construction.

Many Nevada business leaders, especially those in Las Vegas, initially welcomed this proposal, seeing it as yet another example of federal expenditures that would spur economic growth. By 1981 land prices began to increase as speculation in Nevada desert properties took root. It was widely assumed that Nevada's two senators, both recognized for their strong national defense postures, would support the system. With the invasion of Afghanistan by the Soviets and President Reagan's major increases in military budgets, the Cold War seemed to be deepening.

Laxalt, however, was skeptical from the time President Carter announced the grandiose plan. He was unsure if Carter really intended to proceed with the system, even privately expressing his suspicions that the president had picked the most expensive and environmentally damaging system in hopes that Congress would kill it.

In 1980 Congress appropriated initial funding for the new weapons system, but postponed the final decision on the basing mode until after the presidential election. During the campaign, candidate Reagan promised only to review the basing-mode decision. Laxalt did not press for a greater commitment, nor did he express his final position on the matter. In 1981, Laxalt assumed chairmanship of the Military Construction Appropriations Subcommittee—the panel with direct jurisdiction over the basing-mode funding. Republican Jake Garn of Utah was also on the committee. As Laxalt studied the details of the plan, his reservations intensified. He was very concerned, however, of public perception if he attempted to scuttle the MX prematurely, or if he used his influence to persuade the president of his views. Instead, to protect both the president and the review process, he set about to demonstrate that the racetrack basing mode was flawed on its merits.

In line with the commitments he had made during the campaign, the president ordered a Pentagon review of the basing mode. Secretary of Defense Caspar Weinberger told the reviewers they had until July of 1981 to make their recommendations. Laxalt used that time wisely, holding a series of subcommittee hearings in which the military planners as well as opponents had full opportunity to testify. The environmental community, which had always opposed the plan, pressed its case vigorously, especially in hearings that Laxalt conducted in Las Vegas and Reno. Following a series of closed meetings where national security issues were discussed, Laxalt told the press he "wouldn't be surprised" if the panel recommended a different deployment. He now was pushing for reasonable alternatives.

Senator Garn pursued a similar course in Utah. The now-apparent lack of enthusiasm by the two conservative senators whose states would be most directly affected sent a strong message. Local support for the basing mode began to erode in Nevada and Utah alike. Newspapers began publicly opposing the system, and important local political figures joined environmentalists in the expanding opposition. In May 1981, the Mormon Church hierarchy issued a plea to President Reagan not to put the MX system in either Nevada or Utah. Even within the Defense Department opposition to the basing mode grew; Deputy Defense Secretary Frank Carlucci publicly advocated deploying the missiles on submarines, while Secretary Weinberger privately worried that environmental lawsuits could tie up deployment for years.

With the political ground prepared, Laxalt and Garn finished the job. In June 1981, they released a report from the Military Construction Appropriations Subcommittee that called for an alternative basing for the MX. The report rejected the air force proposal for national security reasons, citing recent intelligence estimates revealing that even the proposed 4,600 shelters would be inadequate to meet the Soviet threat. It also expressed doubts that the exact location of the live MX missiles could be kept secret. It released estimates by the Office of Technology Assessment that the projected cost of the system would grow from $43 billion to $83 billion, forcing the Defense Department to cut funds for the procurement of other weapons. Finally, it listed the environmental and socioeconomic impacts of the system, calling them devastating.

The report also highlighted alternatives to the racetrack system, including the deployment of two hundred MX missiles in existing Minuteman III silos that would be protected by a new antiballistic missile (ABM) system. It also called for upgrading the existing Minuteman force, pursuing a better arms control agreement, accelerating research on ABM technology, increasing the percentage of strategic bombers on alert, building a new generation of manned strategic bombers, and upgrading the command, control, and communications network. By proposing reasonable defense alternatives, Laxalt and others were able to preserve their national security credentials while undercutting the MX. In the summer of 1981 the Reagan administration quietly shelved the MX proposal.

In many other instances, Laxalt's interests coincided with the policies of the Reagan administration, a situation that alleviated the need to engage in public policy fights. One example of this was the Sagebrush Rebellion. The rebellion was the reaction of the governments of western states to the perceived anti-West policies of the Carter administration and called for the return of federal land and water to state control. But when Reagan became president and James Watt was named secretary of the interior, the pro-development policies of the new administration defused the need for the Sagebrush Rebellion and the movement became dormant.

By the mid-1980s, Laxalt's senatorial power was such that he could accomplish many of his goals legislatively without resorting to pressure on the administration. In 1983, Laxalt became chairman of the powerful Appropriations Subcommittee with jurisdiction over the Departments of State, Justice, and Commerce and a host of independent agencies. He effectively used that position to secure federal funds for a wide range of projects.

Laxalt has been criticized for not accomplishing more for Nevada when he was in his unique position of power during the Reagan years. Other people would have been more aggressive in similar circumstances. However, that method of operation was not in his nature. He accomplished most of his goals through behind-the-scenes actions, through his own legislative efforts, and by remaining in close contact with the administration. As a result, he never strained his friendship with the president, and they were closer friends when they left office than when they entered.

As the 1984 election cycle began, Laxalt was at the peak of his personal and political career. He was the general chairman of the Republican Party, the chairman of President Reagan's reelection effort, a respected member of the senate Republican leadership, chairman of two legislative subcommittees, and a key spokesman for Republican causes. He served as a conduit between his senate colleagues and the president. He sat in on all the long-term strategic planning sessions of the Reagan reelection campaign, and participated in most of the day-to-day decision meetings. He placed Reagan's name in nomination at the Republican convention, as he had in 1976 and 1980. He ensured that the Republican election committees and the White House worked closely together for the benefit of Republican candidates throughout the nation. His efforts, along with those of the entire Republican political team, were enormously successful. President Reagan was overwhelmingly reelected, winning the electoral votes for all except Walter Mondale's home state of Minnesota and the District of Columbia.

After the successes of 1984, Laxalt once again began to tire of politics.

There were no new heights to climb. His friend was now a lame-duck president, and Laxalt had now logged ten years in the Senate. Never overly interested in the complex legislative process, Laxalt did not look forward to the prospect of endless debate and votes on the Senate floor. Thus, as he began to contemplate a reelection campaign in 1986, many of the thoughts that had persuaded him not to run for a second term as governor resurfaced. It soon became clear that he intended to retire. Many political leaders, both in Nevada and Washington, D.C., tried to persuade him to run again. He listened politely but could not generate any enthusiasm for another campaign or for six more years in the Senate. In the summer of 1985, he retreated to Marlette Lake and had one final series of meetings with his "political family." Almost all of them urged him to run, but in his boyhood sanctuary, he again returned to his independent roots and decided that what was best for him was to retire.

In early 1986 he gave up chairmanship of the Appropriations Subcommittee and increasingly withdrew from his Senate responsibilities. But before he left, he had one more battle to fight. During the spring of 1986, the secretary of energy was required by law to designate three sites in the West for review as a potential site for deep underground storage of high-level nuclear waste generated by nuclear power plants. The secretary was also required to designate a number of potential sites in the East for further study for a second nuclear repository. A number of the potential eastern sites were in states represented by freshmen Republican senators, all of whom were up for reelection in 1986. Those senators vigorously lobbied the secretary of energy, John Harrington, to defer action in the East and instead focus solely on western sites. After months of pressure, the secretary yielded. On the same day that he designated three specific places in the West for site-characterization work, including Yucca Mountain in Nevada, he announced that further exploration of an eastern site would be deferred.

Political leaders in the three western states—Nevada, Washington, and Texas—were outraged. They contended that Harrington was ignoring specific mandates in the law concerning a second site while also inconsistently holding firm on the need to follow the law regarding the first site. The process had become politicized. Following his usual style, Laxalt did not criticize the president or Harrington, even though he was deeply disappointed. True to form, he quietly communicated his deep concerns to his colleagues on the Senate Appropriations Committee. When the committee reviewed the Fiscal Year 1987 Energy and Water Development Bill, which contained the budget for the Nuclear Waste Disposal Fund, Laxalt proposed an amendment that would cut the program's budget from $769 million, as proposed by the department, to $380 million. Laxalt gave a low-key, but passionate, speech in support of his amendment. Rather than criticize the secretary for a bad decision, he argued that the whole program should be reviewed, citing the recent explosion of the space shuttle *Challenger* as evidence that our science and technologies were not perfect. Before the United States committed to burying the "most toxic material on earth," he argued, all the scientific options available needed to be reviewed. In all likelihood, the majority of senators on the committee favored proceeding with the characterization of the western site, if for no other reason than that their own states were off the hook. However, Laxalt made a powerful case, and the amendment passed and was carried through in the final version of the bill, having the effect of considerably slowing the selection of a western site.

It has been argued that Laxalt should have cut a deal with Harrington to gain a bundle of benefits for Nevada in return for accepting the location of the repository. But it must be remembered that Harrington had no authority to offer benefits to Nevada until after the law was amended in 1987, directing the Department of Energy to review only the Yucca Mountain site. In 1986, Nevada was not the only state with a site subject to review, and neither Laxalt nor the administration was in a position to negotiate what would have essentially been a sugarcoated payoff.

On January 3, 1987, Laxalt retired from public life. In 1988 he briefly participated in an exploratory effort to determine if he should become a candidate for the Republican nomination for president, but he failed to raise sufficient money or enthusiasm to convince him to enter the race. He remained active in political circles, helping in the George Bush campaign in 1988 and serving as an adviser to Senator Robert Dole's presidential bid in 1996. He continued to work in Washington as a legislative consultant, but maintained his ties to his home state and his beloved Marlette Lake.

The Laxalt legacy is lasting. By remaining true to his independent instincts, he developed a highly successful political style that enabled him to accomplish a large number of goals he had set for himself. He was never a man defined only by a list of bills passed or policies enacted. Instead, it was always his personal qualities that made him unique. When Laxalt left the Senate, Senator Strom Thurmond paid him the following tribute in the Senate:

> The qualities which his colleagues have come to value most in him are his deep-seated sense of right and wrong; his quick sense of humor; his openness and honesty; and his unfailing loyalty. Our Nation was

founded by men with these qualities—men who were not confined by the stale boundaries of prescription politics. I am told that Senator Laxalt has a sign on the wall in his office which reads: "There is no limit to what a man can do or how far he can go as long as he does not mind who takes the credit."

Throughout his career Paul Laxalt remained true to his Nevada roots. He found in politics an outlet for his considerable talents and energies, and his accomplishments helped sculpt the shape of the New Nevada for the better. But he never let his success or popularity cloud his own view of himself and his Nevada. He always kept his political career within a healthy perspective that grew out of the values he learned as the child of two hard-working Basque immigrants.

Steve Wynn

"I Got the Message"

BY WILLIAM N. THOMPSON

The slides were stunning. The audience sat in awe as the captivating speaker described a "new level" in gaming resorts. I sat with them at the International Gaming Exposition being held in Atlantic City in 1987. Next to me was Arnie Wexler, chairman of the New Jersey Council on Compulsive Gambling. On the dais was the glowing chairman of the Golden Nugget, uttering a rapid series of staccato-like sentences proclaiming his new project as the ultimate in entertainment experiences. Tigers and waterfalls, dolphins and volcanos, multimillion-dollar cottages for high rollers, and an atrium with a tropical forest. Misty air with the fragrances of piña coladas. Hundreds of elegant suites, crystal-chandeliered ballrooms, and a complete warehouse on premises. This would be the pinnacle facility for Las Vegas, a town known for its exaggerations. The image that the speaker described stunned even this audience of hardened gaming moguls and was soon to become the reality of Steve Wynn's extravagant new resort hotel-casino, the Mirage. Arnie Wexler just smiled and shook his head in amazement. "I think he'll do it. This man will do it. He can pull it off!"

Many explanations may be offered for why people gamble. Some suggest that gamblers—at least those with patterns of habitual gambling—are seeking a magical escape from the tedium and boredom of depressed daily living. Somehow by hitching their wagons to the magical carousel or roller coaster of gambling they can, even if for only mere moments, reestablish a world of dreams that left them as they entered adulthood. But what does a society as a whole do when it has fallen into the tedium and boredom of mundane routine? Some suggest that members of society seek an escape from that life by identifying with magical individuals who rise above the confines of ordinary ways of doing things. By hitching their wagons to these individuals there is an escape, if only temporarily, back to a time when dreams and promising futures gave meaning to life. Several scholars have examined the

12

special kind of leader who can rally the people with extraordinary images and promises, and they have used a word to describe the leader. The word is *charisma.*

This essay explores the concept of charisma in order to analyze a major contemporary leader in one of the nation's most rapidly growing industries: gambling. Las Vegas is an appropriate place to analyze such leadership, because unlike many other large industries, casino gambling is a relatively new industry. It has also continually encountered opposition that threatened its very existence. Casino gambling has been in a sixty-five-year struggle to maintain its mere legality, let alone its legitimacy in American society. Ever since legal gambling appeared in Las Vegas during the early years of the Great Depression, the industry has periodically faced severe challenges that required strong leadership to right the foundering ship and set it again on course.

Las Vegas faced such a crisis during the early 1980s. Following an extended period of growth, the city was hit hard by a severe economic recession that came immediately on the heels of the opening of casino gaming in Atlantic City. Nevada's monopoly had been shattered, and Atlantic City threatened to drain off hundreds of thousands of visitors—and untold millions of dollars in revenue—annually. Further, many other state governments were seriously examining the possibilities of taking the plunge into casino gambling as a quick fix to their own economic malaise. Twenty-nine states had already tested the temperature of the gaming waters by establishing state lotteries. As Las Vegas gaming revenues fell absolutely for the first time in more than three decades, massive shock waves rippled through a stunned Nevada political and economic leadership. The future looked problematical at best. But at this very juncture—when prospects seemed as dim as at any time since the early 1950s when the sensational Kefauver hearings probed organized crime's presence in Las Vegas—a single man emerged who provided the charismatic leadership that led to a stunning turnaround of Las Vegas's fortunes. That man was Stephen Alan Wynn.

After Nevada legalized gambling in 1931, the gambling tables in back rooms of bars and saloons were moved to the front, and signs were put on the façades of buildings announcing to residents what all had known before: Gambling was going on inside. Initially, there was little effort to attract tourists or out-of-state gamblers. For more than a decade, construction workers building Hoover Dam, the workers at the new Basic Magnesium Plant, and army air force personnel stationed at Nellis Air Base provided sufficient clientele for this small, start-up industry. Many Las Vegans feared that a gaming economic boom would disappear after the war and that their city would return to its previous existence as a mere desert outpost, a water stop on the San Pedro, Los Angeles, and Salt Lake Railroad. No one foresaw the arrival, in the years immediately following the war, of a small group of investors intent on capitalizing upon legalized gaming in ways that Nevadans had never anticipated. Those visions included large tourist resort hotels that featured lavish casinos.

It would be difficult to put the label "charismatic" on Benjamin "Bugsy" Siegel, but he did what other charismatic leaders do. He provided energy, he provided an idea, and he coordinated resources so that the idea could become a reality. He envisioned a luxurious resort casino, on the highway to Los Angeles, that would attract Hollywood celebrities who in turn would attract high-stakes gamblers. In 1946, he completed the construction of the Flamingo begun by Billy Wilkerson, setting in motion the process of turning Highway 95 into the world-famous Las Vegas Strip. Others soon followed, and the small Las Vegas Chamber of Commerce even launched a publicity campaign to attract visitors and developers. Soon thereafter the Desert Inn was built, and in short order the Sahara, the Sands, the Dunes, and the Riviera appeared. The new hotel-casinos were no longer drab local joints with stereotypical western decor. They were plush international tourist destinations—an essential ingredient of the New Nevada—and they attracted a large, growing, and affluent clientele that changed forever the face of Nevada and the shape of its primary industry.

Nevadans welcomed Siegel and those who followed after him because they brought essential managerial expertise and investment capital. The fact that many of these persons were identified as having close associations with major crime syndicates was of little concern so long as they remained law-abiding citizens in Nevada. Federal authorities might have relentlessly pursued many organized-crime figures who played prominent roles in Las Vegas gambling circles, but the primary concern of Nevada's political leadership was to establish an unquestioned legitimacy and integrity for its lucrative new gambling economy by expanding the scope and authority of its regulatory operation.

As long as major banks would not provide capital for construction and operation of new hotel-casinos, and as long as state law prevented corporate ownership of gambling enterprises, the future of Nevada gaming was problematical. Some predicted its ultimate demise. For nearly twenty years the state government struggled, with limited success, to control its dominant industry. Then in 1966 a magical person appeared in the form of the eccentric but highly esteemed Howard Hughes. This famous industrialist-entrepreneur-investor had been forced to sell his holdings in Trans World Airlines because of a federal antitrust action, and he needed to reinvest the money quickly in order to avoid exorbitant income and capitals gains taxes.

Hughes moved into the top floor of the Desert Inn and began buying casino properties. Like magic, the industry-threatening specter of organized crime was reduced to one of relatively minor proportions. Hughes's lofty reputation as a responsible business executive provided Nevada casinos a new legitimacy within the state and across the land. While many still considered Howard Hughes to be a dashing, charismatic capitalist (as perhaps he was in earlier years), by 1966 he had degenerated into an eccentric recluse, living a most unusual lifestyle that bordered on the macabre. He did not put any of his energy into gaming development; he only acquired properties. In this regard he was once more up against federal antitrust laws, and Las Vegas faced the prospect of inadequate capital for its industry. This time, however, the state was able to attract public corporation participation, partly because of the reputation Hughes brought to gaming and mainly because it changed its licensing laws in 1969. Almost overnight corporate America controlled many large casino properties. Corporations also built even larger casino-hotels—the International (soon the Hilton) and MGM Grand (later Bally's). The intervention of the charismatic Hughes had transformed the nature of Nevada's casino industry, substantially reducing the unsavory influence of organized crime and providing a new sense of legitimacy and public acceptance.

By the early 1980s the expansion and enthusiasm generated by Howard Hughes had run its course. On one hand, the mobsters had lost much of their control to large, out-of-state corporations, but the new management demonstrated a marked lack of imagination. Concerned with the bottom line, corporate managers had introduced cost-conscious accounting practices into their operations. Fearful of making expensive mistakes, they shunned innovation and tended to standardize their gambling product. In a word, they had bureaucratized an enterprise that had been attracting customers who had hoped to find magic in their lives. As long as Nevada was the only major casino venue in North America, the customers would keep coming. But in 1978 casino gambling had begun in Atlantic City, New Jersey. Then came a severe economic recession in 1980 and 1981 that greatly compounded Nevada's (and Las Vegas's) problems. For the first time in over thirty years, Nevada's gambling revenues went down in terms of constant-value dollars, and the slippage continued into the middle of the decade. Consequently there was little interest in building new properties or making major new infusions of capital into the Las Vegas casino industry. Ominously, innovation and excitement along the Strip was focused on Circus Circus, a company that went public in 1984 and earned its reputation as a provider of bargain packages for down-market customers.

It was precisely at this critical juncture in Las Vegas's history that Steve Wynn emerged as a major player. Several antecedent events may have suggested that he was going to be a strong leader. He was born in Utica, New York, on January 27, 1942. His nuclear family was critical in his development. Stephen was the grandson of a traveling vaudeville performer and the son of Mike Wynn, a small-time gambling entrepreneur who was required to operate on the margins of the law, if not the margins of society. His mother, Zelma, commented, "If you ran a bingo parlor, some people looked at you as if you were a bookie." Steve Wynn's own personality suggests that the excitement of entertaining and gaming may have been ingrained in his genetic makeup. However, Wynn's tie to gaming was more than just genetic. His exposure to bingo facilities, other gaming, and the personalities of a marginal gaming industry began early in his life.

His father's business activities required his frequent absence from the home, but this may have made him only a stronger role model for his son. It did make Stephen, the only child for ten years, the center of attention in the household. His father was very conscious of his duty to support and provide for his family, and his mother sought to indulge all of Stephen's needs and desires. He was sent to private schools and treated as a very special person by his parents. All parents should make their children feel special and important, but Steve's parents did so in spades.

What appears to be a defining moment, one that is prominently mentioned in most profiles of Steve Wynn, occurred in 1952. He has commented upon it in several personal interviews. When Steve was just ten years old, his father took him to Las Vegas, where Mike explored the possibility of establishing himself as a bingo operator. Steve saw the vast expanses of desert and sagebrush, the starkly beautiful mountains, the shimmering blue waters of Lake Mead. He rode horses and breathed the dry crisp air of the Nevada desert. But most important, he witnessed the action of Las Vegas. It apparently left an indelible imprint upon this impressionable youngster. After graduation from a private military academy, Wynn attended the University of Pennsylvania, where he studied chemistry and for a time gave serious thought to a career in medicine. However, he graduated with a degree in English literature and in the process took several courses in the Wharton School of Business. He briefly contemplated pursing a career in the law, but found himself inexorably gravitating toward his father's profession. Steve Wynn seems to have been destined for a career in gaming.

The habitual gambler is likely to experience the excitement of the game early in life and, while first participating, is likely to achieve a win that provides such a feeling of pleasure that he cannot quit playing. A similar experience may have occurred on Wynn's initial visit to Las Vegas. His was not a gambling win, but a sense of extreme pleasure in knowing that there is a unique place where one belongs. Like the gambler who constantly chases one game after another, win or lose, seeking always to find the magic of that first-win sensation, Steve Wynn may still be chasing after a feeling he experienced in 1952. Like the habitual gambler, he may never recapture that feeling, and so he may never be able to stop the chase. He has told interviewers that he is always "running scared, straight ahead."

While Steve may have found his dream, his father did not have a winning experience in Las Vegas. Mike's bingo establishment within the Silver Slipper Casino lost out to competition from the more well-heeled Last Frontier next door. He also lost his gaming profits through his own gambling. (Steve once told a reporter: "My father made a nice living from bingo, but he'd lose all his money playing gin or betting on baseball. And God forbid if there was a crap game in the vicinity.") Mike was given further bad news when the Nevada Gaming Control Board denied him a gaming license in April 1953. According to John Smith's *Running Scared,* the board was not able to resolve concerns about some of Mike's associations in East Coast gaming. His ventures in casino bingo operations were successful, but his bingo trade in the East fell short of establishing his own credentials as a top entrepreneur. But the short side that was concealed as marginal success was more than offset by personal gambling losses.

Michael Wynn's personal drive for the golden ring ended prematurely. Heart failure led to his death on an operating table in 1963, at the age of fifty-five. A business opportunity, as well as family responsibility, was handed over to his son, a twenty-one-year-old Ivy League college graduate. The weight of responsibility was made heavier when Steve married Elaine Pascal, a graduate of George Washington University, just two months after his father died. Someone had to manage a string of bingo halls. But more than an opportunity or a necessity, a rekindled dream was placed directly in front of Steve Wynn. He was not destined to be a physician, a literature teacher, or a lawyer. He was destined to chase his childhood dream and achieve the success that eluded his father. Perhaps now the mission was clear in his mind: He was going to Las Vegas. And he would not only make it in Las Vegas, he would make it big in Las Vegas.

A mission, a dream perhaps, but things do not just happen. Most dreamers who chase games in Las Vegas, seeking to repeat early feelings of excitement, fall flat. While they try and try again, eventually most find only depression and despair at the end, and resources—money and energy—dry up before the big win occurs. But this does not happen for everyone. Steve Wynn did not avoid setbacks—he has had several; but so far, he has been able to land on his feet when his career has taken a tumble. Much of the mythology of the man has been attributed to miracles of recovery that occurred when his falls seemed destined to lead to total failure.

Steve Wynn has been able to achieve a string of business triumphs despite being somewhat restricted by retinitis pigmentosa, an incurable eye disease. Because of his limited range of vision, he is unable to drive a car by himself. The disease may progress, but he has refused to permit it to restrict his life, although he routinely attempts to conceal its limiting effects. In some ways this limitation might propel his ambition. He certainly expresses a desire for visual perfection with his personal appearance and his properties. He is always impeccably dressed (even when purposely informal), and his properties rate kudos from architectural analysts and the general public alike for their good taste and attention to the smallest of details in fixtures and furnishings. Paint lines are exact in corners, and brass railings are always polished. Wynn is known for having a sharp temper, and invariably the story is told that he expresses loud verbal displeasure when he observes that one lightbulb is burned out in a casino sign containing hundreds. As a blind person is often credited with having a sixth sense, Steve Wynn's limited range of vision seems to give him a heightened sense of detail.

His physical limitations are outwardly considered to be only an inconvenience. They do not keep him from rigorous physical activity. He especially enjoys downhill skiing. One particular episode has added to his legend. During a trip to his family lodge in Sun Valley, Idaho, Wynn miscalculated a steep slope and curve and shot off a cliff, landing sixty feet below. Rescuers hurried to the scene, fearing the worst, but found Wynn merely shaken up, with a few sore spots and in good spirits. Within a few days he was at the slopes again—back on his feet.

Wynn brought his new family—wife, Elaine, and daughter Kevin (born in 1966; a second daughter, Gillian, was born in 1969)—to Las Vegas in 1967. Through contacts gained by work in his father's bingo halls, Wynn was given an opportunity to make a 3 percent investment in the Frontier Hotel and Casino. Subsequent investments increased that stake to 5 percent. The opportunity must have been especially sweet, considering his father's sour bingo experience competing with the Frontier back in the 1950s. With the investment came a job as a slot manager. Wynn's new associates, however, were not all the most reputable people in gaming. Some were exposed in a cheating scheme and later subjected to federal criminal indictment. Wynn, however, was untainted in the investigation, which occurred after the Frontier, and Wynn's portion of it, was sold to Howard Hughes. When questioned about the associations in later licensing hearings in New Jersey—detailed hearings that lasted for three weeks—Wynn was cleared of personal wrongdoing.

A bright star was rapidly emerging on the Las Vegas scene. In 1971 Wynn purchased a large block of Golden Nugget stock, won a place on the corporate board, and in 1973 emerged as the new chief executive of the downtown Las Vegas property. He was just thirty-one years old. He constructed a new hotel tower and transformed an ordinary (or worse) property into the most fashionable downtown casino. From his position as CEO of the Golden Nugget he masterminded the construction and operations of the Golden Nugget of Atlantic City in the late 1970s, a casino that soon became, by all measures, the most successful on the East Coast.

Wynn benefited greatly from loyal friends who played important roles in his commercial activities. Two such individuals were E. Parry Thomas, president of Valley Bank of Nevada, and investment mogul Michael Milken. Thomas helped Wynn obtain a liquor distributorship after he left the Frontier, a position that enabled him to establish many important contacts within the Las Vegas entertainment and gambling community. More important, Thomas helped Wynn make a critical connection with Howard Hughes, also a client of Valley Bank. Hughes had a reputation for acquiring—but never selling—property. Thomas and/or Wynn found out that Hughes was paying a high rent for property next to his Landmark Hotel and Casino that was used for parking space for Landmark patrons. Hughes owned a strip of property next to Caesars Palace (conveniently located at the city's busiest intersection), which Caesars was renting for its patrons' parking. But Hughes was taking in less from Caesars than he was paying out to rent the Landmark parking area. Caesars had attempted unsuccessfully to buy the land from Hughes for approximately $1 million. Wynn found the owner of the Landmark parking lot and in 1971 executed an option to buy the land.

Wynn then approached the Hughes organization and suggested a land swap. Hughes went for the deal. Financing for Wynn's purchase was arranged by Parry Thomas. Wynn then started to play high-stakes poker. He turned down an offer from Caesars that would have given him a modest profit. Instead he initiated a process to win a license for a newly constructed casino that would abut Caesars. He filled out all the application materials and went through the full planning process to win all necessary building permits. He even had a contractor break ground before he extracted the price he wanted for the land: more than $2 million. Wynn's personal profit was in excess of $700,000. He used this bonanza to greatly increase his holding of the Golden Nugget stock.

As a shareholder and board member of the Nugget, Wynn had learned (he probably had the information well before) about mismanagement and inside thievery at the property. He confronted the president and board chairman, Bucky Blaine, with the information and threatened to expose him if he did not make a settlement to leave the company. Blaine left quietly, and Wynn moved into the chairmanship.

Wynn originally met Milken through Stanley Zaks, Milken's cousin and a college friend of Wynn's. Wynn and Milken were a natural mix. Milken made the arrangements with various financial houses to sell high-interest-bearing ("junk") bonds, and Wynn closed the deals with personal presentations, where he could exercise his considerable talents of communication and persuasion. The first deal they worked together resulted in the financing of the Golden Nugget Atlantic City. Later they worked together to attempt a takeover of MCA Corporation, which owned Universal Studios in Hollywood. In 1984 Wynn bought more and more MCA stock, but at crunch time he was short of his goal. He could have been ruined, but Milken, who engaged the assistance of Ivan Boesky, was successful in selling the stock to an unsuspecting investor public.

Wynn escaped from this delicate situation financially intact. These financial dealings, however, helped earn Milken and Boesky felony convictions. Again, federal investigators could find no wrongdoing on the part of Wynn. Fortunately for Wynn, the criminal actions against Milken did not prevent him from putting together one more, quite legal, investment package involving junk bonds that financed the $620 million Mirage. While Boesky and Milken went to prison, Wynn remained firmly on his feet.

The 1980s also brought Wynn together with Frank Sinatra, probably the most dynamic entertainer ever to play Las Vegas. On a personal-handshake deal, Sinatra agreed to be Wynn's personal entertainer. He gave shows for small selected audiences at the Golden Nugget properties, and he mingled with the guests at special events such as sports parties or golf outings. Sinatra also made a series of television commercials featuring a supporting actor named Steve Wynn. As a "straight man" for Sinatra, Wynn came across as a sweet, loveable, clean-cut young casino executive. The advertisements ran nationwide for more than a year. What the reputation of Howard Hughes had done for Las Vegas's respectability in the 1960s, when it needed it the most, the Wynn-Sinatra advertisements did for the casino gaming industry twenty years later.

Despite Wynn's financial success, his dreams continued to grow far beyond the limits of his financial resources. However, in 1986 he was given a golden opportunity when the management of Bally's perceived that the only way it could defend itself from a hostile takeover by Donald Trump (owner of two Atlantic City casinos) was to purchase a second casino of its own. Atlantic City rules had restricted owners to holding only three licenses. Bally's wanted the Atlantic City Golden Nugget, and they wanted it quickly. They agreed to pay Wynn an exorbitant sum for the property—well above its appraised value—and they did so.

Steve Wynn was thus free to make his defining Las Vegas move. It came at just the right moment for a city that had been on the defensive for several years. The move, of course, was the creation of his dream property: the Mirage. It was the first new casino property built on the Las Vegas Strip in sixteen years. Almost instantly, the Las Vegas community was transformed and reenergized by this spectacular new property. Development money suddenly flowed into Las Vegas. The Mirage brought a new popular, but still high-roller, casino into Las Vegas along with the world's top magic team, Siegfried and Roy, in a production considered by some to be the greatest stage extravaganza in entertainment history. The front exterior of the Mirage featured a waterfall with an "erupting volcano" shooting flames fifty feet into the air at all hours of the evening. The back exterior included a dolphin tank and arena. Inside was a shark tank. The interior also featured a tiger cage adjacent to a shopping mall, along with top-grade restaurants and state-of-the-art convention facilities.

A new standard was set for the Strip, and a new psychology of pride and growth took over the town. Others followed Wynn's example. The Flamingo expanded, the Excalibur opened, Circus Circus grew some more, the Luxor's pyramid created another notable Strip landmark, and Kirk Kerkorian set his sights on creating the world's largest hotel-casino complex, the new MGM Grand with 5,009 rooms. Throughout Las Vegas a succession of large new casino properties opened, their arrival obscured only by the incredible megaproperties appearing along the revitalized Strip. Not to be outdone, of course, Wynn followed with his own Treasure Island, located next to the Mirage, and his next dream property, the Bellagio (originally called the Beau Rivage), a 3,000-room upscale hotel-casino to be located on a seventeen-acre island in a fifty-acre artificial lake on the Strip where the elegant Dunes once stood. Wynn proclaimed the Bellagio (roughly translated, it means "elegant relaxation") would be "the single most extravagant hotel ever built on Earth." Estimated cost: $1.2 billion.

The 1990s has thus become a decade of unprecedented growth for Las

Vegas. It seems to know no limits. There is no question but that this incredible era would not have happened without the impetus provided by the insatiably energetic, charismatic Steve Wynn, the son of a marginal bingo operator.

Wynn soured on Atlantic City after winning a difficult fight for relicensing in 1986. He jumped at the chance to cash in on an offer from Bally's to buy the Atlantic City Golden Nugget and to concentrate his efforts on building the Mirage. Wynn was disappointed with what he considered a hostile regulatory atmosphere in New Jersey, but he returned a decade later when the political and regulatory atmosphere was more attractive. In the meantime, his absence from Atlantic City provided him an opportunity to concentrate his energies on Las Vegas.

The Mirage opened and experienced what seemed to be a stunning success. Then reality set in. The debt load of the property and the interest rates of the junk bonds were very heavy. Even if they were not going to bring down the property, these financial obligations would certainly restrict the Mirage Inc. from expanding in new directions. The company was holding close to $1 billion in debt. Wynn solved this financial bind by offering new sales of equity shares and using cash-flow revenue to accelerate bond payoffs. New investors jumped at the chance to have a "piece of the action" in the most profitable casino in Las Vegas. Wynn could only pull off such a deal because he was recognized as a "winner." Common stock of Mirage Inc. became a standard holding for the most prestigious of investment fund portfolios, a surefire indication of the value attached by Wall Street to Wynn's expanding operation and his leadership.

From the Mirage, Wynn moved next door and created the Treasure Island, a modestly priced addendum to his high-roller property. Soon he bought the Dunes and cleared the property for construction of the Bellagio, due to be completed in 1998—the year also scheduled for Wynn's return to Atlantic City and the opening of a $600 million resort located on 178 acres of prime urban property. The license hearing for this casino lasted only three hours. Atlantic City (and the state of New Jersey) desperately wants him and his financial wizardry back; consequently the regulatory atmosphere has become decidedly more friendly.

As his power in Las Vegas increased, Wynn became more visible as a community leader. His primary focus has been the University of Nevada, Las Vegas, and his large presence has been especially felt since his wife assumed the leadership of the UNLV Foundation, the institution's fund-raising arm. The Wynns have sponsored many scholarships and have used their influence to benefit the university's efforts to become recognized nationally for academic accomplishment. They also made their opinions on certain university policy questions known to university officials. In 1983 the Wynns befriended the new university president, Robert Maxson, who came from the University of Houston with a reputation as an aggressive academic leader. Maxson's exuberant and outgoing personality was akin to Steve Wynn's, and his activist posture made it clear that he was seeking an opportunity to display his own version of charisma as he undertook the building of a bigger and more prestigious university. Benefiting from the Wynns' protective guidance, Maxson's star quickly soared.

For several years Maxson enjoyed the status of a brilliant community leader who was doing great things at UNLV. Maxson's reputation, however, suffered a severe blow when he became embroiled in a raging controversy with Jerry Tarkanian, the popular basketball coach who won a national championship in 1990. Wynn staunchly supported Maxson throughout this prolonged and embittered battle that deeply divided the Las Vegas community. After Tarkanian's forced (and acrimonious) departure, Wynn apparently assisted Maxson in raising the funds necessary to hire Rollie Massimino away from Villanova University, where he had won a national championship in 1985. Unfortunately for Maxson, his new coach's tenure was beset by a series of embarrassing academic problems and revelations about a "secret" supplemental contract that paid him an additional $375,000 per year beyond his lucrative announced salary of $511,000. Although Maxson was able to escape Las Vegas in the spring of 1994 in a dignified manner by taking the presidency at California State University at Long Beach, Massimino was forced to depart ignominiously six months later amid a public furor when details of his secret salary were revealed. Wynn apparently was deeply involved supporting Maxson in this brutal struggle, but he remained unscathed by it all. Although many careers were ruined or severely damaged in the fray, once again Wynn emerged on his feet, ready for new challenges, seemingly oblivious to the fact that many bodies were scattered about the Maryland Parkway campus of the university whose academic reputation he had hoped to enhance.

After Maxson's departure, Wynn continued his role as a major benefactor of the university. He also was recognized as a generous contributor to many other social and cultural causes in the community. His attachment to the educational and arts establishments probably demonstrates that he finds personal gratification in being identified with those things that contribute to the quality of life in a community. In turn, the identification supports his image as a concerned representative of the gaming industry, just as his advertisements with Frank Sinatra supported the image of a clean-cut gaming executive in the early 1980s.

Often on the edge of defeat, Steve Wynn seems always to come out a winner, even when he may not think so. Wynn may have smarted over a series of defeats in attempts to win licenses in new jurisdictions, yet each defeat has proven to be a blessing, enabling him to move to greater heights on the Las Vegas Strip. For a time he contemplated expanding into Connecticut, but he faced adamant opposition from Governor Lowell P. Weicker as well as a $600 million down payment in order to open a casino. He wisely opted not to become involved, preserving his resources for investment elsewhere.

Wynn has a good magic act in Las Vegas. He has shown that his act can work in Atlantic City, too. But would it be successful everywhere? In Las Vegas he is firmly on his feet, and that is not a bad position in which to be. Wynn has come up short in seeking to win approvals for operation agreements to run Native American casinos. However, clear "victories" in obtaining these permits would have exposed him to requirements for detailed interactions with a very confused National Indian Gaming Commission and also some very disorganized tribal partners. Licensing victories would not have guaranteed success; more likely they would have guaranteed constant frustration, perhaps major financial setbacks.

Denial of a gaming license in Great Britain has kept Wynn out of the clutches of what has been called the most strict regulatory environment in the world. One might wonder how the dynamic public persona that is Steve Wynn would have operated in a London venue that prohibits advertising and requires tourists to wait two days before they can make wagers. Similarly, rejection of his attempt to win approval for a megacasino entertainment complex in Vancouver, British Columbia, also kept Wynn out of the complex arena of Canadian politics and allowed him to avoid having to sell his style of gaming to a staid, conservative community. Siegfried and Roy, blackjack, and a thousand lights certainly could have produced millions of dollars in British Columbia, but there also would be untold numbers of headaches because the government of British Columbia would have been his partner in the enterprise. Private gaming operators in Canada are not allowed to own and operate slot machines.

Rejection of his bid to get into the murky and highly politicized waters of New Orleans gaming was perhaps Wynn's greatest blessing. He joined with Promus Inc. (Harrah's Casinos) in seeking a license in the Big Easy, but a city decision favored a proposal from Caesars and entrepreneur Chris Hemmeter.

In a later phase of the complex process, the state and city awarded the project jointly to Harrah's, Hemmeter, and several local investors. The project subsequently became mired in the morass of Louisiana politics. Costly overruns have doubled its initial price tag to over $850 million. Unable to secure continued financing, the project team led by Harrah's applied for Chapter 11 bankruptcy rescue. In the meantime two Louisiana riverboat casinos owned by Hemmeter have also failed. Wynn clearly was the winner for having lost out in his New Orleans bid. Once again, he emerged squarely on both feet.

Certain societies are more open and receptive to charismatic leaders than are others. It can be suggested that Las Vegas offers such an environment. The core values of Las Vegas reflect a history of an isolated desert area that at first attracted nomadic Native Americans with its groundwater and later itinerant prospectors seeking quick wealth from mining. Latter-day sojourners have also been nomadic people seeking a string of successes at craps tables or three sevens on the lower line of a progressive slot machine in order to provide magic for their lives. The supporting cast of local residents was always open to different ways of doing things, since its cultural history provided no set rules or expectations. The residents also seemed to be passively waiting for magic things to happen. Wynn's own words sum it up: "In some ways, Las Vegas is psychologically still the Wild West. The town is the closest thing to an unstructured society that exists anywhere in the world."

Public corporations were precluded by Nevada law from operating casinos until 1969. While corporations have now built very large casinos, private groups—the Binions, the Engelstadts—still have a major presence in the industry. Corporations within the industry now seem receptive to innovative personal leadership, as open competition still welcomes imagination even if many Wall Street investors shy away from it. Nevertheless, the first wave of corporate leadership in the casino industry did seem to stifle that imagination by trying to impose values of Wall Street and the Harvard Business School onto the gambling floor. Traditional thinking in corporate gambling restricted the creative impulse. Wynn suggests that this made his task as an emerging leader so much easier. "There was this sameness . . . on the Strip. Las Vegas was like the portrait of Dorian Gray. The world had been moving by for twenty years, but everything here stayed the same. You didn't have to be a genius to be a top dog; all you had to do was walk into the present."

Las Vegas could easily have suffered through the doldrums of the mid-1980s and drifted into a serious economic decline in the 1990s. Las Vegas had a serious need for bold, charismatic leadership, and Stephen Alan Wynn provided it. Other creative entrepreneurs followed in his footsteps, but there can be no assumption that the energized transformation his leadership and new properties have brought to Las Vegas would have been achieved in his absence.

Charismatic leadership, however, demands continuing victories. Once institutions are established, they tend to lapse into a routine and may slowly drift into complacency, especially if their leaders go on to new and different challenges. America's business history is littered with examples of once-dominant companies losing their competitiveness and creativity after enjoying spectacular success. One of the major problems confronting a complex, bureaucratic organization is finding a successor for the departing charismatic leader. As of this writing, it is apparent that Steve Wynn has no natural successor. If he departed prematurely there would be a tremendous void left not only in his vast entertainment empire but in the community of Las Vegas as well.

Like many charismatic leaders, Wynn has been criticized by some for surrounding himself with a group of loyal administrators who often appear to be serving as their boss's cheerleaders. Although Wynn has attracted several of the top young executives who clearly have the capacity to operate during periods when Wynn is temporarily absent, gaming industry analysts have serious doubts as to what will happen when he departs permanently. There is no clearly identified successor waiting in the wings, and many fear that Las Vegas will suffer a tremendous leadership void whenever he departs.

Despite his reputation as a demanding executive with a penchant for angry outbursts and an almost obsessive attention to detail, Wynn has enjoyed a high degree of employee support. His properties have experienced what is probably the lowest turnover rate of any Las Vegas casino—less than 15 percent annually. His employees are considered to have among the highest levels of morale in the industry. Operations at his casinos are carried out with top professionalism in an industry known historically for its "seat of the pants" style of management. No other operator of Las Vegas casinos has devoted as much time and resources to training. This is especially true in the area of customer service. Although succession will constitute a major crisis for Mirage Inc., the new leadership will benefit from an organizational structure that has been carefully established and fully implemented. The possibilities for continued charismatic leadership by Wynn's properties after his departure seem to be good, because of the structure that has been put in place. As a charismatic leader, Wynn has projected images and methodologies that the casino industry has desperately needed. With these structures in place and with a quality team of top executives, it is apparent that he has also gotten the message that someday Las Vegas will go on without him.

In the fall of 1989 the International Gaming Exposition was meeting in Las Vegas. It was holding a gala dinner and ball at Caesars Palace in honor of the first year's inductees for the Gamblers Hall of Fame. Steve Wynn was present to make the induction speech on behalf of the late Jay Sarno. Sarno had greatly enhanced the concept of "Las Vegas" by developing the first "themed" casinos: Caesars Palace, with its magnificent fountains, Cleopatra's barge, and Roman architecture; and Circus Circus, with its trapeze acts and arcade of games. Wynn likes to say that Sarno was the real development genius of Las Vegas. Indeed, he was a critical "idea" man, but the reality is that Sarno could not follow through and make his properties successes, as the subsequent owners of each property did. Sarno had liked the dynamic young Wynn, and the two became close friends. With great animation, Wynn related a conversation he once had with Sarno. After Wynn had taken over the Golden Nugget in downtown Las Vegas, he decided to change its motif from neon lights to white marble and golden metal fixtures. He was proud of his new sign, which, unlike its gaudy predecessor, proclaimed the existence of the Golden Nugget with a confident, elegant tone. Wynn told of taking Sarno downtown and showing him the sign. He recalled that "Jay looked at me and sighed. Jay said, 'Steve, Steve, ya gotta nice sign, but Steve, Steve, Steve, ya gotta do something with waaater.' " Wynn turned his face upward and looked into the ballroom chandeliers and shouted, "Jay! Jay! I Got the Message!"

William Raggio

Personality, Power, and Politics

BY ROBERT E. DICKENS

The normal pattern for a successful career of an ambitious politician is to seek office at the national level after serving an apprenticeship in local or state government. Bill Raggio of Reno followed a different path, demonstrating that an individual can gain a local power base and accumulate and wield extensive influence and greater power by first mastering the vagaries of county-courthouse politics and the inner workings of the Nevada State Legislature. Recognized as a potential major player in Nevada politics as early as 1960, the personable and ruggedly handsome Raggio earned national recognition as a Washoe County district attorney for his vigorous prosecution of high-profile cases. When his effort to ride his image as a crusading district attorney into a United States Senate seat failed in 1970, he won election to the Nevada State Senate in 1972 and established himself as an astute political operative whose fingerprints can be found upon nearly every major piece of legislation and every important appropriation measure to come out of the legislature in the last quarter of the twentieth century.

A dedicated, albeit nondoctrinaire and pragmatic, Republican in a state long dominated by Democratic registration majorities, Raggio's deft political touch enabled him to set the agenda for state government, deflecting both the social and fiscal crusades of ultraconservatives in his own party as well as occasional spending attacks upon the state treasury by liberal pressure groups. He did so by dint of hard work and the utilization of his superb skills of negotiation and persuasion, which he perfected as a high-profile prosecuting attorney. Raggio emphasized a fiscal conservatism that was mitigated by a strong commitment to Nevada's public schools. Naturally dedicated to rigorous law enforcement, he was in the forefront of the enactment of unforgiving criminal codes and the construction of new prisons. At the same time he evidenced awareness of the importance of diversifying the state's gambling-dominated economy, which contributed to his in-

13

sistence upon major increases in the funding for Nevada's university and community college system and the initiation of several economic development programs.

Bill Raggio's Nevada is one that has maintained close ties to the verities and values that he learned growing up within the protective cloak of a traditional Catholic family in the small city of Reno during the lean years of the Great Depression. His own educational experiences and his instinctive pragmatic approach to problem solving led him to accept as a legislative leader the challenges confronting a state that was becoming increasingly urban and culturally diverse. To understand Bill Raggio's political career is to understand the transition from the Old to the New Nevada. Political commentator and columnist Jon Ralston aptly summed up Raggio's contribution as that of "a masterful political genius who revels in the intricacies of the political process, sizes it up, knows all the moves in advance and uses his gifted foresight to look to future solutions."

William J. Raggio Jr. was born on October 26, 1926, the only child of William Sr. and Clara Cardelli. Both parents were natives of Nevada, their families having emigrated to the United States from northern Italy in the 1880s and 1890s, settling in the rugged desert valleys of the Carson and Truckee Rivers of western Nevada amid the foothills of the Sierra Nevada. The Raggio family story begins with Benjamin A. Raggio, born sometime in the 1860s in Genoa, Italy. Ambitious but frustrated with the political and economic instability of his native country, he emigrated to the United States in 1886. He became a ranch hand in northern Nevada, married Angelina Avansino, and eventually operated his own ranch in the desert foothills northeast of Reno. Ben's grandson would often cite this story of migration, hard work, and success as exemplary of the American Dream.

When it came to politics Benjamin defied the norm for Italian Americans, being a lifelong Republican. "He hated, really hated, FDR. I do not know why," Bill recalls. Perhaps the American West, with its frontier tradition and deeply entrenched individualism, provided different political perspectives than most Italian immigrants faced in urban settings, but his grandfather's commitment to the Grand Old Party became an important part of Bill Raggio's cultural inheritance.

Raggio's recollections of his youth evoke images of a sturdy middle-class life not dissimilar to those painted by Norman Rockwell. Walter Van Tilburg Clark's 1945 classic novel about Reno, *City of Trembling Leaves,* describes this environment as bounded by the ranching valley on the east of it and the yellow hills with a few old mines on the north, [and] is drawn out of the influence of the university and Peavine [mountain] into the vortex of the race track. The race track was alive only two or three weeks out of a year, yet it seems a fast-moving place. The trembling of the leaves in its sphere rises easily into a roaring through tall Lombardies set in rows in dust and open sunlight. This quality of thick hasty brightness persists clear down through the quarter, where the trees close in and the small, white houses fill the blocks, in the lumber yard beyond, and even down to the Western Pacific Depot on the grimy edge of Fourth Street. It is a theme almost strident, and saved from being as intolerable as persistent [train] whistles only by the yellow hills, like cats asleep in the north, and by the greater and darker Virginia Range in the east, through which the Truckee cuts it red and shadowy gorge.

It was in this setting that Benjamin's son, William, a young bank teller, and his wife, Clara, started their marriage in 1923 and their family with the birth of William Jr. on October 26, 1926. Bill Raggio was raised in the modest neighborhood located just southeast of the University of Nevada campus. His was a normal childhood, not unlike those of millions of other youngsters growing up during the Great Depression years of the 1930s. Reno in the 1930s and 1940s fostered traditional American values that emphasized personal discipline, hard work, an unquestioned faith in God, self-improvement through education, and patriotism. These were the truths that underpinned young William's march toward adulthood.

His high school years were overshadowed by the Second World War. Reno's reputation as a gaming and divorce capital was acknowledged, but the glitzy image was not reflected in its neighborhoods or in the house on Maple Street. Reno's racy reputation obscured the powerful influence of the beliefs and values that were to be found in all small American towns. The Raggio family took far greater comfort in the local emphasis upon the widely proclaimed counterimage of Reno as a "city of churches." Bill attended Orvis Ring Elementary School, Northside Junior High, and Reno High School, then located adjacent to downtown Reno.

As Allied troops assaulted the beaches of Normandy on June 6, 1944, a young, strong, healthy male high school graduate in that pivotal year faced the inevitability of military service. Raggio attended one semester at nearby University of Nevada, until he was called to duty as a candidate U.S. Naval officer.

The navy continued his education and training at Louisiana Tech in Ruston and then at the University of Oklahoma. Raggio describes this time of his life and the possibilities it held for him as equally bleak. By the time he transferred to Oklahoma, however, he had been identified as possessing leadership potential and was channeled into the U.S. Marine Corps officers candidate school. As a marine lieutenant, his military training grew more intensive; he recognized that he was being prepared to participate in the much anticipated invasion of Japan in late 1945.

On May 5, however, the Nazis surrendered; and in July, President Harry S Truman approved the use of nuclear weapons upon Japan. The terrifying realities of Hiroshima and Nagasaki precluded the need for Raggio, and some 2 million other equally relieved young Americans, to assault the shores of Japan. For the next eighteen months, however, Raggio remained on active duty, stationed at Quantico Marine Base in Virginia. In December 1946 he left the armed services and enrolled in the University of Nevada for the spring semester of 1947. He joined Alpha Tau Omega social fraternity, long recognized on the campus for producing future political leaders.

He also maintained a special interest in Dorothy Brigman, the daughter of a local physician, whom he had dated since high school days. They both graduated from the university with the Class of 1948 and married that same August. By September they had taken a third-floor apartment in San Francisco. Dorothy's wages as a department store clerk and a stipend from his paternal grandmother combined to enable Bill to attend the University of California Boalt Hall and subsequently graduate from the Hastings College of Law in 1951.

After considering several options, the young couple returned to their hometown, where Raggio first opened a small office and later assumed a position as an assistant district attorney for Washoe County. He was attracted to the position simply because it "seemed like the kind of place I wanted to work." Raggio recalls his view of the office as nonpolitical, and he quickly demonstrated a natural inclination for his work, his forceful speaking skills and his thorough trial preparation enabling him to build a strong reputation as an up-and-coming prosecutor with definite political potential. In 1958, when District Attorney Jack Streeter opted not to run for reelection, Raggio entered the race and won decisively. He insists that he initially had no political aspirations:

> I had no intention of running for office. I just wanted to be a good lawyer. The political bug did not hit me until Jack Streeter appointed

me deputy district attorney, making me the likely candidate for district attorney in 1958. I never really had an interest in a political career. I did not envision myself as anything other than a good prosecutor.

Dorothy Raggio proudly adds that "Bill was such a good, 'stand-up' attorney. I attended many of his trials. He was so good at it—his dress, manner, stature—there have not been any as good here since."

Raggio enjoyed a growing local reputation as a no-nonsense prosecutor, possessed of a strong determination to put criminals in jail and to protect public safety. He believed his primary role in presenting his cases was to educate the jury and build a consensus among its members. In his eighteen years as a prosecutor, he refined this skill to a fine art. He would later comment that as a leader of the state senate he found himself drawing upon these same essential skills, educating a legislative committee toward the end of building a workable consensus among often headstrong and disagreeable legislators.

From the beginning as district attorney he never backed away from using the power at his command to achieve his objectives. He attracted considerable local attention when he impaneled the Washoe County Grand Jury and used it regularly to secure indictments; previously, use of the grand jury had occurred only rarely in Washoe County. During a series of interviews conducted in 1996, Raggio reflected that his use of the grand jury may have been the basis upon which his public persona and career were built. Perhaps, but early in his career as district attorney, Raggio became engaged in two high-profile, controversial cases that did not require the use of a grand jury. Together, these established his reputation as a tough and creative advocate of law and order, Nevada style.

As the Truckee River cuts through the Virginia Range east of Reno, the boundaries of two Nevada counties meet along the bottomland at the Triangle Ranch just north of the meandering river. It was there in 1955, just over the boundary into Storey County, that Joe Conforte opened the renamed Mustang Ranch, an enterprise that would soon become Nevada's most famous brothel. For complex reasons—and his friends and foes advanced many theories—the new district attorney grimly set his sights on this inviting, high-profile target, even though it lay beyond his Washoe County jurisdiction.

Raggio's tenacious struggle to close the Mustang Ranch made him a household word throughout Nevada and attracted considerable national attention. Although Raggio carefully stayed within the letter of the law, he nonetheless stretched his authority and the law to the outer limits. In so doing he gained much more politically than he lost. Residents in Washoe County overwhelmingly opposed legalized prostitution. Raggio also understood that Renoites had long lived with the unsavory national reputation that gambling and easy divorce had given their town. That Nevada even permitted a local county option on sex-for-hire only added to their discomfort. In moving against Conforte, he was reacting to not only his own values but also those of his constituents. That he did so with flamboyance and an inordinately fierce determination only added to his political reputation.

For reasons nestled deep within the historical context of Nevada's mining and ranching frontier period, the state legislature has never repealed the law that permits counties to legalize prostitution. Nevada's rural "cow counties" have resolutely fended off reform efforts to repeal the law, arguing that the revenue generated is worth the inevitable criticism. Only the two urbanized counties, Clark and Washoe, have failed to exercise the option. So, in dealing with Conforte, Raggio was confronted with the conflicting facts that legalized prostitution was a creature and fact of public policy, but also a burden to Reno's delicate sensitivities.

Navy veteran Joe Conforte arrived in Reno in 1955 after a sleazy past that included working the streets of the Bay Area as a small-time hustler. Conforte, a native of Boston and also the descendant of Italian immigrants, left the navy in San Francisco in 1946 and remained there to seek his fortune. After frequent encounters with vice squads in Oakland and San Francisco, he opted to ply his primary trade of pimp in the nearby state of Nevada, where prostitution was legal. The Storey County commission, eager for new sources of revenue, readily agreed with Conforte's suggestion that he be charged high license fees. Appreciative commissioners granted him a license, and he moved a few mobile homes onto the Triangle Ranch, located just beyond the Washoe County line. In the fall of 1955 he opened the doors of the trailers for around-the-clock business. His operation proved to be a lucrative one, and Conforte found himself presiding over a thriving trade that attracted a diverse clientele of tourists, truck drivers, servicemen on leave, and, he noted with wry satisfaction, many locals from nearby Washoe County.

Much to the consternation of many Reno and Sparks residents, the ranch actually was located much closer to their communities than to Virginia City, the seat of Storey County. Further, this small town, once the booming hub of the nineteenth-century Comstock mining bonanza, where prostitution had openly flourished, was cut off from the Mustang Ranch by rugged mountainous terrain. As many a male visitor to Reno's casino learned, the Mustang Ranch was situated just ten miles distant—within range of an affordable taxi ride. So the man Bill Raggio came to detest—"a pimp from San Francisco"—

operated his business with a distinct flair under the nose, but definitely beyond the legal reach, of the Washoe County district attorney.

Or so he thought. True to his tacky profession, Joe Conforte presented the socially conservative citizenry of Reno with a colorful and flamboyant image. He apparently assumed at first that most Nevadans approved of prostitution and its practitioners. When he recognized that the citizens of Reno were chagrined by his high-profile enterprise, Conforte decided to rub it in. He assaulted the sensibilities of Renoites as he drove around their city's downtown casino district in a large Cadillac convertible, smoking large cigars, enjoying the company of his "working girls." He loved to pay his tab in the town's best restaurants and bars by pulling several large bills off of a bulging roll of cash.

He thoroughly enjoyed his new role as cynical rogue, reveling in the fact that his presence and behavior offended local residents. The more uncomfortable and irritated they became, the more ostentatious his behavior became. Conforte even sought to play the role of a benefactor of the poor. Each Thanksgiving and Christmas he made large—and highly publicized—donations of fresh turkeys and other foodstuffs to the needy of Washoe County, his donations often exceeding those extended by local service clubs.

Conforte's open and defiant flouting of local proprieties could not last for long. Many of Reno's leading citizens, including Bill Raggio, were proud descendants of Italian immigrants who had migrated to northern Nevada during the late nineteenth century. Many had now moved into positions of community and business leadership. These Italian Americans were repelled by the garish behavior of a Sicilian pimp, whose every mocking of local values reflected upon their efforts to rise above the mythologies of the Italian Mafiosi. These were respectable and hard-working Americans with roots now reaching deeply into the community. They naturally resented the image cast by this descendant of dubious (and detested) Sicilian parentage. When Conforte attracted the attention of national media, their desire to silence this uninvited pariah intensified.

Many of Bill Raggio's friends and associates urged him to use his powers as district attorney to investigate the legality of Conforte's operation, apparently assuming that the brothel entrepreneur was closely tied to the growing and highly publicized Mafia presence in Las Vegas. According to journalist Gabriel Vogliotti, several Reno attorneys and other well-connected men discovered that they could irritate Raggio with jokes and comments about Conforte; these good-natured but sharply barbed comments undoubtedly grated upon the young descendant of hard-working and respectable Genoese immigrants.

It did not take long for this aggressive defender of law and order to take action. Shortly after he won election in 1958, Raggio bluntly informed Conforte that he could not enter Washoe County, even for purposes of shopping or entertainment, because Raggio had formally declared him a public vagrant. Raggio based his surprising action on a nineteenth-century Nevada law that established that any man who frequented a house of prostitution was to be considered a vagrant.

The incredulous Conforte reportedly snorted to a reporter, "Vagrants are bums, and every year I've given as much to charities as Raggio earns!" But the battle was joined, with Conforte threatening Raggio's family and soon plotting to silence his oppressor by nailing him in a crude sting operation. He arranged for the sister of one of his female employees to retain Raggio as her attorney in a contrived divorce proceeding (at this time Washoe County district attorneys were still permitted, even expected, to conduct a private legal practice to supplement their small county paycheck). The woman then privately alleged that she had been sexually assaulted by the district attorney during one of their conferences. A meeting was set up in the Riverside Hotel, during which Conforte sought to goad Raggio into suggesting an illegal solution to the allegations. For more than an hour, Conforte attempted without success to extract from Raggio a self-incriminating bribe offer.

Fully expecting such a setup, Raggio had secured the services of a private investigator and went to the session with court-ordered recording devices. In the meeting, convened by Conforte's attorney, an offer was made to head off any public revelations of the young lady's allegations if Raggio would agree to end his vendetta. Raggio was expected to stop his enforcement of the vagrancy law and permit Conforte to visit Reno without being harassed by law enforcement officers. Raggio was also to publicly apologize to Conforte.

Conforte's crude but clear extortion attempt had been captured by Raggio's concealed taping system. Raggio had cleverly reversed the sting. With Conforte's self-incriminating efforts to bribe the Washoe County district attorney captured on tape, Raggio moved quickly and decisively. He had Conforte arrested and jailed, and he let it be known that he was not prepared to grant any quarter to his cornered prey. In February of 1960 he obtained a conviction on the vagrancy charges, and Conforte received a thirty-day jail sentence. In June of that same year Raggio appeared as a star witness while Reno attorneys John Bartlett and Harold Taber pinch-hit for Raggio as prosecutors. After a sensational, five-day trial, Conforte was found guilty of extortion and was sentenced to spend a year of his life in the state prison in Carson City.

By the time Conforte took up his twelve-month residency in the state penitentiary, however, Raggio had landed on the front pages of the nation's papers when he presided over one of the most aggressive, if not humorous, actions ever taken by a Nevada law enforcement officer. He did so under the guise of an obscure 1949 state court decision that affirmed that some events that routinely occurred in Nevada's legal brothels were "public nuisances." When the Nevada Supreme Court concurred, this curious legalism became part of the state legal code. Consequently, Raggio determined that this decision made brothels, although legal, a "public nuisance." Raggio thereupon persuaded some Storey County officials, including District Attorney Robert Moore, that drastic action had to be taken. Hence they appeared at the Mustang Ranch on the evening of March 24 with Washoe County sheriffs and several members of the Sparks Fire Department.

After Raggio had declared to an invited group of reporters and photographers that the facility had been legally determined to be a "public nuisance," and after care was taken to ascertain that no employees, customers, or pets remained inside, the firefighters poured gasoline over the mobile homes that had been connected permanently into a complex of lounges, bars, and "cribs." They then proceeded to torch the place. As photographers snapped pictures, many with the handsome profile of the determined Washoe County district attorney outlined in the evening shadows by the soaring flames, the brothel was reduced to a heap of charred rubble. Raggio had carefully followed the letter of the law in devising and carrying out his plan, emphasizing to the press that the officials of two counties had simply been "assisted by the Sparks Fire Department in abating a public nuisance."

Many individuals with political aspirations covet but never achieve name recognition. From that day forward, however, Raggio had no such problem. To many Washoe residents he would be remembered first and foremost, as one interviewee delicately put it in a 1996, as "the guy who burned down the whorehouse." There is no question that Raggio had established himself in the minds of many Washoe County voters as a no-nonsense enforcer of the law; a few civil libertarians, of course, were not so certain and expressed reservations about the use of gasoline as the best means of abating a public nuisance.

From the distant perspective of 1996, Raggio looked back ruefully upon the torching of Joe Conforte's place of business, granting that this one episode forever seared his name into the public consciousness. "I would like to be known for my overall record," he told this writer, "the things I've done to make things better in Nevada. And look, there are substantial achievements. The universities, the community colleges, finding the money to reduce public school class size, accountability initiatives, and buildings all over the state. It was not easy finding that money and creating a fair tax base. But most people remember only the brothel. I hope they remember the rest of my record as well."

In February of 1960, about the time Raggio was preparing to rid Storey County of its public nuisance, the United States hosted the Winter Olympics at Squaw Valley, California, located within an hour's easy drive of Reno. One athlete liked the area so much that she decided to become a permanent resident. She was Sonja McCaskie, a skier from Britain. By 1963 she had taken up residence in a working-class Reno neighborhood. She worked in "the clubs." She skied and dabbled with her hobby of photography. Neighbors also noted that on many evenings she entertained male visitors.

In that year Thomas Lee Bean was an eighteen-year-old sophomore at Wooster High School and lived in the same neighborhood as McCaskie. To his fellow students he seemed distant and aloof. Two years older than most members of his class, he frequently seemed lost in his own world, his mind not focused upon his studies. He was most assuredly a loner. Those who attended classes with him remembered his small, piercing blue eyes and his cold, penetrating stare. Anyone who knew him understood that he was not bound for college, yet he showed only disdain for vocational courses. What teachers and students did not know was that he had spent several months at the state reform school in Elko. His record there indicated that although he was "of average intelligence" he was nonetheless "a retarded reader."

Late on the evening of April 5, 1963, he returned to a familiar neighborhood house, one that he had visited previously. He had been there before to watch through a bedroom window while Sonja McCaskie entertained her visitors. This evening he patiently waited for a guest to depart, despite the bitter cold of an early spring night. Sometime after midnight he quietly entered the house by the back door, found McCaskie sleeping, and proceeded to strangle her with a homemade garrote while raping her. Forensics experts at trial indicated that her strangulation lasted for at least eleven minutes, during some of which time she was certainly conscious and aware of her assailant, although her most primal fears could never have matched the horrid reality of this brutal murder. More than three decades later, while recalling the case, Raggio visibly shuddered: "She was raped before and after death. She was also dismembered. Her heart was found in a separate room." The court record adds a tone of finality: "The victim had been raped, her body mutilated, dismembered and placed in a wooden chest."

District Attorney Raggio visited the blood-smeared crime scene and wishes to this day he had not done so. Sonja McCaskie's brutal murder became one of Reno's most famous—and gruesome—murders. For a brief time the police were stumped. There were no apparent leads. But then they discovered that one piece of property was missing. McCaskie had recently purchased a sophisticated twin-lens reflex camera. The purchase receipt with its serial number was inside the empty camera box that detectives discovered on a closet shelf, but the camera was nowhere to be found. The day following the grisly murder, the expensive camera was located in a downtown pawnshop. The name on the ticket was that of Thomas Lee Bean.

Bean was arrested and questioned. Police records indicate that Bean was a willing and helpful suspect, voluntarily offering information, readily providing a full confession. He even accompanied police officers to the scene of the murder, describing in detail and demonstrating how he committed the crime. He led investigators to corroborating evidence that further established his guilt. At one point he apparently attempted to create his own death sentence. A police report observes that after being fingerprinted and footprinted at the police station, he suddenly bolted from their control and out the door. The officers gave chase, and even fired a few shots at their fleeing suspect. But Bean was quickly recaptured, and he plaintively asked, "Why didn't they hit me? Why didn't he shoot to kill me? I just wish you would have killed me."

Although the evidence was overwhelming, Raggio prepared for the trial with his usual careful attention to detail. He prepared his prosecution under intense media scrutiny and public interest. Although Raggio's methodical but dramatic presentation of his evidence resulted in the outcome that he desired—a first-degree murder conviction with a penalty of death in the state prison's gas chamber—the Bean case would continue to dog his career for several more years. The bloody murder scene he visited would be forever etched in his mind. This case is the primary reason he has consistently supported the death penalty. He laments the impact of the case on the community, his family, and himself, recalling that the pressure to convict the killer was intense. "It was a small town. It was scared. People you saw every day and had nothing to do with my office, yet knew me, would talk to me about it. You had to listen. They were frightened. Their kids were frightened. They wanted to know if I thought it would happen again."

He recalls, "I am proud of having personally prosecuted all the murder cases in my office. This trial took a lot of preparation. The jury agreed that Bean was guilty and that he deserved the death penalty." But Bean never visited the gas chamber, as the presiding judge ordered. He remains incarcerated in the Nevada State Prison. In 1970, the Nevada Supreme Court reversed Bean's death sentence, doing so while Raggio was pondering his political options. Would he run for the United States Senate or for governor? On learning of the reversal, Raggio called a television press conference and excoriated the court. The reversal was, he said, "judicial legislation at its very worst. This is the most shocking and outrageous decision in the history of the Supreme Court of this State. It's unexplainable, and in my opinion totally uncalled for."

His outraged comments may have been partially motivated by his political future, as opponents charged, but they also came from the heart. He had won his victory in court based upon the evidence. The Supreme Court, however, was not in a forgiving mood. In a subsequent disciplinary hearing before the court, it was concluded that "maximum dissemination was given his views. His comments were frequently repeated in the press and on television during the weeks and months to follow. The public was quick to respond. This court became the center of the controversy. Essential public confidence in our system of justice may have been eroded. Standards of propriety and honor require the lawyer to uphold the respect due courts of justice." The court thereupon "reprimanded" Raggio for his "intemperate" comments.

During a 1996 interview—a full quarter of a century later—Raggio continued to reveal the anger he felt at both the reversal and the subsequent reprimand. While the court's punishment suggests his remarks were politically motivated, Raggio's continuing disbelief suggests that his reaction was that of a tough prosecutor taking exception to *Witherspoon* v. *Illinois* (1968), which retroactively applied reforms to death-sentence convictions previously entered and upon which the Nevada court based its reversal. Given the lingering emotional impact of the Bean case on Raggio, it is little wonder that he criticized the Nevada Supreme Court's reversal; in his mind, the death penalty was precious little justice for the brutal rape and homicide of Sonja McCaskie.

Dottie Raggio fondly recalls her husband's career as a prosecutor. "He was so good at presenting his case to the juries and court. He looked and dressed like a district attorney. You could take one look and you *just knew.*" Others concurred. In the wake of the highly publicized Bean case, Raggio was named the nation's outstanding prosecutor in 1964. In 1966 a third term as district attorney was ensured, and in 1968 he became president of the National District Attorneys Association. It appeared that greater political opportunities were forthcoming for this hard-driving, forty-four-year-old district attorney. The time had come to consider statewide office.

In the 1960s the Nevada Republican Party was split between ideologically driven conservatives and moderates who placed high priorities upon economic growth and feared the volatility and instability fermenting in their party's right wing, which had emotional ties to McCarthyism and the John

Birch Society. The 1964 Nevada Republican Party convention included a critical vote on a hotly contested resolution, the effect of which was to muzzle rightist splinter groups and mediate disputes between the far right and more centrist factions. The influence of the troublesome John Birch Society was effectively excised by the moderates, led by Lieutenant Governor Paul Laxalt. In a 1996 interview, Laxalt recalls this as the moment when support for his 1966 candidacy for governor solidified. He would retain a firm grip upon the state Republican Party until he left the United States Senate in 1987. His influence remains to this day.

In 1966, while Raggio was easily elected to his third term as Washoe County district attorney, Paul Laxalt defeated incumbent governor Grant Sawyer in his bid for a third consecutive term. In his one term Laxalt continued to consolidate state control over gaming by developing a regulatory capability that is today an international model, made possible corporate ownership of gaming, created the state community college system, established the University of Nevada School of Medicine and the Desert Research Institute, and launched a bistate initiative to conserve and manage Lake Tahoe. Laxalt's ambitious agenda dominated the state's Republican Party, providing a complex scenario in which Raggio attempted to expand his political horizons.

Raggio first tested his statewide appeal in 1968 when he entered the Republican primary election for the United States Senate. He lost by a narrow margin to Lieutenant Governor Ed Fike, taking solace in his strong statewide showing and the fact that he would have been a distinct underdog to Democratic incumbent Alan Bible. He spent the next two years contemplating his next move; the unexpected announcement by Laxalt that he would not seek reelection pulled Raggio toward entering the gubernatorial primary, even if it meant a rematch with Fike. He also was receiving substantial encouragement to run for the United States Senate. Which way to go?

At this juncture, national political considerations overshadowed political decision-making in Nevada. In November of 1969 President Richard Nixon had suffered a major political setback when segregationist federal district judge Harold Carswell of Florida, his nominee for a seat on the United States Supreme Court, was rejected by the United States Senate. During the confirmation process, Nevada's Democratic senator Howard Cannon had been courted by the Nixon White House with a pledge to pressure the state's Republican Party not to put up a viable opposing candidate if Cannon supported the Carswell nomination in the Senate Judiciary Committee. After apparently indicating his acceptance of this offer, Cannon voted against

Carswell in committee. Nixon and his domestic office staff went wild, vowing vengeance.

In 1970 the White House intervened in the selection process of a candidate, ostensibly seeking someone strong enough to beat Cannon. The Las Vegas Democrat, however, was a formidable candidate, having used his office to secure for Nevada substantial military expenditures and other hefty chunks of federal pork. Hawkish on Vietnam, recognized as a strong advocate of large defense appropriations, and generally conservative on social issues, Cannon would be a tough foe for any Republican.

At a critical juncture in the spring of 1970, the White House asked Laxalt to arrange for Fike and Raggio to be in Carson City to take a conference telephone call from the president. The implication was that Nixon himself would make a strong request regarding which office each man should seek. When the call from the White House came, however, it was Vice President Spiro Agnew who informed the group that the president was requesting that Fike seek the governorship and that Raggio take on Cannon. Raggio was clearly disappointed, because he had much more interest in the governorship than in the United States Senate. He also reasoned that he had a much better chance of defeating former schoolteacher and welfare administrator Mike O'Callaghan (whose superb campaigning skills were not yet readily apparent) than he did an incumbent senator. Bowing to the pressure from the White House, however, Raggio agreed to the arrangement, but commented in a 1996 interview that he felt betrayed by the Nixonians. "I felt the president asked me to do what turned out to be the biggest mistake of my political life." More than a quarter century later, Raggio leaned across his desk and asked with a tinge of bitterness, "You remember Agnew, don't you? He had some serious problems of his own. I never should have listened to him."

Thrust into a campaign not of his choosing and where he was the clear underdog, Raggio nonetheless waged a strenuous campaign. The White House did send several cabinet members to Nevada to help out in the race; even Ely-born Pat Ryan Nixon, despite her well-known aversion to political campaigning, visited her native state on Raggio's behalf. Governor Laxalt did his part as well, even providing Raggio with a pair of cowboy boots to wear while campaigning in Winnemucca. Laxalt already recognized Raggio for his affection for fashionable clothes. "I wonder if those boots are still around," Laxalt wryly commented during an interview in 1996. "I don't think I've seen them since."

It would have taken more than western garb to defeat Cannon, but the most unsettling event of the campaign occurred when the White House undercut Raggio's campaign just at the time it seemed to be gaining momentum. In the wake of the national outrage over the killing of four Kent State University students by Ohio National Guardsmen in early May, Nixon sought to soften public criticism by sending a blue-ribbon committee to Vietnam. Among those whom Nixon asked to travel to the war zone was Howard Cannon. "There I was near the end of the campaign," Raggio fumed during a 1996 interview, "using Cannon's record on domestic and foreign policy against him, and Nixon decides to send him to Vietnam on a fact-finding mission. The White House pulled the rug out from under me, even though they had persuaded me to run." Raggio attributes his 24,000-vote defeat in November to voter perception, based on the Vietnam mission, that Nixon preferred Cannon to him. Apparently Nixon had neglected to recall Cannon's vote against Carswell. To this day Bill Raggio has not forgotten the duplicity of his own party's president that not only deterred him from the gubernatorial race but also contributed to his defeat by Howard Cannon.

Raggio's disillusionment with national politics, however, set the stage for a distinguished career in the Nevada State Senate. It contributed to his determination to establish a new political base in the legislature, to set his facile mind and political acumen to work as a pragmatic conservative on the mounting problems facing a rapidly growing state. Although embittered at the time, and not recognizing that he was entering state government on the eve of a national political trend that would witness the slow devolution of power away from the Beltway to state and local governments, he decided to run for the state senate in 1972. He used his law office in downtown Reno not only as the place where he earned his living but also as a venue for expanding his political power statewide as he acquired clout in Carson City. When he left the district attorney's office, Raggio left criminal law behind, concentrating in private practice on banking, corporate, tax, and gaming law. He accepted appointment to several corporate boards, and in 1993 became the senior partner in the firm of Vargas and Bartlett.

His distrust of Nixon and his top associates was, of course, confirmed by the forced resignation of Agnew under a plea bargain with Department of Justice officials and the revelations of Watergate that forced Nixon's own departure in August of 1974. Raggio also tended to view the ethical collapse of the Nixon administration from the perspective of eighteen years in the district attorney's office. He would practice law and continue his political career as a member of Nevada's biennial "citizen's legislature." Once he got over the hurt of the Senate campaign, Raggio recognized that many of Nevada's leading political figures—from both parties—were men of high caliber who eschewed national office and focused their talents upon state and local matters. He thus tended to emulate the likes of such respected legislators as Carl Dodge, James Gibson, Lawrence Jacobsen, and Joe Dini. He would from time to time flirt with the possibility of running for governor or Congress, but in the end he found himself content with becoming a dominant figure in the state senate. After the disappointment of 1970, he would never again seek statewide office.

In 1972, Raggio easily won election to the Nevada State Senate at a time when Republicans were a distinct senate minority. Venerable Carl Dodge recalls that "Bill wanted to be a party leader more than anyone I ever saw" and that he chafed under his party's minority status. Raggio recalls those early years when he was hopelessly outnumbered by Democrats on the senate floor as "not much fun, especially when you are one of a minority of four." Several legislators and party activists interviewed for this essay observed that Raggio quickly realized that knowledge is indeed power, and he entered each session armed with facts and figures on all major issues. He also recognized that he could have considerable influence in shaping the biennial state budget, the central document that drives policy. His legal expertise—especially with jury trials—soon translated into a mastery of parliamentary mechanisms and backroom consensus-building that ensured he would be able to influence greatly, if not control, the legislative process when he rose to the post of senate minority leader in 1981.

As minority leader Raggio came to each biennial session well versed on all major issues. He reviewed the budget and the performance of state agencies in minute detail, listened attentively to the testimony of state and local officials seeking approval of their budget requests, and, according to Dodge, "devoted considerable thought to what it would be like to be majority leader." During some of those many years spent in the minority, Raggio found himself able to work with two distinctly different Democratic leaders. The first was the flamboyant and often irascible Floyd Lamb, who presided over the Senate Finance Committee with flair and occasional vindictiveness. In 1977 the studious and impeccably fair Jim Gibson replaced Mahlon Brown as the Democratic senate majority leader, and Raggio established an effective working relationship with this dedicated legislative leader, learning much about the importance of establishing bipartisan trust and cooperation on major issues. Throughout the 1980s the number of Republicans in the senate steadily increased, and in the election of 1986 they gained a clear majority. At the age of sixty-three, a major leadership opportunity had finally arrived for

Raggio. In the 1987 session Raggio chaired the powerful Senate Finance Committee and assumed the position of majority leader.

Raggio immediately set the tenor for the senate. Throughout his senate career he had been recognized for his gentlemanly demeanor, his ability to remain unruffled in times of great stress, even for his impeccable dress, complete with stylish suits and French cuffs. No cowboy boots, no public bluster, no frontier bawdyisms. The days of burning down brothels and of publicly berating the state's highest court were now in the distant past. His legal background and his moderate conservatism, coupled with his reserved personality, led him to emphasize the importance of decorum, of respecting the integrity of state officials, of following established procedure and process. In a time when the media delighted in reporting conflict and disagreement, and when some legislators took special delight in humiliating and harassing bureau heads appearing before their committees, he sought to create a professional environment. Raggio appreciated the importance of dealing with adversarial positions behind closed doors, of finding a common ground for compromise whenever possible, of avoiding embarrassing name-calling and finger-pointing. He discovered that most men and women in the legislature responded better to calm reasoning and humor than to bombast and bluster. His was a leadership that exercised power with finesse.

Legislative insiders noted with incredulity his ability to work with the mercurial Democrat assemblyman Marvin Sedway, who for years chaired the powerful Ways and Means Committee. A dedicated, often militant urban liberal from Las Vegas, Sedway's animated demeanor was accentuated by a large and often unkempt beard and frequently abrasive style. He certainly added verve and excitement to the biennial sessions in Carson City; among his many habits was chain-smoking cigarettes and periodic absentmindedness when he became engrossed in a debate. One time Sedway became so engaged in the give-and-take that rather than lighting a cigarette he ignited his beard.

Certainly there were no greater contrasting styles than those of Raggio and his Democratic counterpart in the assembly. Every two years they were thrust into the situation of having to negotiate with each other the final details of the all-important state general-fund budget. Every single line had to eventually receive the blessings of both men. The session in 1989 proved to be a difficult time for them. With money tight and demands for enhanced funding of many state agencies being forcefully pressed by lobbyists and public support groups, they found themselves at loggerheads over university and public school funding, welfare and medical care, prison construction and law enforcement, among other contentious things. For days, and then weeks, the two men clashed, until eventually they hammered out a budget.

Following that troubled time, however, Raggio and Sedway were determined not to have to endure a repeat performance in 1991. They and their wives found themselves together on a two-week tour of the soon-to-be-dissolved Soviet Union. As the trip progressed, the two men tended to gravitate to each other, discovering that they in fact did share Nevada's betterment as their bottom-line agenda. In this distant foreign land a friendship took root. Marvin Sedway died in 1990. It was Nevada's misfortune to not witness Sedway and Raggio collaborate in helping to bring Nevada into the twenty-first century.

The 1990 elections saw Nevada voters gravitate toward the Democrats, and much to his disappointment, Raggio was returned to his role of minority leader. He thereupon devoted extensive time and effort to mobilizing a statewide Republican drive to recruit strong senate and assembly candidates and to support them in the 1992 fall elections. His efforts through the Senate Republican Leadership Caucus—his creation—were rewarded. Despite Bill Clinton's surprising victory in Nevada over George Bush, the Republicans regained control of the state senate. Raggio continued to use the caucus to influence political events, and in years when the legislature was not in session, it provided a Republican presence in molding and responding to state political issues while a strong and politically savvy Democrat, Bob Miller, was in the governor's chair. Observing Raggio's discreet but firm leadership of the caucus has led Nevada's premier political journalist, Jon Ralston, to conclude that the Reno attorney has emerged as a "master of the legislative process as he orchestrates issues, procedures, timing, and dominates the institutional culture of the Senate."

Raggio's complex mind allows him to simultaneously plan the close of one legislative session, shape upcoming elections, and develop scenarios for the next session. During the 1991 session, revenue forecasts were set at unrealistically high levels. Consequently, both the Senate Finance Committee and Assembly Ways and Means Committee authorized 1991–1993 expenditures that substantially exceeded revenue, which declined because of an economic recession. Especially concerned that the state's system of higher education would suffer from a proposed deferral of building maintenance, Raggio quietly suggested the use of bonding authority to provide funds to accomplish improvements to campus facilities. In the end-of-session flurry, only the most astute legislative watchers noticed this innovative approach.

The combination of overbudgeting and a fall in tax revenue created a twenty-four-month period in 1991–1993 during which all governmental agencies had to reduce expenditures. More than 270 state employees of the executive branch were laid off. Although the combined efforts of the university system and the executive branch mitigated much of the human impact, Nevada faced serious problems. It was obvious to Raggio that an adjustment in state fiscal policy was needed.

During the 1993 session, therefore, he introduced legislation creating the Nevada Economic Forum. Revenue forecasts would henceforth be subjected to impartial data developed by a technical advisory group far removed from the influence of partisan interests. Forecasts would be presented to and reviewed by five forum members, three appointed by the governor and one each by the speaker of the assembly and the senate majority floor leader. The forum's mission is protected from political interference, and it has the authority to establish a revenue projection against which all expenditures must be authorized. The procedure was first used in 1995, and has provided a much more rational and stable system of state budgeting in the 1997 legislative session.

As a senate leader Raggio has become a master of the "end game," the final hectic weeks of a legislative session in which most significant decisions are made. In 1995, final levels for more than 80 percent of the general-fund budget were completed during the last five days of the session—a push of eighteen-hour days and stop-and-go floor sessions, choreographed to balance the agenda of one legislative house against that of another until all details of a biennial budget are resolved. Without a priori consent on how revenue would be forecast, and with one chamber's claims competing against the other, fiscal staff members found themselves caught squarely in the middle. In this difficult environment, pressures for adjournment increased the likelihood of error and stalemate. The cumulative effect has been protracted conflict, longer sessions, and increased public and press ridicule. The creation of the economic forum, although highly technical and not widely appreciated, provides a structure and coherence to the appropriations process. It is typical of Raggio's systematic approach to the legislative process.

Raggio is widely regarded as a strong consensus builder in the often acrimonious legislative environment. He has held together unlikely coalitions to set the stage for northern Nevada's management and conservation of water resources. He has long struggled to maintain civility and balance in resolving tax-formulae and revenue-allocation disputes between Reno and Las Vegas, although he was unable to fend off in 1993 a reallocation of revenue between Clark and Washoe Counties in an extremely contentious north-south battle.

He had managed to delay passage of the Fair Share bill in 1991, but the determination of the Clark County delegation, spurred on by angry and insistent Clark County voters, proved decisive. The definition of an equitable allocation of state general-fund revenue among competing appropriation sectors and regions of the state—a legacy of the Fair Share battles—remains a challenge on the state's policy agenda, most notably in 1997 infrastructure-financing conflicts. Although a dedicated consensus builder, Raggio does know how to use the power at his command. As political scientist Michael Bowers comments, "As majority leader, Raggio has managed to advance Republican issues and protect the interests of northern Nevada by delaying, forcing compromises, and killing bills in the senate in spite of Clark County's majority." His budgetary and procedural expertise is surpassed only by knowledge of his opponents' vulnerabilities.

To most observers, however, he wields a hammer. In the closing days of the 1995 session, in a typical demonstration of his use of his power, Raggio forced a vote in the assembly on a Republican welfare measure before he would permit a vote to occur in the senate on a Democratic bill on an unrelated matter. But Senate Minority Floor Leader Costandina Titus of Las Vegas, often heard during legislative sessions venting her frustration with Raggio's exercise of power, observed in a 1996 interview (a nonlegislative year, so partisan differences had waned) that Raggio "is highly respected by enemies and friends. I don't know anyone better at boxing people in before folks realize it. His style [is] different than mine; Bill does not rule by consensus, but by force, such as by the campaign finance power of the Senate Republican Leadership Caucus. Raggio does not hesitate to use it."

In 1991, when terminally ill Democratic senator Nick Horn chaired the Senate Finance Committee, a Democratic assemblywoman from Las Vegas expressed her frustration at failing to achieve senate consent to an Assembly Ways and Means initiative by saying into an open microphone, "We can wait. We will still be here when you die." Raggio was one of the first to react by objecting to this breach of civility and decorum and by demanding that an apology be delivered on the floor of the assembly the next legislative day. A reluctant apology resulted, although without an admission of responsibility. Raggio remembers who said what as much as the "faithless apology."

Raggio also found ways to keep in touch with his constituents. In 1989 he vigorously opposed special legislation greatly enhancing legislative retirement packages when the bill was being surreptitiously slipped through the system, its existence not even discovered by the media until the last possible moment. Despite great pressure from his peers to climb aboard this special-interest bandwagon, he was one of a handful of legislators who voted against the bill. In a subsequent special session, he had little difficulty in obtaining repeal of this extremely unpopular law. Voters reacted with indignation in 1990 and defeated several legislators who had voted for it.

Raggio is a man who practices the art of surprising humor. In 1970 then University of Nevada, Reno, political science professor Joe Crowley wrote to the editor of the *Reno Gazette Journal*, puckishly protesting senatorial candidate Bill Raggio's public comments about language sometimes employed in college classrooms. In 1995, during the heat of the debate over high education funding, state senator and majority floor leader Raggio, with a devilish glint in his eyes, and by this time a long-standing good friend of the president of the University of Nevada, Reno, told Crowley that "the letter you wrote about me to the editor cost me the election against Cannon!"

Raggio is a man who combines his humor with contemporary gender politics. Many women who serve in appointed or elected capacities are inclined to consider him a "good ol' boy" or, as one lobbyist opined, a "sexist dinosaur from another era." Most, however, have been surprised by his mannerly and chivalrous conduct. Raggio is recalled by many lobbyists and other legislative watchers as incredibly charming. "He offers his hand as if to shake yours, turns yours, and moves as if to kiss the back of your hand, only to kiss his ring!" Raggio has been known to publicly kneel, take the hand of a leader of an important constituency, and again "kiss his ring."

Raggio has thus effectively assembled, then wielded, legislative power. His influence has weighed in heavily on all major legislative decisions since the mid-1970s. Frustrated in his bid for national or statewide office, he found in the state senate an ideal outlet for his political ambitions. It was a place where he could have major impact upon the development of his native state, and it was a place were he could get things done. In 1996, at age seventy, he won reelection without opposition, in what could be his last campaign.

His career thus mirrored the most dramatic period of growth in Nevada history. His wife of forty-eight years recalls enjoying most his eighteen years as district attorney, when "he always knew where the trial would end, and how he would present his final, irresistible argument to the jury." But Dottie Raggio has also marveled at the equanimity he has displayed during his quarter century in the legislature. When Raggio filed for reelection in 1996 and no opposition emerged, he proudly proclaimed his political invincibility to Dottie. Her reply perhaps put the future of Nevada politics into sharp relief: "My God, Bill, has it occurred to you that no one else wants the damn job?"

Sue Wagner

Triumph over Tragedy

BY PATRICIA FERRARO KLOS

The news spread throughout Reno and across the state with lightning fast speed that warm Labor Day afternoon in 1990. Sue Wagner, the fifty-year-old state senator from Washoe County, considered one of Nevada's most popular public figures and someone with a seemingly unlimited political future, had been critically injured in the crash of a small airplane. The accident occurred shortly after takeoff from the Fallon airport when state treasurer Bob Seale's twin-engine Cessna 411 went into a stall and crashed near Soda Lake. Rescue workers found a devastating scene. Seale suffered from multiple injuries; his wife, Judy, had died from massive injuries to her head and spinal column; and Seale's aide Brian Krolicki and Wagner's aide Stephanie Tyler suffered less serious injuries. Wagner was unconscious and had sustained severe injuries to her head, neck, and spinal column. Only a rapid transfer of her broken body by a medical helicopter to the trauma center in Reno saved her life. This extraordinarily cruel twist of fate was not lost on anyone familiar with her family history: Her husband, Peter, had been killed ten years earlier in another airplane crash.

After spending weeks in intensive care units in Reno and the University of California Hospital, Wagner began the long and arduous fight to regain her health. She endured a series of surgeries, which have left only five vertebrae in her spine. Two steel rods run from her neck to her waist; she has plates and wires in her neck; a patch on her skin secretes medication to relieve pain. By the time she was able to communicate with friends and advisers, she had received the Republican Party's nomination for lieutenant governor in the primary election held the day after her accident. Just as she found the strength to continue her political career in the Nevada State Legislature after her husband's death, once again Wagner determined not to permit a devastating accident to end her political career. She had found in politics an outlet for her enormous energies and strong interest in public policy; politics provided a means of

14

satisfying her need to serve her community. She remained on the ballot for the general election, somehow finding the physical and mental courage to leave the hospital's rehabilitation center for brief campaign appearances to dispel rumors that she was mentally impaired. To the surprise of no one, she defeated Las Vegas Democrat Jeanne Ireland by almost twenty thousand votes.

Wagner thus became the first woman elected to the state's second-highest office. Octogenarian Maude Frazier, a veteran educator and Democratic legislator, had served in the office for a few months in 1962 after being appointed by Governor Grant Sawyer to fill Lieutenant Governor Rex Bell's unexpired term after his death from a heart attack. Wagner's stunning victory had little, if anything, to do with a sympathy vote, because she had arrived at this stage of her career with an exceptionally strong record as a legislator. In the previous fifteen years she had built an enviable reputation as a fair-minded, courageous political leader, an independent woman who never hesitated to vote her conscience regardless of party dogma or public opinion. Ever since she first appeared in the Nevada assembly in 1975, Wagner had shown no fear of challenging conventional political values, and voters of both parties recognized that hers was a career dedicated to principle rather than expediency.

Wagner's reputation was one that most politicians crave but never achieve; it had already provided her with several opportunities to run for higher office. Over the years her name was widely discussed in speculation about races for governor and the U.S. House of Representatives and Senate; in 1988 the National Women's Political Caucus advanced her name to George Bush as a potential vice-presidential candidate. Up until this point she had not actively pursued these possibilities, primarily because of her heavy responsibilities as a single parent. And so in 1990, with her children, Kristina and Kirk, in college, she was in a position to consider higher office. The lieutenant governorship seemed to be the logical stepping-stone; her campaign had scarcely begun when she found herself in excruciating pain, barely clinging to life in the Washoe Medical Center's critical care unit.

Wagner's determination in carrying out her responsibilities as lieutenant governor did not surprise her many friends and supporters. They knew that she was in constant pain, that blurred vision complicated reading, that the lengthy sessions spent presiding over the state senate sapped her energy, and that the endless meetings were extremely enervating. Thus her many supporters were not surprised in early 1994 when she announced that she would not seek reelection or, as some hoped, the governorship. She opted to leave political life, at least temporarily, in an effort to deal with the continued health problems resulting from the crash. It was the right time, she felt, to take a step back, to assess her life and contemplate the future. She had helped break down many unwritten but nonetheless powerful barriers that confronted talented and qualified women seeking careers in public service in Nevada. She did so with such extraordinary grace and courage that her achievements seemed nothing out of the ordinary, even natural. Never one given to rhetorical excess, Wagner led by example. In so doing she not only advanced her own career but did much to obliterate the practice of sexual discrimination in Nevada public life.

On Tuesday morning, December 5, 1995, Nevadans picked up their morning newspapers to discover that Representative Barbara Vucanovich had announced her retirement from Congress. Within hours telephones were ringing across the state urging Wagner to reenter the political arena; she admitted to all that she wanted to serve in the House of Representatives, and for several weeks it looked as though her name would appear on the ballot. However, by the end of the month she disappointed many supporters by announcing that she would remain on the sidelines. Her statement to the press reflected her moderate political stance in the face of a conservative Congress: "I'm a results-driven person. You have to give a little. But I don't think that's the kind of House of Representatives I'd be elected to. This is not the job for me at this time." Only Sue Wagner knows all of the reasons for the decision of January 1996 that disappointed many Nevadans, but her statement that "this is not the job" at least implied there could be something in the future.

Sue Wagner had no such lofty dreams on January 20, 1969. On that day she and infant son, Kirk, flew from Tucson to join Peter Wagner in Reno to establish a new life. She was merely concerned about getting her household in order and establishing herself in a new community. Peter, the proud possessor of a recently earned doctorate in electrical engineering and atmospheric physics from the University of Arizona, was eager to begin a career as an environmental engineer with the Desert Research Institute. As they drove to their new home in Stead, they listened on the radio to the inauguration of Richard M. Nixon. Sue listened with more than casual interest to the celebration heralding the return of the Republican Party to power, because she had been raised in a politically active family. Her membership in the Grand Old Party came naturally: Her parents were rock-ribbed Republicans of conservative New England stock. Her deep interest in the political process came from her father, Raymond Pooler, a pharmacist by profession who had also been a Republican activist and chairman of the Republican Central Committee in his native state of Maine.

Ray Pooler's strong interest in politics clearly influenced his daughter, and she graduated with honors from the University of Arizona in 1962 with a major in political science. Two years later she earned a master's degree in history from Northwestern University and did additional graduate study at Ohio State University. Her father had been forced to leave the often cold, damp climate of the small seaport city of Portland, Maine, in 1950 for Tucson on the recommendation of his physician, who suggested that the warm, dry air of southern Arizona would assist him in dealing with chronic lung problems. Sue Pooler arrived in Arizona as a fifth grader and immediately plunged into the activities of her elementary school. Her down-east accent apparently made an instant impression upon her new classmates, who insisted that she often speak to the class. "The kids gave me all the reports to read: the sports reports, the weather reports, all the reports. I thought I was really popular, but they were just having a kick because they had never heard such a funny sounding girl in all their lives." Sue did not become embarrassed. Instead she capitalized upon every opportunity to demonstrate her academic skills to her classmates and teacher. "It really didn't bother me at all."

From early childhood it was apparent that Sue Pooler Wagner was not likely to shun the spotlight, never one to refuse an opportunity to be a leader. And she always held a strong interest in entering politics. As a young girl she had met and talked several times with the pioneering United States senator Margaret Chase Smith; she knew that if a conservative state like Maine could produce such an outstanding woman political leader, then she, too, could aspire to a career in public service. "I never realized at the time that she was such a pioneer; I just assumed lots of senators were women." As a college student in the 1960s, the formative years of the modern women's rights movement, Wagner perceived that opportunities for women in public life were going to improve, however slowly that might happen.

The family environment in which she was raised, as well as the education she received, produced a pragmatic political leader who willingly supported social reform as a means of preserving the best of American values and traditions. Thus her political views, while considered to be too progressive or liberal by conventional Republican standards in Arizona and Nevada, come directly out of the mainstream of the Republican progressive tradition that has its roots with such leaders as Theodore Roosevelt, Robert LaFollette, and Hiram Johnson. Always pragmatic and attentive to the views of others—and after assuming public office and listening to the views of her constituents—Wagner never hesitated to tackle controversial issues and demonstrate a courage and intelligence reminiscent of her role model, Margaret Chase Smith. Thus Sue Wagner pursued an independent course as a Nevada political leader, never hesitating to take a leadership position on controversial or even unpopular issues.

All the more remarkable is the fact that her support for significant social reform did not damage her political stature as an elected representative of conservative Republican legislative districts located in a conservative town in a conservative state. Her demonstrated independence only enhanced her reputation as a political leader. Her record in Nevada politics is replete with examples of strong support for advancing women's rights, providing adequate legal protection for children at risk, increasing funding for public and higher education, extending the scope of environmental protection, securing the constitutional rights of incarcerated persons, and expanding campaign accountability. Although she at times offended both the traditional "good old boy" system and conventional political wisdom, Wagner never suffered a defeat while representing conservative southwest Reno districts as assembly-woman and senator. In fact, she never attracted serious opposition after she won her first campaign in 1974.

Another rising political star in the legislature, Richard Bryan of Las Vegas, first met Sue Wagner when he was campaigning door-to-door in Reno in 1974 for Democratic candidates. He spoke with her in the driveway of her home in southwest Reno, where she was playing a fierce game of basketball with neighborhood children. Bryan later recalled his impression of a bright, competitive individual, and his interest intensified when he learned she was a Republican candidate for the state assembly. She had decided to run for Assembly District 25 only after she and her husband had thoroughly explored the prospects of providing for their two young children. Peter encouraged her to take the plunge, and they worked out the details of balancing family and careers.

Although she loved her family dearly, Wagner found the role of housewife to be incomplete for someone with her education and, especially, her compelling interest in public affairs. Hers was the dilemma endured by many modern women caught between the pressures of domestic and public life. "In those days, when the kids were very young, the big thrill of my week was when *Time* magazine arrived on Thursdays. I adored my kids then and now, but I was bored to death." She had found time to squeeze in many hours as chairwoman of the Reno Blue Ribbon Task Force on Housing and as a member of the Mayor's Citizen Advisory Board. These were, however, merely volunteer roles with limited responsibilities. She found herself desiring a more substantive involvement. She worked hard as a volunteer on Pat Hardy Lewis's campaign for city council. Lewis's victory in 1973 proved to be a precedent, since she was the first woman elected to the Reno City Council. "I started out as a volunteer, but by the time it was over I was essentially in charge of the campaign," Wagner recalls. "After Pat's election, she appointed me to several committees. The next year I decided that I had to get more directly involved."

Like many other legislative candidates in Nevada, where all politics is indeed personal, she compensated for lack of campaign funds (her campaign budget was just $1,600) for television and radio exposure by knocking on doors in her predominantly Republican district. She simply outworked her two male opponents in the primary—Ted Moore and Alex Kanwetz—impressing voters with her enthusiasm, knowledge of the issues, sincerity, and good humor.

This neophyte politician began her successful career in the year Richard Nixon was forced to resign the presidency—not exactly a good time to be campaigning as a Republican, even in a district with a heavy Republican registration. She vividly recalls the television sets blaring out news about the Watergate hearings that summer as she and her cadre of volunteers, largely friends from the Reno chapter of the American Association of University Women, went door-to-door to talk with voters. One of the questions most frequently asked by skeptical voters was "Why do you want to leave your two small children at home to serve in the legislature?" She obviously answered those questions to the satisfaction of the voters.

After cruising to victory in the general election, Wagner took her seat in the 1975 Nevada State Legislature. From the first few days she stood out from other freshman legislators, establishing herself as a lawmaker who was not bound by either tradition or rigid party discipline. "As soon as she arrived in Carson City," then state senate leader Bryan recalls, "we knew she was a rising star. She quickly became an able legislator. She was bright, made educated decisions, and clearly earned everyone's respect."

Wagner's early years in the assembly were boosted by her friendship with two other female legislators, Democratic senator Mary Gojack of Reno and then-Republican assemblywoman Jean Ford of Las Vegas (Ford later switched parties). Partisanship notwithstanding, these women found that they had much in common. They found themselves gravitating toward issues that were often derisively dismissed as "radical feminist" by many of their male peers. Wagner relishes the story of the morning she stopped to get gasoline before her daily commute to Carson City: "I was at the service station getting a fill-up when the attendant noticed my license plates that identified the owner of the vehicle as a 'State Assemblyman.' 'Hey, what's your husband's name?' the attendant asked. I'd had it. I looked him straight in the eye and said, 'Sue.' And then I drove off."

Wagner established herself in the public mind by focusing on the Watergate-inspired issue of campaign reform. In public hearings and in her comments on the floor of the assembly, she sharply criticized the way political campaigns in Nevada were financed and conducted. She sponsored thirteen separate bills that closely regulated the use of campaign signs, greatly expanded requirements for the reporting of campaign donations and expenditures, and demanded strict accountability of expenses for primary and general elections. Eventually, eleven of those bills were enacted and signed into law by Governor Mike O'Callaghan. Richard Bryan recalls the impression Wagner made in that first session: "She was everybody's favorite, regardless of party affiliation."

Her reputation as a hard-working and responsible assemblywoman established, Wagner waltzed to easy reelection in 1976, encountering only token opposition. In the 1977 legislature, she began to tackle what were increasingly referred to as "women's issues." She sponsored a bill mandating testing of newborn babies for genetic metabolic disorders, a treatable and curable medical problem if detected immediately. Her interest in this particular issue was stimulated by her own daughter's disorder; Wagner was jubilant when the bill was enacted.

This modest beginning soon led to her tackling a myriad of issues that had become part of her agenda. She forthrightly spoke out in defense of the right of women to obtain an abortion during the first trimester of pregnancy, a position that found her the subject of considerable criticism among conservative circles within her own party. She also embraced foster care reform, the rights of female victims of abuse and violence, and the inherent rights of incarcerated pregnant women and mothers. As she spoke out, Wagner found herself flooded with invitations from various women's groups to speak. Often aligned with the liberal Mary Gojack on these issues, Wagner moved well beyond not only her party's legislative leadership but that of most male Democrats as well.

Such was the case when the Equal Rights Amendment came before the Nevada Legislature. She found herself walking a very thin political line, because opposition to the ERA was clearly the dominant view in District 25. Already skilled in the fine art of political maneuvering, she balanced her support of the ERA and other women's issues with her staunch adherence to fiscal conservatism—undoubtedly a manifestation of her Maine Republican legacy. The ERA had passed the U.S. Congress in 1971, and most political observers expected ratification by the requisite three-fourths of the states without much difficulty. That at least seemed to be the case when, within four years, thirty-one state legislatures had voted for ratification. But then came a furious counterattack launched by longtime conservative activist Phyllis Schlafly and her determined Eagle Forum.

What most political observers thought would soon become the 27th Amendment to the U.S. Constitution readily passed the 1975 Nevada legislature, but the state constitution requires a second passage. By the time the 1977 legislature convened, conservative opponents had mobilized for an all-out assault. Nevada essentially became a bellwether state for ERA opponents and supporters. Wagner and other women's rights advocates were outraged when eleven men in the assembly who had voted for the amendment in 1975 switched their position two years later. Television cameras caught Wagner fighting back tears while commiserating with other supporters in the wake of the decisive vote. Wagner later learned that powerful state senator James I. Gibson of Las Vegas had played a crucial role behind the scenes in producing the stunning reversal by working in concert with his Mormon Church's hierarchy. The church had earlier gone on record denouncing the ERA as a "dangerous step backward in time," and Wagner suggested as much. She told *Ms.* writer Lisa Cronin Wohl that "each of the eleven Assemblymen who switched had made promises to us. . . . There had to be something very powerful to make them change their mind." Wohl, however, was not as discreet as Wagner, writing that Gibson, himself one of the two Nevada representatives to the Council of Twelve, the governing body of the Church of Jesus Christ of Latter-day Saints, had played a decisive role: "Many ERA proponents believe Gibson's heady, and some say dangerous, amalgam of political and religious power was the factor that convinced eleven Nevada legislators—every one of them supporters of the ERA in 1975 and 1976—to vote the Amendment to defeat in 1977."

As the frustration over the ERA reversal slowly receded, Wagner found herself enmeshed in another emotional social issue: the right of women to have an abortion. Ever since the United States Supreme Court had voted 7–2 in *Roe* v. *Wade* in January of 1973 to affirm that right during the first trimester and with some restrictions during the second, the issue had grown in intensity with the passage of years. Wagner was convinced that a majority of her Republican constituents supported the right to choose to terminate a pregnancy, the intensely outspoken opponents notwithstanding. Her perception of Republican ideology was based upon keeping the state as far removed from individual control over people's lives as possible, and thus she soon found herself in a leadership role defending abortion rights as social conservatives in her party launched attack after attack.

By the time serious antiabortion legislation surfaced in the Nevada legislature, Wagner had completed her third term in the assembly and had won election to the state senate in 1980. Among other things, she had found in the give and take of state politics an outlet for the grief that came from the death of her husband in the March 2, 1980, crash of a converted B-26 bomber. Peter

Wagner and two other Desert Research Institute researchers were killed while monitoring weather modification experiments. When the forty-two-year-old scientist/engineer died, he left behind his wife and their children, nine-year-old Kirk and eight-year-old Kristina. Sue Wagner's first option was to return to public school teaching—she had taught American government and American history for three years in Tucson—but that would have forced her out of politics. Thus she was delighted with an invitation from President George M. Hidy of the Desert Research Institute to accept a position as his administrative assistant with the flexibility to take leaves of absence during the biennial legislative sessions.

In 1980 Wagner won election to the state senate, where she joined forces with her friend and colleague Jean Ford. They were confronted by a bill that would have required women to receive permission from husbands, and minors permission from parents, before an abortion could be performed. In their determined opposition they were joined by many moderate groups and were bolstered by a strong editorial in the *Reno Gazette Journal* that denounced the proposal as "a ludicrous bill of hodgepodge overregulation" and suggested that "this bill should be—well—aborted." Adding a sardonic twist to the debate, Ford and Wagner jointly introduced an amendment that turned the central feature of this proposed legislation back upon the men's so-called advise and consent requirements. Their tongue-in-cheek amendment would have required a man to receive his wife's permission before obtaining a vasectomy, even requiring that physicians certify in writing the patient's age and marital status before performing the procedure. Further, before taking out the surgical kit, physicians were required to explain to the patient the possible long-term psychological damage they might suffer from having a vasectomy; Ford and Wagner even tacked on a provision requiring males under the age of eighteen to receive parental permission for a vasectomy.

Their amendment amused some and irritated others. Of course it died a predictable death, but the embattled women had made a telling point about the inherent inequities they perceived in this legislation. Nonetheless, the male-dominated legislature passed legislation requiring parental notification, a law later declared unconstitutional by the United States Supreme Court.

Throughout the 1980s Wagner provided statewide leadership in deflecting similar initiatives. This effort culminated in 1990, when a statewide, nonbinding referendum in the form of Ballot Question #7 passed by a substantial margin. Voters reaffirmed support for the essential tenets of *Roe* v. *Wade,* thereby providing Wagner with confirmation of what she had long believed, despite the ever present pressure from social conservatives and unsympathetic, male-dominated legislative majorities: Nevadans did in fact support a woman's right to have an abortion. She also took satisfaction in enactment of legislation she sponsored in 1987 mandating a sex education program in the public schools.

Although Wagner found herself assuming a leadership role on issues of particular concern to women, she was by no means a one-dimensional legislator. This, in fact, proved to be a major factor in her growing statewide reputation as a legislative leader. Central to her interests was making good on a campaign promise to reform state campaign financing laws. Although she and fellow reformers met strong opposition, they did manage to chip away at the edges of the issue. She began introducing campaign reform legislation in 1975 and was still introducing legislation to address finer points in 1989. Her legislation included everything from setting limits on legislative campaign expenses for primary and general election periods combined (in 1975), to introducing a bill (in 1985) to revise provisions for reporting campaign contributions, to a bill (also in 1985) to prohibit certain contributions and donations during sessions. These, as well as many other technical bills, passed into law. Her stance on political contributions and campaign ethics led to the formation of a Commission on Ethics, which she and Senator Thomas "Spike" Wilson of Washoe sponsored and took effect in July 1985. She went on to serve as the commission's first chairperson.

By the mid-1980s Wagner had established herself as one of the most respected and influential political leaders in the state. Her appeal as a moderate Republican enabled her to reach beyond partisan boundaries. She had chaired with distinction the Senate Judiciary Committee and served as vice chair of the Legislative Commission and as an active member of the Government Affairs Committee. In 1988 she was honored by the National Republican Association as the Outstanding Legislator of the Year. Not surprisingly, her name surfaced many times in political speculation about higher office; more than once she opted not to pursue invitations from prominent party leaders to run for Congress or statewide office.

Although the responsibilities she carried as a single parent had forced her to defer such attractive possibilities, in 1990 she decided to seek the position of lieutenant governor. When Attorney General Brian McKay, a popular Republican, unexpectedly announced that he planned to return to private practice and would not run for governor against incumbent Robert Miller, as most pundits had expected, Wagner was pressured by many leading Republicans to seek the governorship. She declined, noting that she still faced considerable parental responsibilities and implied that the lieutenant governorship seemed to be a logical step. Four years later, she and her friends privately reasoned, might be a likely time for her to take the next step and seek the governorship.

Thus what seemed to be a sensible decision turned into a personal nightmare. The crash of Bob Seale's small aircraft following a Labor Day celebration in Fallon instantly and tragically changed Wagner's life and political career forever. Wagner lay unconscious as Stephanie Tyler walked from the crash for help. The next day both Seale and Wagner won easy primary victories as they lay in Washoe Medical Center. After it was determined that Wagner would eventually recover, more or less, she and Seale both determined to remain in the fall campaign; both were easily victorious.

Wagner faced a lengthy and painful rehabilitation. By the time the legislature convened in mid-January 1991, she had already undergone a series of difficult surgeries in which her spine had been permanently fused. In 1992 she elected to undergo an arduous thoracic spinal reconstructive surgery at UCLA Medical Center that would require yet another round of post-operative physical therapy. Prior to this she had contracted a rare and sometimes deadly virus known as Guillain-Barre, or French polio. The virus set her back several months and seriously complicated her recuperation.

Nonetheless she presided with dignity and good humor over the daily sessions of the state senate and even managed to infuse enthusiasm and meaning into the two commissions she chaired, tourism and economic development. In these roles she brought expanded responsibilities to the lieutenant governor's office.

Nevada's Commission on Economic Development grew out of the 1983 legislature, in which Wagner and her colleagues charged the commission with seeking ways to diversify and expand Nevada's economy beyond the traditional venues of gaming, tourism, agriculture, and mining. Wagner's chairmanship from 1990 to 1994 gave birth to "Focus 2000—a plan for the '90s." Gaming had sprung up across the United States on Indian reservations and along the Mississippi River, a development that forced rethinking of Nevada's economic base. The Focus 2000 program began to attract California industry; established "Quick Start/Job Training," a vocational program funded with state money; initiated rural development grants for industrial sites and tourism; attracted federal dollars and assisted firms in obtaining federal grants; enlarged Nevada's Motion Picture Division; and used the North America Free Trade Agreement (NAFTA) to Nevada's advantage by matching Nevada firms with international buyers and distributors.

In a January 1992 speech to Western Industrial Nevada, Wagner quipped that California businesses were writing "escape plans" and that only Utah and Hawaii did not have some sort of gaming. "So, where do we start?" She had to operate with a minuscule $50,000 budget. "With less money, we'll just have to work smarter," she observed. Las Vegas political columnist Jon Ralston took notice, writing in May of 1994 that Wagner was giving the office a sharp focus and, by chairing both Economic Development and Tourism, was promoting trade and tourism nationally and internationally.

Nevada had become the fastest growing state in the nation. Its 1980 population of 800,508 grew to 1,201,833 by 1990. With growth came new problems: more non-English-speaking residents, fewer homeowners, more low-income families, heavy pressures upon educational and medical facilities, and increased juvenile delinquency, divorce, and crime rates. Additional residents did not necessarily produce more tax dollars, but they did increase demand for public services. From all parts of the state's political spectrum came the same solution: Increase economic activity through strategies designed to reduce the state's reliance upon tourism and gaming.

Wagner targeted the Motion Picture Division. She saw Nevada's geographic and cultural diversity as a perfect setting for the production of films. Did they want ski slopes? Wide-open spaces? Rocky canyons? Cattle ranches? Casinos? Nevada had it all, almost right next door to Hollywood. In the early 1990s several feature films were shot on Nevada locations: *Honeymoon in Vegas; Sister Act; Cool World; Honey, I Blew Up the Kids; Universal Solider; Roadside Prophets; The Bodyguard; Blood In Blood Out; Best of the Best II; Pure Country;* and *Indecent Proposal.*

The Motion Picture Division attracted millions of dollars, but Wagner wanted a firmer base. She called for the establishment of filmmaking curricula at the two state universities to establish a technical base, and she personally visited Los Angeles to sell the product. In September 1994 two missions were planned for Los Angeles, where she met with executives and producers involved in selecting filming locations.

The passage of NAFTA gave Wagner an opportunity to promote Nevada businesses in Mexico. The Las Vegas newspapers quoted the Nevada congressional delegation as being opposed, but Wagner disagreed and again took her show on the road. The United States Department of Commerce sponsored *Representaciones Commerciales,* which Wagner and her representatives attended in Monterrey and Mexico City. She was the only elected official in attendance, which made a positive impression on all attendees. Upon her return she mentioned that few Mexicans realized they could gamble and ski in Nevada. "I think this points out that the international visitor needs to know more about Nevada destinations on a regional basis." The *Reno Gazette Journal* heralded her as "a one-woman whirlwind as she heads out of office. [S]he is working wonders for Nevada."

Sue Wagner determined not to allow physical impairment to keep her from her personal mission: making the office of lieutenant governor work for the people of Nevada, the same people for whom she had initiated legislation for twenty years. She had come to know and understand Nevadans from Laughlin to Elko, from Ely to Carson City; therefore, her tourism commission promoted such diverse programs as Elko's Cowboy Poetry Gathering, Fallon's Silver State Rodeo, the Wells-to-Wendover National Motorcycle Race, and the Winnemucca Mule Show and Races.

Although she refused to ask for any special consideration, those who worked closely with her understood that the pain and periodic weakness that afflicted her were taking a terrible toll. Thus when Wagner announced early in 1994 that she would not enter the race for governor, but also would not seek reelection, her friends were disappointed but not surprised. Very quickly the tributes came rolling in. Republican senator Kay Bailey Hutchison of Texas wrote, "You will be missed during your sabbatical, and hopefully it will be a short one." Harriet Woods, president of the National Women's Political Caucus, wrote, "It would be great if you could become part of our leadership with whatever time and energy you have available." However, no one expressed their regrets more sensitively than Faith Greaves, University of Nevada, Reno, Office of Communications: "Thank you for all you've done for this state, but especially for all you've done for Nevada women. One day they'll get it. I think. I hope. I pray." Nevada's Democratic governor Bob Miller perhaps best summarized the bipartisan sentiment when he said that Wagner was "one of the best, if not the best, public servants I have ever known."

Wagner has said that she loves the political process, the give and take of crafting and enacting legislation, of negotiating for a purpose, the intricacy of the legislative committee system, the unpredictability arising from the interaction of complex political personalities. As she left political office in January 1995, Wagner found herself in a position not unlike the one she encountered when she entered state politics two decades earlier. She easily made the transition back into private life, but did not leave politics, since she assumed responsibilities as associate director of the Great Basin Research Center located in the Department of Political Science at the University of Nevada, Reno. She moved into the academic world with the same enthusiasm as she had entered politics, teaching courses in politics, directing student interns during legislative sessions, and assisting in the development of applied research projects. In 1997 she was appointed to the Gaming Control Board, so speculation continues regarding her political future. Whether or not she ever again seeks elective office, she has already established herself as the most important woman in twentieth-century Nevada political history.

Jerry Tarkanian

Nevada's Special Rebel

BY RICHARD O. DAVIES

For nearly twenty years Jerry Tarkanian was Nevada's most famous resident. He appeared frequently on national television, relentlessly pacing the sidelines, chewing on a towel as he focused his attention upon the play of his powerful Runnin' Rebels. He had an unforgettable television persona. His morose, hangdog expression, made more poignant by deep-set, dark eyes and shaved head, became familiar to sports fans everywhere. The more he won, the more agonized he seemed to become. When Tarkanian left his high-profile position at the University of Nevada, Las Vegas, in 1992, he had reached the pinnacle of his intensely competitive profession. He had done it all. No other coach of the modern era could equal his 83 percent lifetime winning percentage. His teams had racked up nine consecutive conference championships while routinely earning high national rankings. The Rebels appeared in twelve NCAA postseason tournaments, hustled their way to four Final Four appearances, and captured the national championship in 1990.

He was a sportswriter's dream. His teams not only won, but did so in flamboyant style, and off-court events often made for even better copy. The controversy surrounding his program was frequently as intense as the play of his team on the court. He spoke in a voice that had the timbre of a high squeak. The closely cropped hair and rumpled clothes revealed a man comfortable with himself, intently focused upon his craft to the exclusion of other worldly concerns. He let his record speak for itself. This doleful but unrepentant man, nervously chewing on a white towel before seventeen thousand screaming fans in cavernous Thomas and Mack Center and a national television audience of millions, became an overwhelmingly popular, if improbable, icon for an underdog state.

Tarkanian was hailed by his many supporters as the person who brought fame and fortune to UNLV. But throughout his tenure at UNLV he also was the target of intense criticism that labeled him a renegade coach who routinely flouted the ethi-

15

cal standards of his profession. His triumphant reign at UNLV thus did not lead to the elevated status of an athletic prince enjoyed by such peers as Dean Smith, Mike Krzyzewski, and John Wooden. Ultimately, he was forced to resign his position amid serious allegations that cast a very long shadow over him and his university.

A profound ambivalence about his methods and professional ethics hovered over Tarkanian throughout his turbulent two decades at UNLV. This ambivalence replicated that with which many Nevadans viewed their state. They tended to accept Tarkanian in much the same way they warily embraced their primary industry: as a mixed blessing. Casino gaming providing plenty of jobs, the foundation for a rapidly growing and diversifying economy, and a lucrative source of state tax revenue that made it possible for Nevadans to forego state income and inheritance taxes and to keep property taxes relatively low. Conversely, however, gaming also contributed substantially to a social environment in which divorce, crime, drug dependency, alcoholism, high public-school dropout and low college attendance rates, and other social pathologies flourished. Similarly, Nevadans were excited by Tarkanian's teams and proud of the national attention he brought to UNLV and Nevada. But as the years went by, the questioning of his methods and ethics intensified to the point that his forced resignation was received by many Nevadans with a distinct sigh of relief.

Early on, most Nevadans instinctively embraced Tarkanian, drawn to his down-home but stubbornly rebellious nature. They had long felt victimized by what they perceived as a sanctimonious puritanism that piously condemned and poked fun at a state and its people where gaming was the primary industry, where some of its leading business and social leaders were widely reputed to have strong mob connections, where prostitution was not only legalized but practiced openly, whose first—and lasting—national image had been that created by easy divorce laws that once attracted estranged movie stars to Reno, and whose major industry grew out of heavy investment and management by organized crime. Thus when the investigators from the NCAA first came calling, seeking to expose wrongdoing, old-time Nevadans naturally placed them in the same category as they had federal investigators during the 1950s and 1960s. In was within this context that Tarkanian's fans hung upon him the nickname "Tark the Shark," suggestive of traits widely respected by the "wise guys" who plied their trade on the Las Vegas Strip.

For much of his tenure at UNLV Tarkanian was the most popular local celebrity in a town that thrives on celebrities. Whereas Jerry Tarkanian would never have been welcomed as a coach on many college campuses, he received a genuinely warm reception in Las Vegas. From the early days of his tenure as the head basketball coach at UNLV, he and his Runnin' Rebels embodied the spirit of the city they represented: swaggering, brash, openly defiant of regulations, unawed by established authority, fully prepared to accomplish high goals in unconventional ways, and beyond all else, dedicated to the proposition that winning—and winning big—is the only thing that really counts. He and his teams were indeed rebels, appropriate representatives of a community long recognized for doing things in its own unique way.

Jerry Tarkanian came to Las Vegas in 1973 intent upon building a national basketball power. He brought with him an impressive portfolio as a championship-caliber coach, most recently having built a highly successful program at Long Beach State. He came to Las Vegas because he realized that unusual opportunities awaited him at a fledgling state university that was often derisively referred to by locals as Tumbleweed Tech.

It was that unflattering image of Nevada's new university that prompted a group of well-connected boosters to seek out Tarkanian as the school's new basketball coach. They recognized the public relations potential to be derived from the existence, in their image-conscious city, of a prestigious university. The lack of community and legislative support for UNLV deeply bothered faculty and administration, but it especially rankled among those business leaders who perceived the importance of a respected university being located in Las Vegas. At a time before gaming had gained substantial national acceptance, they envisioned UNLV as providing cultural ballast to the glitzy, sometimes sleazy, reputation that surrounded Glitter Gulch. Understanding that it takes decades, if not longer, to build reputations for academic excellence, these boosters opted for a quick fix, seizing upon the strategy used by such universities as Ohio State, Oklahoma, and Michigan State, where the parade to national academic recognition was led by powerful football teams. The cost of building a national football power, however, seemed too daunting. Such an enterprise might take decades to accomplish, if it happened at all. They turned instead to basketball, a much less expensive proposition, where one or two top players could turn a losing program into a national contender.

Academic vice-president Donald Baepler provided the campus link to the boosters. A prominent research biologist with a doctorate from the University of Oklahoma, he acutely appreciated the potential inherent in such a quick-fix strategy. He later recalled, "The decision was that we wanted to have an athletic program that was good enough to pull the public closer to the university. Early on, there was a conscious effort to get the community involved with the university because we needed to get that public support in order to get things off and running, and reach a measure of academic credibility. . . . It was very difficult to get the legislature to take us seriously. And we wanted academic communities outside Nevada to take us seriously too."

Thus in the spring of 1973, a group of determined UNLV boosters essentially preempted the campus search process for a new head basketball coach. They did not want merely a winning basketball program. They wanted—even expected—a basketball program that would bring national recognition to the university and a reputation upon which the university's academic reputation could also ride toward national prominence. Central to their strategy was creating an image of academic respectability that would soften the unflattering image that afflicted Nevada and its largest city. "For a town whose main industry is tourism, you can't do it any better than this," one of the boosters later recalled. Sig Rogich, whose skills as a public relations guru later led him to serve as a media consultant for President George Bush, recognized the connection: "For us to appear in every newspaper in America every day with the University of Nevada, Las Vegas, it might just prompt someone in a windstorm or a rain storm in Buffalo to visit the town. For a town that's selling its name, and spending millions of dollars to do it, the University of Las Vegas on the front of jerseys and in box scores was the right kind of name for us to be successful."

Jerry Tarkanian did not arrive at UNLV in 1973 simply as a promising basketball coach. He was part of a much bigger strategy. "Did we want to use athletics to establish UNLV as a university?" Baepler rhetorically asked. "You bet."

Las Vegas is a city that embraces winners and discards losers. In forty-two-year-old Jerry Tarkanian the boosters thought they had found themselves a big winner. In 1961 Tarkanian began his college coaching career at Riverside City College. The Tigers lacked a winning tradition and stimulated no campus or community interest. They played before rows of empty seats; no one seemed to care. Tarkanian's modest salary and minuscule operating budget defined basketball's place in the grand scheme of things at this commuter junior college. His predecessor had won only one conference game the previous season, and Tarkanian's success at nearby Redlands High School had prompted a job offer that came without even the trappings of a formal search process. Tarkanian professed surprise when he was offered the job, but in fact no well-established coach had expressed much interest. Although Tarkanian's late hiring precluded recruiting new players, his first team responded to his intense coaching style by compiling a 14–13 record. It would be the closest he ever came to a losing season as a college coach.

During the seasons that followed Tarkanian established himself as an exceptional coaching talent. His penchant for working at his profession year-round, never taking vacations, became a hallmark of his entire career. His only interest, other than family, was basketball. He had no hobbies, once remarking that he never hired an assistant coach who owned a set of golf clubs or a recreational vehicle. "Our assistants are here to work with the kids, to be available. I've never played golf and I won't hire a coach who does."

His deep understanding of the complexities and nuances of basketball resulted from a lifetime of playing and observing the game. At Fresno State College in the early 1950s he played sparingly as a part-time starter, but he impressed his coaches and teammates with his ability to analyze the technical aspects of the game. Throughout his career he continued to learn and to adapt to changes in the game. His teams were always recognized for their mastery of fundamentals; they were equally recognized for their thorough preparation and ability to mesh as a team. But his success resulted from important factors beyond the technicalities of coaching; he was a master motivator, capable of getting the best from each player, no matter what their psychological makeup.

Most college coaches say that recruiting the right players is 75 percent of the effort required to produce a championship team. In a sport where one or two exceptionally talented players can turn a mediocre team into a championship contender, Tarkanian had few, if any, equals as a recruiter. For starters, he worked year-round at recruiting, overwhelming rival coaches with his tireless effort. He haunted the playgrounds and high school gymnasiums of Southern California, building an invaluable network among coaches, players, and the many hangers-on who naturally gravitate to the fringes of the game. His engaging personality enabled him to communicate his understanding of the problems and needs of youngsters, especially those from poor and disadvantaged backgrounds.

His reputation as a coach who cared for his players even after their eligibility had ended spread through the California hoops network. If any one aspect of his career stands out, it is the loyalty that he inspired among his players. Tarkanian's willingness to take a chance on players other schools routinely overlooked—the high academic risk, the unpolished but promising athlete, the poor, the uncultured, and, especially, the black athlete—enhanced his reputation throughout serious basketball circles. Not long into his college coaching career, Tarkanian began to find himself being contacted by top-flight players who had heard of his reputation and wanted to play for him.

In just his second year at Riverside, his first crop of recruits—all of whom came from nearby towns—powered the team to a 32–3 record, ending the season with a narrow loss in the finals of the California junior college tournament. The following year, with the school's two thousand–seat gymnasium packed for every home game, Riverside won thirty-five straight games without a single loss and captured the state championship.

That he won his first championship with four blacks in the starting lineup did not go unnoticed. Although Tarkanian began his college coaching career during the defining years of the civil rights movement, one of the major unwritten rules of coaching that remained in force across the country was that at least three starters had to be white, and never should a coach have five blacks on the floor simultaneously. Tarkanian was quick to defy tradition and conventional thinking. He recognized ability, not skin pigmentation. This dramatic departure from racial convention established Tarkanian in the black community as a coach who not only talked about equal opportunity but actually practiced it. This reputation would pay great recruiting dividends later in his career.

Tarkanian did not consider himself to be a civil rights pioneer. He simply dipped into the best talent pool available. Discrimination was never part of his makeup, and being the son of struggling Armenian immigrants made him an instinctive champion of the underdog. Born in 1930, he lived his early years in Euclid, Ohio, an industrial suburb of Cleveland, where his parents worked hard to survive the early years of the Great Depression by operating a small grocery store. As a young boy he learned about the slaughter and persecution of Armenians by the Turks. The murder of several members of his own family had prompted his parents to seek refuge in the United States. When Jerry was ten, his family moved to Pasadena, California. He graduated from the local high school, where sports had absorbed his energies. When he enrolled in Pasadena City College the major attraction was not academics, but basketball.

In five years at Riverside, Tarkanian produced a mind-boggling 147–23 record. He won four conference and two state championships and then moved on to Pasadena City College, where he continued to work his special brand of hoops magic. He rebuilt a team that had won only five games the previous season and garnered another state championship as his team went 35–1. The next year his team lost in the state tournament finals.

His teams were anything but the prototypes of the run-and-gun teams he later produced at UNLV. He played his own special version of a matchup 1–2-2 zone defense that enabled his often undersized players to prevent many close-in shots and to rebound effectively. He also ran orthodox, conservative offenses that emphasized ball control and careful shot selection. What distinguished his teams from others was not the style of play, but rather the level of team discipline, extensive preparation, and mastery of fundamentals. It was in his demanding, three-hour practices that he made precise execution of all phases of the game second nature to his players. Time and again he would interrupt a practice session to give an extended lecture on the importance of attention to the smallest of details. Precise team execution and proper individual fundamentals—not merely wins and loses—were the benchmarks he employed to evaluate his teams as well as his own coaching performance.

In 1968 Tarkanian accepted the head coaching position at Long Beach State College. For the third time in eight years he took over a program that had suffered through years of mediocrity. Long Beach State endured the role of stepchild to the highly visible programs at UCLA and USC. During his five years at Long Beach he operated on a parsimonious $3,000 recruiting budget; nonetheless, he lured many top players to his program by dint of his personality and hard work.

Once ensconced at a four-year program, Tarkanian never forgot his roots as a junior-college student and player. He engendered heavy criticism from academics, the media, and other coaches by recruiting primarily junior-college players, who were considered damaged goods by many university coaches. Soon Tarkanian's approach provoked complaints that he was running a "renegade" program built upon less than stellar students. He saw it much differently. By dipping into this large pool of talent, he not only attracted players with considerable game experience but also provided disadvantaged and/or academically deficient youngsters an opportunity to obtain a college education. Because many of these recruits also happened to be black, the rumors and criticisms mounted as rapidly as the number of Long Beach victories.

In five years at the helm of the 49ers, his teams produced a 122–20 record; in his third season his team made the 32-team NCAA tournament field. Efforts to schedule USC and UCLA, however, were summarily rejected. It was clear that Tarkanian definitely marched to a different beat than his rival coaches. All five starters on this 1970 team were not only junior college transfers, but also black.

Beneath Tarkanian's reliance upon junior-college transfers rested his own experience as a struggling student and athlete. "It comes down to the fact that I like J.C. kids because I was one of them. In fact, it took me three years to get out of Pasadena City College, so I never considered myself a brilliant student. I was like a lot of J.C. kids in that my main concerns were playing basketball and finding the next party. And I continued to struggle in school at Fresno State until I met Lois [his wife] and got my priorities in order. Then I went from a barely average student to an excellent one, a guy who even earned his master's degree with honors." His talented recruits helped him produce stellar

25–4 and 26–3 records during his final two years at Long Beach; with those seasons came rankings in the nation's top ten and additional invitations to the NCAA tournament.

Tarkanian's philosophy might have troubled many traditionalists, but it only added to his attractiveness for the UNLV boosters in search of a new coach. Like Tarkanian, Las Vegas had an image of rebelliousness and nonconformity, but what the boosters liked most was his decade-long record as a winner. In three successive college coaching positions he had taken teams with losing records and no basketball tradition and produced superior teams. In a time before affirmative action policies that require universities to ensure equal opportunity for all candidates through elaborate search processes, the UNLV boosters, working with Vice-President Baepler, targeted Tarkanian as their man. "We knew the numbers and there wasn't anybody else in the picture," Baepler recalls.

For his part, Tarkanian was ready to move, discouraged by a lack of fan response in Long Beach and an administration that did not reward his achievements with increased budgetary support. When the insistent Las Vegas boosters offered to double his $27,000 Long Beach salary, provide him with additional income from a radio show, and for good measure facilitate the purchase of a house at cost, he and his wife decided to cut their lifelong ties with Southern California. He was ready to try to work his magic at yet another school that lacked a winning basketball tradition.

The dreary image of Tumbleweed Tech was about to end.

Tarkanian did not miss a beat as he recruited a bevy of junior-college transfers that included such standouts as Ricky Sobers, Glen Gondreszek, Jackie Robinson, Eddie Owens, and Lewis Brown. They were the first of what would become a steady stream of high-quality players to UNLV. As the years unfolded Tarkanian's network expanded nationwide. Contrary to popular myth, his recruits were seldom among the nation's most sought-after players. With a few notable exceptions—Larry Johnson, Stacey Augmon, Reggie Theus, and Sidney Green—his greatest players were not widely recognized as "can't miss" "blue chippers." Rather, they were good players whose potential he recognized, but whose talents had to be nurtured and developed after they arrived at UNLV. Seldom did his recruiting classes compare to such established programs as UCLA, North Carolina, or Kentucky.

Although Tarkanian's much ballyhooed home opener against Texas Tech resulted in an embarrassing 82–76 loss, his first UNLV team ended the season 20–6. Tarkanian became the toast of the town. In his second season he found himself with a team that lacked height and strength—his center was just six-foot-seven—but possessed superb speed and athleticism. Although Tarkanian had enjoyed great success with his patented system that emphasized slow-paced, disciplined play, he now abandoned it for a new, up-tempo style. His zone defense—which had been emulated by many an impressed coach—was scuttled in favor of a full-court-pressure, trapping man-to-man defense designed to take advantage of his team's quickness. "I figured that if we got the bigger teams running, it would take away their size advantage. Rather than work the ball around the perimeter, I wanted us to get the ball up the court as fast as possible, and then take a quick jumper before the defense could set up. Speed would be the determining factor[;] . . . rebounding became more of a matter of hustle and quickness than size in our style of game."

For all their bravura, coaches are a doggedly conservative bunch. Most readily imitate successful systems but are chary of innovation for fear of suffering embarrassing failure. What Tarkanian did by completely changing his style of play after more then fifteen years in the coaching profession was truly remarkable. One of basketball's most respected coaches and theoreticians, Pete Newell, later commented in frank admiration about the risk that Tarkanian took: "For years Tark was the best zone coach in the country. He had a very controlled offense. In one year, he ripped up his whole book of coaching and tried something entirely new. There aren't many coaches who would have the courage to try that." As befitting the primary industry of his adopted state, Tarkanian was not afraid to take a major gamble upon which his professional future rested.

Thus was born the Runnin' Rebels. The new, up-tempo style became an immediate hit in Las Vegas. Runnin' Rebels basketball also set a new standard for the college game, producing many attempts, often futile, at emulation. Tarkanian's revamped team went 24–5 and frequently scored more than 100 points. During that pivotal season, the Rebels ran up a new collegiate record by scoring 164 points against Hawaii-Hilo before 2,500 incredulous Hawaiians. As his new approach received extensive national publicity, Tarkanian found himself besieged by prospects who wanted to play in his exciting system.

UNLV boosters were thrilled. The frequent appearance of the Rebels on television produced the recognition they craved. Their new coach not only had established a winning program and snared considerable national attention, but had done so with a highly entertaining style of play that provided Las Vegas with a special identity. The Runnin' Rebels aptly symbolized the frenetic lifestyle of America's most controversial city. As Tarkanian recalls,

"The fans went nuts. . . . They just loved how we ran." The flashy style of the basketball team aptly reflected the pace of life in the city that never sleeps: aggressive, hustling, fast-paced, intent upon winning.

In 1975 the run-and-gun Rebels made their first appearance in the NCAA tournament. In 1976 the team averaged 110 points a game, before the introduction of the shot clock in college basketball; in 23 games that memorable season the Runnin' Rebels scored over 100 points. In 1977, just Tarkanian's fourth year on the job, they powered their way through the NCAA tournament behind the long-distance shooting of Sudden Sam Smith and the hustling defense and scoring of Ricky Sobers and Reggie Theus before narrowly losing to traditional national power North Carolina 84–83 in the national semifinal game. UNLV had been transformed into a major college basketball power.

Although things were going Tarkanian's way on the basketball court, elsewhere ominous problems began to appear. During his final year at Long Beach the NCAA had conducted a probe of the schools' football and swimming programs, and it added the basketball program to its inquiry shortly after Tarkanian left for Las Vegas. Although some believed that UCLA athletic director J. D. Morgan had blown the whistle, it seems that a newspaper column Tarkanian published in the *Long Beach Independent Press–Telegram* in January of 1973 prompted the investigation. He questioned the integrity of the NCAA's rules-enforcement establishment, charging that it treated the elite athletic schools with deference while hammering newer programs (such as Long Beach State) that were on the rise. "It's a crime that Western Kentucky is placed on probation but the famous University of Kentucky isn't even investigated," he fumed. "The University of Kentucky basketball program breaks more rules in a day than Western Kentucky does in a year. The NCAA just doesn't want to take on the big boys."

Tarkanian's questioning of the integrity of the NCAA would not go unnoticed, and the athletic director at Long Beach soon received a curt letter from Warren Brown, the assistant executive director of the NCAA. Three months later, and just four days after Tarkanian publicly accepted the UNLV position, the NCAA announced its probe of his Long Beach program. A year later the Long Beach basketball program was hit with a major set of sanctions, including a two-year ineligibility for the NCAA tournament and a ban on television appearances. The NCAA specified twenty-three violations that had occurred on the departed Tarkanian's watch.

Even more ominous for Tarkanian, within a week after he accepted the UNLV position, the NCAA enforcement branch announced that it was reopening a dormant investigation into the UNLV basketball program. To Tarkanian, this was no mere coincidence but proof positive that he was being singled out by the director of rules enforcement, David Berst, and executive director Walter Byers for special treatment. Was he the target of a special vendetta? In his autobiography published in 1995, Byers denies any such motivation, but his animosity is evident for the coach who he claims "beat the system." Did Tarkanian break the rules? "Of course he did," Byers fumes. "Anybody who studied the case knows he broke NCAA rules."

Tarkanian became the first coach to challenge openly what many coaches had long believed to be highly selective rules-enforcement policies of the NCAA. Tarkanian's pivotal newspaper column contained nothing new; he merely put into print what many coaches believed. As Tarkanian's challenge to the NCAA took on a new level of importance, he expanded his criticism to include the informal system of rules enforcement by which NCAA staff determined which cases to investigate, conducted its own investigation in a manner that protected its sources from disclosure, and recommended sanctions to a committee appointed by the organization.

For nearly three years the NCAA hovered around Tarkanian's rapidly ascending program, and in February of 1976 it charged UNLV with ten "major" violations that it said had occurred since Tarkanian's arrival.

Thus was the battle engaged. It proved to be a protracted war of attrition that waxed and waned for thirteen years—even reaching the United States Supreme Court—before a contentious compromise was reached in 1990. Tarkanian's reputation took a major hit with the announcement of the charges in 1976. He decided to fight. In a strategy not dissimilar to his full-court pressing defense, Tarkanian launched an aggressive counterattack, calling into question the integrity of the leadership of the NCAA. The allegations themselves were relatively humdrum stuff and certainly were subject to different interpretations. The NCAA contended that improper airline tickets had been issued to recruits and players; that a player had been reimbursed in cash rather than by check for an airline trip, that players received free clothing from a local booster-clothing merchant, and that players received free lodging and free meals at Strip casinos, arranged by a booster. Most serious was the charge that Tarkanian and/or his staff had arranged for a player to receive a B in a course he did not attend.

A protracted and acrimonious battle followed. Tarkanian lost no opportunity to denounce his accusers. The NCAA's chief investigator, David Berst, in turn caustically referred to Tarkanian as a "rug merchant," a not-so-subtle, disparaging ethnic comment about his Armenian heritage. UNLV's officials concluded from their own investigation that the charges lacked credibility;

they found many discrepancies in the NCAA evidence and publicly said so. Consequently, the collegial concept upon which the NCAA was established was for the first time seriously challenged. Donald Baepler, having been elevated to the presidency of UNLV, walked a fine line, but it was clear that he believed his coach's version of the truth and not that of the NCAA. For example, although the instructor who allegedly gave player David Vaughan a passing grade in a sociology course denied under oath the complete substance of the allegation, provided documentation as to Vaughan's regular attendance, and submitted evidence that the student himself did the work required in the class, the NCAA nonetheless found Tarkanian and UNLV guilty of this charge.

UNLV's internal investigation was conducted by its administrative leadership with the guidance of prominent Las Vegas attorney Samuel Lionel. They concluded that UNLV and its head coach were being treated vindictively. An appeal that pointedly challenged the accuracy of the allegations, and by implication the integrity of the NCAA enforcement staff, was submitted to and summarily denied by the NCAA. UNLV's vice-president for administration, Brock Dixon, concluded that the evidence supporting the NCAA's case was "clearly in doubt" and that the NCAA's "standards of proof and due process were inferior to what we might expect." He concluded, "In almost every factual situation delineated by the NCAA, the university's own investigation has been able to find a substantial body of conflicting evidence."

In an emotionally charged hearing held in Nashville in the summer of 1977, UNLV's administration and Tarkanian responded to the allegations, mounting a spirited defense led by its attorney. However, Lionel was operating not in a courtroom, but in an administrative hearing, where rules of evidence are not as formal as in a court of law. Under established NCAA policy, Tarkanian was denied an opportunity to confront those who had presented evidence against him; he was even denied the names of the informants upon whose testimony Berst and his staff had based their case. As Tarkanian told anyone who would listen, he was being judged by a committee of the same organization that was bringing charges against him. And in the spirit of American litigiousness, he demanded the rights of due process.

Ultimately, the NCAA committee that heard the charges did what it had always done before: It accepted as valid the charges presented by the infractions committee, finding that Tarkanian's actions indicated "a disregard for the Association's governing legislation" and that he had exacerbated the situation by "encouraging certain principals in the case to provide incorrect information related to violations of NCAA regulations." Although the charges—if true—were anything but earth-shaking in the world of big-time college athletics, the penalty imposed was mind-boggling. It required that Tarkanian be completely removed from any contact with the UNLV basketball program for two years.

Brock Dixon advised Baepler that although "we could wish for standards of due process and evidence far superior to that which we have observed," UNLV had no choice but to comply. As a voluntary member of the NCAA, UNLV had to accept the penalty or withdraw its membership, an unrealistic and impractical alternative for a school set upon a course leading to the Final Four. Thus did Baepler reluctantly order Tarkanian suspended.

Much to the surprise of the folks at NCAA headquarters in Shawnee Mission, Tarkanian hustled into a Nevada state court, where he quickly obtained an injunction ordering UNLV to reinstate its coach. Clark County district judge James Brennan also issued an extraordinarily sharp rebuke of the NCAA: "The evidence the NCAA presented was 100 percent hearsay without a scrap of documentation in substantiation. The evidence shows that every fundamental principle pertaining to the plaintiff's due process rights were violated." He denounced the NCAA for conducting a "Star Chamber" proceeding that was based upon "lies, distortions and half truths" that resulted from David Berst acting like "a man possessed and consumed with animosity toward the plaintiff." Tarkanian's critics, however, were quick to denounce Brennan's decision as politically inspired. As an elected judge, they charged, Brennan was sensitive to the political clout possessed by Tarkanian's supporters. In Las Vegas, Rebel basketball had become a political issue possessed of high visibility.

The NCAA appealed, and the case entered the labyrinth of the Nevada state court system (where it remained for nearly eight years), then headed into the federal courts. Tarkanian's unprecedented response had clearly put the association on the defensive. By bringing suit over his denial of due process, Tarkanian had gained a distinct advantage in the court of public opinion. He never had to sit out the two-year suspension. Thus, much to the chagrin of Berst and Byers, Tarkanian continued to coach with the full support of the Las Vegas community, the courts of Nevada, and his university's administration.

Nevadans overwhelmingly supported Tarkanian. Those with long memories recalled the 1950s investigations conducted by Senator Estes Kefauver into alleged mob influence in Nevada and a later vendetta conducted against the state's primary industry through the FBI by Attorney General Robert Kennedy. Both of these assaults from afar had struck most Nevadans as unfair and politically inspired. They tended to view the NCAA's informal system of justice as yet another attack upon the state's integrity. Conversely, the NCAA viewed Tarkanian as a pariah: "Tark was walking testimony to the modern redefinition of institutional control of athletes," Walter Byers later wrote. "He did what he wanted to do: his university did what he wanted it to do."

As the NCAA's appeal of the court order reinstating Tarkanian slowly wound its way through the courts, Tarkanian blithely went about his business of winning basketball games and appearing in the NCAA's special party, the March basketball tournament. Tarkanian's impact upon Las Vegas was never more clearly felt than in 1983, when the enormous, 17,000-seat Thomas and Mack Center was constructed on the western edge of the UNLV campus. It quickly became known as the Shark Tank. Enthusiastic fans, many of whom could never obtain tickets in the 6,000-seat Convention Center, now poured into the new facility to watch the exciting Rebels run. A student in a resplendent red and grey shark costume prowled the sidelines at games. Visiting teams were often awed by a dazzling fireworks and light show, in the darkened, packed arena, that included the ominous theme song from the shark-infested movie *Jaws*. By the time the pregame show was over, many visiting teams had their confidence shaken, even before having to confront Tark's swarming full-court press.

And so in the Shark Tank the beat went on. UNLV won the Pacific Coast Athletic Association/Big West Conference championship nine seasons in succession. Between 1983 and 1986 the Rebels reeled off stunning season records of 28–3, 29–6, 28–4, and 33–5. In 1987, the Rebels, led by center Armon Gilliam and guard Freddie Banks, stormed to a 37–2 record and the Final Four, only to lose, 97–93, in the semifinal round to eventual national champion Indiana. For Las Vegas residents, the Runnin' Rebels had become the biggest act in town. Front-row seats in Thomas and Mack became the ultimate status symbols in a status-conscious town. The glitterati of Las Vegas society made it a point to be seen on "Gucci Row" for the big games. Tarkanian's salary skyrocketed to six figures, making him the highest-paid employee in the state of Nevada. His contracts guaranteed him 10 percent of revenues received by UNLV for NCAA postseason tournament appearances, an incentive that paid him handsomely. Lucrative Nike athletic shoe endorsement contracts, a summer basketball camp, radio and television shows, a newspaper column, a lengthy number of commercial endorsements, and his own business enterprises swelled Tarkanian's income well beyond the $203,000 university salary he earned in 1991.

Tarkanian's popularity reached its highest point in 1990 when his team, led by future professional stars Greg Anthony, Stacey Augmon, and Larry Johnson and supplemented by a powerful supporting cast, stormed through the NCAA tournament, climaxing a 30–1 season by overwhelming a talented

Duke team by the humiliating score of 103–73. It was the most lopsided score in the tournament's sixty-year history. When Tarkanian and his players witnessed the hoisting of a special commemorative banner to the rafters of Thomas and Mack the following season, the letters NCAA before the words *National Champion* were pointedly omitted.

As his string of championship seasons unfolded, Tarkanian continued to build his public image. To his many supporters he was the master recruiter who could identify raw talent among society's less fortunate and turn them into stars with his brilliant coaching. *Sports Illustrated* called him "the Pied Piper" who possessed a special recruiting touch. He was often considered to be an informal social worker who gave society's rejects a second chance to earn an education (and incidentally play basketball). He had become known as the "Father Flanagan" of the college basketball world, defender of the poor, the outcasts, the victims of discrimination.

This benevolent image, however, conflicted sharply with that held by his many critics, including several vocal UNLV faculty members who viewed his notoriety as damaging to their university's national reputation. Tarkanian's predilection for recruiting players with suspect academic skills, even some with police records, produced profound skepticism. Allegations of illegal recruiting, cash payments to his players by boosters, lucrative jobs that required little or no work, out-of-season practices, and the provision of luxury automobiles for players by boosters routinely made the rounds. Tarkanian, of course, denied all.

Tarkanian's program—although immensely popular in Nevada—operated under a heavy cloud of suspicion and innuendo. The turning point had its origins in 1983 with the appointment of Robert Maxson to the UNLV presidency. The new president arrived from the University of Houston amid rising community expectations for UNLV and a healthy skepticism about the credibility of its basketball program among faculty leaders. Deeply concerned about image and public relations, Maxson understood the significance of the controversy already swirling around the UNLV basketball program.

Maxson initially received an enthusiastic public response. His strong emphasis upon academic excellence resonated well among the Las Vegas citizenry as he proclaimed his goal of transforming UNLV into a "great urban university." Although he praised his controversial basketball coach with the right audiences, accompanied the team to tournament games, and used home games for the purpose of entertaining university friends and legislators, Maxson understood that Tarkanian presented an image problem for UNLV in some influential quarters. For several years, Maxson apparently gave Tarkanian the benefit of the doubt, all the while keeping a close watch on the program.

Above all else, this Arkansas native with the soft southern accent was an astute practitioner of the art of public relations. He vigorously pursued external funding that produced a flurry of favorable media coverage, all of which prominently featured Maxson's role in securing a new grant or gift. He toured the state proclaiming UNLV's virtues, and within a short time produced an astounding turnabout in public perception of his institution. Carefully courting the movers and shakers in Las Vegas, especially casino magnate Stephen Wynn and his high-profile wife, Elaine, Maxson succeeded where his predecessors had floundered. He mobilized public support behind UNLV as a place where serious academic work took place, proudly quoting a national news magazine's description of UNLV as one of America's "up and coming" public universities. Some skeptics, however, recognized that Maxson possessed an ego as big as the state of Texas, from whence he had come. Could he, they wondered, share for very long the spotlight with the likes of Las Vegas's most popular resident, Jerry Tarkanian?

The answer to that intriguing question cannot be answered with certainty. Maxson certainly coexisted with Tarkanian for several years and took drastic action only when serious revelations about the basketball program surfaced. It is also true that the relationship between Maxson and his coach slowly deteriorated and eventually became ensnared in a series of tragic events that produced truly a circus atmosphere. Ultimately, a series of questionable Tarkanian deeds produced a groundswell of faculty and public reaction that Maxson could not ignore.

Central to this relationship was the long-standing legal battle between UNLV and the NCAA. While his coach spoke only of the organization with contempt, Maxson correctly recognized the importance of his institution being in good standing with intercollegiate athletic's ruling body. In 1988, the United States Supreme Court finally brought the NCAA-UNLV-Tarkanian legal tussle to a nonconclusive ending with a narrow 5–4 decision upholding the NCAA position that as a private organization it was not bound to provide formal, due-process standards in its in-house deliberations. The 1977 infractions report, complete with the sanction requiring Tarkanian sit out two seasons, was once more back on the NCAA table. The infractions committee, now operating with a completely new membership, took several years to ponder its next move. It eventually proposed that the issue be resolved by forbidding UNLV to participate in the 1991 postseason tournament—a recommendation that would have denied the Rebels an opportunity to defend their 1990 national championship. This proposed resolution produced another outcry in Las Vegas. Maxson and his administrators eventually negotiated a compromise that moved the postseason ban to 1992, by which time Larry Johnson, Stacey Augmon, and company would have completed their eligibility and taken their above-the-rim show to the National Basketball Association.

By this time, however, Tarkanian's own long-running act was beginning to wear thin. His relationship with Maxson had grown markedly less cordial. Tarkanian and his friends picked up reports of negative comments about the basketball program that Maxson was said to have made in private meetings; then Maxson appointed an interim athletic director, Dennis Finfrock, whose antipathy for Tarkanian was well known. Tensions between Maxson and the basketball program crested in 1990 when members of the national championship–bound team boycotted a team meal scheduled with Maxson; they openly mocked his southern accent and told anyone who would listen that they distrusted him and his motives.

The catalyst to this deteriorated relationship was the celebrated Lloyd Daniels affair. In 1986 Tarkanian demonstrated extremely bad judgment in recruiting the six-foot-eight Daniels, a sensational prospect whose playground reputation in New York City was compared to that of the legendary Lew Alcindor and Connie Hawkins. His court skills were as widely known as his academic deficiencies. As one sports columnist cruelly wrote, Daniels could do everything with a basketball except autograph it.

Daniels was obviously a severe academic risk, certainly not the type of student a university seeking national academic stature would admit. It was widely rumored that Daniels could not read; his academic transcript revealed that he had bounced in and out of four high schools in three states. He had been kicked out of two for allegations regarding marijuana use and theft. Daniel's checkered record was enough to make even the most callous of basketball recruiters blanch. But as Tarkanian pointed out, Daniels had lived on the streets of Brooklyn since his early teens, and he agreed to give this incredible prospect an opportunity to get his life together at UNLV. Could Lloyd Daniels become the ultimate renovation project of basketball's Father Flanagan?

Tarkanian's critics, becoming increasingly outspoken, asked if UNLV would put forth such an effort to recruit a student if he were not one of the nation's hottest basketball prospects. And in a move that produced incredulity across Las Vegas, Daniels was formally adopted by one of Tarkanian's assistant coaches, who provided his new charge with a used automobile and a motorcycle. Tarkanian and his assistant coach, recruiting coordinator Mark Warkentien, professed that their motivations stemmed only from a desire to help a troubled young man obtain a college education; even the most zealous UNLV fan had to pause over that one.

Daniels gained admission to UNLV under a special policy that permitted non–high school graduates to enroll, based upon successful completion of remedial study and the accumulation of a minimum of fourteen junior-college credits. One month after enrolling at UNLV in January of 1987, however, Daniels was arrested in North Las Vegas, where he was videotaped purchasing crack cocaine from an undercover law enforcement officer in a sting operation. At this point even the Father Flanagan of basketball could not protect his prize recruit, who summarily departed for the Continental Basketball League. Unfortunately for Tarkanian's local support base, just prior to the Daniels episode he had brought Clifford Allen to campus, even though the coach had to go behind the bars of a California juvenile detention center to obtain the six-foot-ten prospect's signature on a national letter-of-intent. Once on campus, Allen seldom attended classes and was sent packing before ever playing for the Rebels; soon thereafter he ended up as a resident of a Florida penitentiary.

The Daniels case, coming on the heels of the Allen fiasco, besmirched Tarkanian's image in the eyes of many UNLV fans, greatly troubled faculty leaders, and gave Maxson substantial cause for serious reflection upon the image problems created by his nationally ranked team. When Tarkanian defended his recruitment of Daniels as merely one social work effort that "backfired," he only intensified the criticism. Why did he do it? Was it a genuine concern for an underprivileged black athlete whose life had been warped by the inner-city environment into which he had been born? Or was it a growing arrogance and belief that he was, in fact, beyond the reach and control of the NCAA and his own university?

Tarkanian's handling of the Lloyd Daniels affair had made him vulnerable in the eyes of those who now believed that UNLV would be much better off without him as its basketball coach. Another important factor had also changed: Las Vegas's media no longer gave Tarkanian the benefit of the doubt. Coverage of the Rebels on television and in the newspapers took on a more critical, distanced, professional tenor. Sportswriters, even editorial-page writers, expressed concern about Allen and Daniels and frequently reported sightings of Rebels driving expensive late-model automobiles along Las Vegas streets. Maxson was now hearing more and more from community and faculty leaders that something had to be done to improve the image of UNLV's athletic program.

The resilient Tarkanian overcame the Lloyd Daniels mess with three Final Four appearances and a national championship in the next five seasons. Spectacular winning seasons have a way of diminishing most problems. Then the roof fell in. On Sunday morning, May 26, 1991, Tarkanian was dealt a crushing blow when the front page of the *Las Vegas Review-Journal* featured photographs of three members of Tarkanian's national championship team—Anderson Hunt, Moses Scurry, and David Butler—sitting in a hot tub drinking beer and playing a pick-up game of basketball with an individual who had been convicted on federal charges of fixing college basketball games on the East Coast. Here was incontrovertible evidence that some of Tarkanian's players were consorting with Richie "The Fixer" Perry. University attorney Brad Booke, already recognized as no friend of Tarkanian, tersely tied the situation up in one neat package for the press: "The long-term problems of being associated with such a person far outweigh the problems of an NCAA violation. The name of Richard Perry probably has greater potential for serious and lasting damage to the institution than does the name of Lloyd Daniels."

The photographs set off a firestorm of controversy in Las Vegas. A few days later another picture appeared in the *Review-Journal* showing Perry sitting a few rows behind the Rebel bench at a game—in seats that had been issued to Tarkanian. The town immediately divided into two camps. Tarkanian's supporters counterattacked, demanding to know who slipped the incriminating pictures to the newspaper, eventually offering a reward of $30,000 to anyone who could link the photographs and the leaker to a conspiracy to get Tarkanian fired. Tarkanian's critics responded by calling for his shaved head on a platter. Subsequent news reports added more damage to the situation when it was revealed that Perry had actually brought Daniels to Las Vegas at his own expense to visit with Tarkanian. Tarkanian blandly replied that he knew Perry only as a "commodities broker," and not as someone convicted as the notorious fixer of harness races in 1974 and Boston College basketball games in 1984. An ominous cloud of suspicion now hovered over the program like an impending storm. Questions surfaced about the shocking upset loss suffered at the hands of Duke a few months earlier in the 1991 NCAA semifinal game. The heavily favored Rebels had played without their usual intensity and flair, and their narrow loss dumbfounded both their fans and basketball experts. In the wake of the Perry photographs, the question inevitably arose: Could the impossible—point shaving—have infected the Rebel program? A subsequent confidential investigation, which apparently included FBI involvement, produced no evidence of point shaving. But irreparable damage had been done to the Tarkanian basketball program.

The sensational pictures gave Maxson few options. The very integrity of the university—and his administration—was at stake. The national media swept into town, intensifying an already explosive situation. Rumors and accusations escalated. A series of terse meetings with Maxson and his top advisers readily convinced Tarkanian and his legal advisers that he had little, if any, support among UNLV administrators. Maxson talked glowingly about Tarkanian's coaching accomplishments, and soothingly about Tarkanian's long-term well-being. But he also pointedly noted that he might have no option but to fire Tarkanian if he did not resign. An emergency meeting was scheduled to reassure worried regents, those nine elected custodians of the welfare of the university system who were receiving heated, but sharply conflicting, advice from a polarized community. Public scrutiny intensified as representatives of the national media flocked to Las Vegas. They obviously smelled blood. And their instincts were right, because Tarkanian was suddenly vulnerable. Now it was Tark the Shark's own blood that was in the water.

On June 7, 1991, less than fifteen months after his team had been greeted by an unprecedented Las Vegas parade crowd estimated at 400,000 when it returned from Denver with the NCAA championship trophy, the embattled coach held a somber press conference to announce his resignation. His voice cracking with emotion, Tarkanian announced that he had agreed to resign as coach and to relinquish his tenured position as assistant athletic director, effective the end of the 1991–1992 season. He and his lawyers had extracted from Maxson the right to coach one more season. Tarkanian's "final lap around the track," ironically, would be played under NCAA probation stemming from the 1977 case: no television appearances, no opportunity to compete for the Big West title, no possibility of accepting a bid to compete in the NCAA tournament.

Tarkanian still wanted to prove himself as a coach. In the autumn of 1992 he became the head coach of the San Antonio Spurs of the National Basketball Association, but it would be a brief tenure. After his team struggled to an early season 9–11 record, tempestuous owner Red McCombs summarily fired him. Ironically, one of his reserve players at San Antonio was Lloyd Daniels. In 1995, at age sixty-five, Tarkanian accepted the head coaching position at the school where he had once been a substitute guard, Fresno State. He was swept into the position by waves of fan support—and promises of enormous financial support—that overwhelmed a reluctant university administration. Tarkanian once more took over a team that had fallen upon hard times, but he resolutely vowed to take his alma mater to the top of the national rankings. In his first season at the helm, using players inherited from a team that had won only eight games the previous season, Tarkanian once more demonstrated his coaching expertise, posting a 20–10 regular season record. Although not given an at-large bid to the NCAA tournament, his team won two games in the postseason National Invitational Tournament before losing in the quarterfinals. Those experts who closely monitored college basketball reported that he was landing some of the nation's most sought-after recruits and predicted a speedy rise to national prominence.

In 1996–1997 his team once more enjoyed a 20-win season, but the season ended on a distinctly sour note amid a series of headline-making allegations regarding point shaving by two Bulldog players. The *Fresno Bee* reported disturbing contacts between the players and known local gamblers—including one individual who allegedly was $41,000 in debt to a Las Vegas casino. The *Bee* had already reported a series of encounters between other Fresno State basketball players and local law enforcement officers. Once more Tarkanian found himself under attack from faculty and community leaders for the types of players he was recruiting and his lack of vigilance in monitoring their behavior and off-campus associations. True to form, Tarkanian denied any wrongdoing and publicly condemned the media for its unfairness in reporting its findings. Ultimately, the FBI did not indict any of the suspects.

In April of 1998, after his team lost a close game in the NIT semifinals, Tarkanian enjoyed one of his greatest triumphs when the NCAA settled without admission of wrongdoing a lawsuit brought by Jerry and Lois Tarkanian in 1992 in which they charged that the organization had fabricated evidence and systematically harassed him ever since his days at Long Beach State. The settlement was for a staggering $2.5 million and was the first such settlement in the NCAA's history. To most observers it gave credence to Tarkanian's long-standing complaints about the NCAA's enforcement staff. "We feel vindicated," a relieved Tarkanian told the press. "They've never paid money to anybody. That says a lot about our case. All I can say is that they beat the hell out of me for twenty-five years." But his detractors were quick to point out that the surprising settlement came immediately on the heels of another flurry of news reports of alleged criminal behavior by two additional members of his Fresno State players.

His successful legal action notwithstanding, the several highly publicized brushes with the law involving his recruits during his stewardship of his alma mater's basketball program raised haunting questions that would not go away.

At the age of sixty-five Tarkanian had sought redemption in Fresno, but his last hurrah in college coaching seemed destined to enhance further the ambiguous legacy he had established in Las Vegas.

But there was no question that Tark the Shark—for good or for ill—was once more back in the swim of things.

COMMENTARY ON SOURCES

1: SAGEBRUSH AND CITIES

The standard overview of modern Nevada is found in Russell Elliott, with the assistance of William Rowley, *A History of Nevada* (Lincoln: University of Nebraska Press, 1987). See also James W. Hulse, *The Silver State: Nevada's Heritage Reinterpreted* (Reno: University of Nevada Press, 1991), and *The Nevada Adventure,* 6th ed. (Reno: University of Nevada Press, 1990), a popular and time-tested text that provides important insights and perspectives. Hulse also offers a "tough love" commentary, written from his background as a native of the mining town of Pioche, Nevada, and as a lifelong resident of the state, in *Forty Years in the Wilderness: Impressions of Nevada, 1940–1980* (Reno: University of Nevada Press, 1986). For the relationship of Nevada to Western American history, see Michael Malone and Richard Etulain, *The American West: A Twentieth-Century History* (Lincoln: University of Nebraska Press, 1989), and Gerald D. Nash and Richard Etulain, eds., *The Twentieth-Century West: Historical Interpretations* (Albuquerque: University of New Mexico Press, 1989). Gilman Ostrander, *Nevada: The Great Rotten Borough, 1859–1964* (New York: Knopf, 1966), provides a hypercritical view of Nevada's first century from the perspective of a disbelieving midwesterner. See also Michael W. Bowers, *The Sagebrush State: Nevada's History, Government, and Politics* (Reno: University of Nevada Press, 1996), and Don D. Driggs and Leonard Goodall, *Nevada Politics and Government: Conservatism in an Open Society* (Lincoln: University of Nebraska Press, 1996).

The editor drew heavily upon the insights provided by several scholars who have addressed specific topics: Carl Abbott, *The New Urban America: Growth and Politics in Sunbelt Cities* (Chapel Hill: University of North Carolina Press, 1981), and *The Metropolitan Frontier: Cities in the Modern American West* (Tucson: University of Arizona Press, 1993); Eugene P. Moehring, *Resort City in the Sunbelt: Las Vegas, 1930–1970* (Reno: University of Nevada Press, 1989); Jerome E. Edwards, *Pat McCarran: Political Boss of Nevada* (Reno: University of Nevada Press, 1982), and "Gambling and Politics in Nevada," in *Politics in the Postwar American West,* ed. Richard Lowitt (Norman: University of Oklahoma Press, 1995), 147–61; Wilbur Shepperson, ed., *East of Eden, West of Zion: Essays on Nevada* (Reno: University of Nevada Press, 1989), and with Ann Harvey, *Mirage-Land: Images of Nevada* (Reno: University of Nevada Press, 1992); Gary E. Elliott, *Senator Alan Bible and the Politics of the New West* (Reno: University of Nevada Press, 1994); John M. Findlay, *People of Chance: Gambling in American Society from Jamestown to Las Vegas* (New York: Oxford University Press, 1986); Mary Ellen Glass, *Nevada's Turbulent '50s: Decade of Political and Economic Change* (Reno: University of Nevada Press, 1981); A. Costandina Titus, *Bombs in the*

Backyard: Atomic Testing and American Politics (Reno: University of Nevada Press, 1986); and William Rowley, *Reno: Hub of the Washoe Country* (Woodland Hills, Calif.: Windsor Publications, 1984).

2: MAUDE FRAZIER

Maude Frazier's "Autobiography" is available in typescript in the Special Collections of the University of Nevada, Las Vegas, Library. A short account of her life by Mary Ellen Glass appears in *Notable American Women: The Modern Period: A Biographical Dictionary,* ed. Barbara Sicherman and Carol Hurd Green (Cambridge: Belknap Press of Harvard Univesity, 1980), 248–49. Frazier's accounts of her work as deputy superintendent of public instruction are available in the Biennial Reports of the Superintendent of Public Instruction for the years 1921 through 1926. See also unpublished commentaries on her life and career by Elbert Edwards of Boulder City, a close friend, and historians Mary Ellen Glass, Eugene Moehring, and Michael Green. These commentaries can be found in the Special Collections of the University of Nevada, Las Vegas, Library.

3: MOE DALITZ

This study has relied primarily on books and journal articles written by journalists and academicians, newspaper articles, interviews, and a videotape. Hank Messick's *The Silent Syndicate* (New York: Macmillan, 1967) is an important source. Based upon newspaper articles and information gained from many anonymous sources, it provides a detailed and, for the most part, convincing picture of organized crime and political corruption primarily in Ohio, Michigan, and Kentucky. Messick also discusses the dealings of midwestern syndicate criminals with their counterparts in other parts of the country from the 1930s through the 1950s. Robert Lacey, *Little Man: Meyer Lansky and the Gangster Life* (Boston: Little, Brown, 1991), also presents useful information about the relationships among syndicate criminals of different geographic and ethnic backgrounds. Daniel Bell, "Crime as an American Way of Life," in *Organized Crime,* ed. Nikos Passas (Brookfield, Vt.: Dartmouth Press, 1995), 81–104, is useful. James O'Kane, *The Crooked Ladder: Gangsters, Ethnicity, and the American Dream* (New Brunswick: Transaction Books, 1992), helped to provide a conceptual framework regarding immigrants and crime as a social ladder. Eugene P. Moehring, *Resort City in the Sunbelt: Las Vegas, 1930–1970* (Reno: University of Nevada Press, 1989), was a valuable source of information about Las Vegas during the time of Dalitz's major involvement in Las Vegas gambling. Ed Reid and Ovid Demaris, *The Green Felt Jungle* (New York: Trident Press, 1963), Steven Brill, *The Teamsters* (Cutchogue, N.Y.: Buccaneer Books, 1978), and Robert Laxalt, *The Governor's Mansion* (Reno: University of Nevada Press, 1994), provide perspectives on Las Vegas, and Dalitz's role in it, that differ, to some extent, with the viewpoints of interviews conducted by the author with David Goldwater, Edythe Katz, Allard Roen, Irwin

Molasky, Lou Wiener, Robert Smith, and Rabbi Mel Hecht. Charlie Resnik, ninety-one years old at the time of the interview and a daily visitor to the Las Vegas Hilton Country Club, explained his negative view of Dalitz as well as his personal view of the role of former bootleggers and gamblers in the post–World War II development of Nevada. Others who shared their perspectives on Las Vegas's development, organized crime, and Dalitz were attorneys George Graziadei and Stan Hunterton, B'Nai B'Rith official Burt Black, and Jim Gabriele. "Mob on the Run," a videotape documentary drawn from Ned Day's reports on organized crime in Las Vegas that have appeared in the *Las Vegas Review-Journal,* provides a valuable perspective on a complex and emotionally charged issue.

4: JAMES B. McMILLAN

This article relies heavily upon about thirty hours of interviews conducted by the author with Dr. James McMillan in 1994 and 1995, which resulted in five hundred pages of transcript. The interviews are part of the Oral History Project directed by R. T. King at the University of Nevada, Reno. Three oral histories of importance to the history of African Americans in Las Vegas are Lubertha Johnson, "Civil Rights Efforts in Las Vegas, 1940s–1960s" (University of Nevada, Las Vegas, Special Collections, 1988); Woodrow Wilson, "Race, Community, and Politics in Las Vegas, 1940s–1980s" (University of Nevada, Las Vegas, Special Collections, 1990); and Clarence Ray, "Black Politics and Gaming in Las Vegas, 1920s–1980" (University of Nevada, Las Vegas, Special Collections, 1991). Of value is the collection of oral interviews edited by Elizabeth Nelson Patrick, "Black Experience in Southern Nevada" (University of Nevada, Las Vegas, Special Collections, 1978). Also useful are a series of interviews conducted by Elmer Rusco with Juanita Barr, Charles Kellar, David Hoggard, and Dr. James McMillan, available in the Special Collections of the University of Nevada, Las Vegas, Library.

Several books on race relations provide a national perspective for McMillan's career. Harvard Sitkoff, *A New Deal for Blacks* (New York: Oxford University Press, 1978), analyzes federal policy during the administration of Franklin D. Roosevelt. Sitkoff's *The Struggle for Equality, 1954–1980* (New York: Hill and Wang, 1981) is the standard book for this era. For racial issues during the presidencies of Dwight Eisenhower, John Kennedy, and Lyndon Johnson, see James L. Sundquist, *Politics and Policy* (Washington, D.C.: Brookings Institute, 1968). See also Hugh Davis Graham, *Civil Rights and the Presidency* (New York: Oxford University Press, 1992).

There is no comprehensive study dealing with racial issues in Nevada, but a number of important articles have appeared in newspapers, periodicals, and journals. Roosevelt Fitzgerald's many articles in the *Las Vegas Sentinel-Voice* are an excellent reference. Fitzgerald also made available to the author two unpublished manuscripts in his possession, "The Movies and the Civil Rights Movement" and "The Evolution of a Black Community in Las Vegas." A brief overview is provided by Michael Coray, "African-Americans in Nevada," *Nevada Historical Society Quarterly* 32 (winter 1992):

239–57. For the relationship between race and housing, see Joseph N. Crowley, "Race and Residence," in *Sagebrush and Neon: Studies in Nevada Politics,* ed. Eleanor Bushnell (Reno: University of Nevada Bureau of Governmental Research, 1976), 59–79.

For an analysis of Nevada political leadership and civil rights, see A. Costandina Titus, "Howard Cannon, the Senate, and Civil-Rights Legislation, 1959–1968," *Nevada Historical Society Quarterly* 33 (winter 1990): 13–29; Grant Sawyer, *Hang Tough! Grant Sawyer, An Activist in the Governor's Mansion,* a narrative composed by R. T. King (Reno: University of Nevada Oral History Project, 1993); and Gary E. Elliott, *Senator Alan Bible and the Politics of the New West* (Reno: University of Nevada Press, 1994).

5: William F. Harrah

During the months before his death on June 30, 1978, William Harrah was interviewed extensively by the director of the Oral History Project of the University of Nevada, Reno. The two-volume transcript of those interviews constitutes the primary source regarding the life of an otherwise very reclusive individual. See William F. Harrah, "My Recollections of the Hotel-Casino Industry and as an Auto Collecting Enthusiast" (Reno: University of Nevada, Reno, Oral History Project, 1978). The direct quotations attributed to Bill Harrah in this essay were all taken from his oral history. See also Leon Mandel, *William Fisk Harrah: The Life and Times of a Gambling Magnate* (Garden City, N.Y.: Doubleday, 1981), which is based upon the Harrah oral history but incorporates additional information from interviews with Harrah's sister, key employees, and some of his spouses. Another source on Bill Harrah's life is Robert A. Ring, "Recollections of Life in California, Nevada Gaming, and Reno and Lake Tahoe Business and Civic Affairs" (Reno: University of Nevada Oral History Project, 1973). Unfortunately, this account by Harrah's closest confidant is scarcely more than a paean to the boss by a loyal employee. The most critical treatment of Harrah is Mead Dixon, *Playing the Cards That Are Dealt: From Oral History Interviews with Mead Dixon,* a narrative composed by R. T. King (Reno: University of Nevada Oral History Project, 1992). Dixon was Harrah's attorney and successor as CEO. There is a sense, however, in which the Dixon account is hypercritical. Its metamessage is practically that Dixon was more responsible than Bill Harrah himself for the Harrah's organization's successes. For George Wingfield and the early gambling climate in Reno, see C. Elizabeth Raymond, *George Wingfield, Owner and Operator of Nevada* (Reno: University of Nevada Press, 1992). The material on Harold Smith's life was gleaned from his autobiographical account: Harold S. Smith Sr., *I Want to Quit Winners* (Englewood Cliffs, N.J.: Prentice Hall, 1961).

6: Hank Greenspun

To compress Hank Greenspun's life into a few pages is difficult; summarizing the material on his life and times is no easier. He left behind an autobiography, *Where I*

Stand: The Record of a Reckless Man (New York: David McKay Company, 1966). Like any such work, it is understandably kind to its subject, but it is also highly entertaining and informative. Greenspun also published columns and articles for nearly forty years in the *Las Vegas Sun.* Reading these pieces is crucial for understanding his political and business views and his newspaper's role in them. Two other local newspapers, the *Las Vegas Review-Journal* and the *Valley Times,* treated him in a less flattering light. The same can be said of other Nevada newspapers, especially the *Reno Evening Gazette* and the *Nevada State Journal.*

Several oral histories by the University of Nevada Oral History Project are helpful; see especially the oral histories by Alan Bible, Benny Binion, Robbins Cahill, John Cahlan, Paul Leonard, Jack McCloskey, Joseph McDonald, Charles Russell, John Sanford, and Grant Sawyer.

Secondary sources on Nevada help place Greenspun in the context of Nevada and Las Vegas politics, the journalism profession, and national affairs. For Nevada and Las Vegas, see Eugene P. Moehring, *Resort City in the Sunbelt: Las Vegas, 1930–1970* (Reno: University of Nevada Press, 1989), and Gary E. Elliott, *Senator Alan Bible and the Politics of the New American West* (Reno: University of Nevada Press, 1994). Jake Highton, *Nevada Newspaper Days: A History of Journalism in the Silver State* (Stockton: Heritage West Books, 1990), offers an alternately admiring and highly critical analysis of Greenspun and the *Sun.* Jerome E. Edwards, *Pat McCarran: Political Boss of Nevada* (Reno: University of Nevada Press, 1982), explores in detail the battle between the senator and the *Sun.* Also helpful is Gary Elliott and Candace C. Kant, "Hank Greenspun Meets Joe McCarthy: The *Las Vegas Sun* Challenges First Amendment Violations," in *Battle Born: Federal-State Conflict in Nevada during the Twentieth Century,* ed. A. Costandina Titus (Dubuque, Iowa: Kendall-Hunt Publishing Company, 1989), 196–205. See also A. Costandina Titus, "A-Bombs in the Backyard: Southern Nevada Adapts to the Nuclear Age, 1951–1963," *Nevada Historical Society Quarterly* 26 (winter 1983): 235–54.

Katherine Best and Katherine Hillyer, *Las Vegas: Playtown U.S.A.* (New York: David McKay Company, 1955), is enlightening if at times excessively entertaining. Donald Barlett and James Steele, *Empire: The Life, Legend, and Madness of Howard Hughes* (New York: Norton, 1979), comments unfavorably on Greenspun's relationship with Hughes. Peter Wiley and Robert Gottlieb, *Empires in the Sun: The Rise of the New American West* (New York: Putnam, 1982), examines the growth of Las Vegas and offers commentary on Greenspun's role in it. Ed Reid and Ovid Demaris, *The Green Felt Jungle* (New York: Trident Press, 1963), discuss Greenspun and his relations with the gaming industry, as does Mary Ellen Glass, *Nevada's Turbulent '50s: Decade of Political and Economic Change* (Reno: University of Nevada Press, 1981). See also John M. Findlay, *People of Chance: Gambling in America from Jamestown to Las Vegas* (New York: Oxford University Press, 1986).

This essay draws heavily upon Michael S. Green, "The Las Vegas Newspaper War of the 1950s," *Nevada Historical Society Quarterly* 31 (fall 1988): 155–82, and "*The Valley Times:* A Personal History," in *Change in the American West: Exploring the*

Human Dimension, ed. Stephen N. Tchudi (Reno: Nevada Humanities Council, 1996), 213–32. Several articles regarding Greenspun and his times attest to how thoroughly his reputation envelops and transcends Nevada. See Joseph Dalton, "The Legend of Hank Greenspun," *Harper's* (June 1982): 32–43; Richard Donovan and Douglass Cater, "Of Gamblers, a Senator, and a Sun That Wouldn't Set," *Reporter* (9 June 1953): 26–30; Robert I. Friedman, "Fastest Pen in the West: *Las Vegas Sun* Publisher Hank Greenspun," *Washington Journalism Review* (April 1984): 36–42, 58; J. Anthony Lukas, "High Rolling in Las Vegas," in *Stop the Presses, I Want to Get Off!* ed. Richard Pollack (New York: Dell Publishing Company, 1975), 217–31; M. L. Stein, "Shootout in the Desert," *Editor and Publisher* (19 April 1986): 28, 104–8; and David W. Toll, "Three's Company," *Nevada* (April–June 1978): 18–21.

The author also has profited from conversations with many longtime Las Vegans about Greenspun and the *Sun.* I appreciate Barbara and Brian Greenspun, his widow and son, for sharing their views with me. Several individuals talked with me on the guarantee of anonymity, but the late Bob Brown and the late Adam Yacenda expressed respect for a fellow publisher with whom they often scuffled, Ruthe Deskin provided useful background material and advice, and Ralph Denton, a former Greenspun attorney, informed me about the mysteries of Nevada politics.

7: ALAN BIBLE

This essay benefited greatly from the definitive biography by Gary E. Elliott, *Senator Alan Bible and the Politics of the New West* (Reno: University of Nevada Press, 1994). Also of importance is Bible's oral history, "Recollections of a Nevada Native Son: The Law, Politics, the Nevada Attorney General's Office, and the United States Senate" (Reno: University of Nevada Oral History Project, 1981). The Oral History Project also contains typescripts of interviews with a number of Bible's more notable contemporaries, such as Eva Adams, "Windows on Washington: Nevada Education, the United States Senate, the U.S. Mint" (1968), and Fred M. Anderson, "Surgeon, Regent, and Dabbler in Politics" (1985). Adams served as McCarran's administrative aide and remained on during Bible's first two years before being appointed to the U.S. Mint. Anderson was a strong political ally, having first become acquainted with Bible at the University of Nevada. Several oral histories are important. Robbins E. Cahill, "Recollections of Work in State Politics, Government, Taxation, Gaming Control, Clark County Administration, and the Nevada Resort Association" (1977) provides perspective on Bible's role in regulating gaming as attorney general. Cahill was a member of Nevada's Taxation Committee during the 1950s. The book *Hang Tough! Grant Sawyer, an Activist in the Governor's Mansion,* a narrative composed by R. T. King (Reno: University of Nevada Oral History Project, 1993), recounts Bible's efforts in Washington while Sawyer was governor of Nevada (1959 to 1966). Robert McDonald, "The Life of a Newsboy in Nevada" (1971), describes at length Bible's relationship with Patrick McCarran.

The records for Bible's years in the attorney general's office can be found in the

Nevada State Division of Archives and Records, in Carson City. The Alan Bible Papers are deposited in the Special Collections of the University of Nevada, Reno, Library.

8: ROBERT LAXALT

A good sense of Robert Laxalt may be gleaned from reading his books and articles, since most of Laxalt's works spring directly from his experience and are semiautobiographical. In addition, *The Deep Blue Memory* (Reno: University of Nevada Press, 1993), a novel written by Laxalt's daughter Monique Urza, shares Urza's memories of growing up in the Laxalt family. Laxalt's papers are housed in the Special Collections of the University of Nevada, Reno, Library. This collection includes Laxalt's working drafts and original manuscripts, screenplays of some of his books, published and unpublished stories and articles, correspondence with his agent and publishers, reviews of his books, published interviews, newspaper articles by and about him, campaign material for Paul Laxalt, documents from Robert Laxalt's University of Nevada Press years, family and personal material, memorabilia, and photographs. The library of the Basque Studies Program at the University of Nevada, Reno, possesses a collection of Laxalt family photographs.

Joan D. Morrow's "The Sheepherder's Son" *Reno* (February 1980): 22–24, provides a history of Laxalt's early adulthood, a discussion of his vocation as a writer, and a consideration of his love for Nevada and his Basque roots. An interview with Robert Laxalt by Maria L. Madruga, *Brushfire* (1992): 40–43, explores his writing methods and his advice to aspiring writers. A more recent interview by Bill Martin, "Artitude," *Nevada Weekly* (May 1994): 11–17, focuses upon *A Lean Year and Other Stories* and *The Governor's Mansion* and includes a list of "must read" books recommended by Laxalt. Barbara Land reviews Laxalt's life, work, working habits, and affiliation with the University of Nevada, Reno, in "Midnight Writer," *Silver & Blue* (June 1992): 9, 15.

William A. Douglass's foreword to the University of Nevada Press's special edition of *Sweet Promised Land* (1986) places the book in historical context and traces its impact. An overview of Laxalt's work as director of the University of Nevada Press appears in an article by Chad Jones, "All about the UN Press, plus a Raffle," *Sagebrush* (6 November 1986). A brief summary of Laxalt's publications, awards, and career is on file at the Donald W. Reynolds School of Journalism, University of Nevada, Reno.

Books by Robert Laxalt

(listed in order of date of publication)
The Violent Land: Tales the Old Timers Tell. Illustrated by Richard Allen. Reno: Nevada Publications, 1953.
Sweet Promised Land. 1957. Special edition. Reno: University of Nevada Press, 1986.
A Man in the Wheatfield. Special edition. Reno: University of Nevada Press, 1987.
Nevada. New York: Coward and McCann, 1970.
In a Hundred Graves: A Basque Portrait. Reno: University of Nevada Press, 1972.

Nevada: A Bicentennial History. 1977. Special edition. Reno: University of Nevada Press, 1991.

A Cup of Tea in Pamplona. Reno: University of Nevada Press, 1985.

The Basque Hotel. Reno: University of Nevada Press, 1989.

A Time We Knew: Images of Yesterday in the Basque Homeland. With photographs by William Albert Allard. Reno: University of Nevada Press, 1990.

Child of the Holy Ghost. Reno: University of Nevada Press, 1992.

A Lean Year and Other Stories. Reno: University of Nevada Press, 1994.

The Governor's Mansion. Reno: University of Nevada Press, 1994.

Articles, stories, and chapters by Robert Laxalt

"The Anasazi: Indians of Mystery." *Vista USA* (fall 1980): 13–17.

"Basque Sheepherders: Lonely Sentinels of the American West." *National Geographic* 129 (June 1966): 870–88.

"The California Trail: To the Rainbow's End." *Trails West* (1979): 108–43.

"Chillida at Gernika: Birth of a Monument." Catalog of an exhibition at Tasende Gallery, La Jolla, Calif. 1988.

"Death Valley—Nature at the Limits." *National Geographic Traveler* (autumn 1986): 55–63.

"The Enduring Pyrenees." *National Geographic* 146 (December 1974): 794–819.

"Exploring the Grand Canyon." *National Geographic Traveler* 1 (spring 1984): 22–37.

Foreword. *The City of Trembling Leaves,* by Walter Van Tilburg Clark. Special edition. Reno: University of Nevada Press, 1991.

"From a Balcony in Paris." *Cosmopolitan* (August 1964): 70–75.

"The Gauchos: Last of a Breed." *National Geographic* 158 (October 1980): 478–501.

"Golden Ghosts of the Lost Sierra." *National Geographic* 144 (September 1973): 332–53.

"The Indomitable Basques." *National Geographic* (July 1985): 69–71.

"Land of the Ancient Basques." *National Geographic* 134 (August 1968): 240–77.

"In the Land of the Navajo." With John Stetter. *Vista USA* (spring 1983): 6–9.

"The Melting Pot." In *East of Eden, West of Zion; Essays on Nevada,* ed. Wilbur S. Shepperson. Reno: University of Nevada Press, 1989.

"New Mexico: The Golden Land." *National Geographic* 138 (September 1970): 299–345.

"New Mexico's Mountains of Mystery." *National Geographic* 154 (September 1978): 416–36.

"The Other Nevada." *National Geographic* 145 (June 1974): 733–61.

"Pity the Gambler." *Bluebook* 98 (April 1954): 32–38.

"The Sheepmen." *Nevada* 37 (April–June 1977): 22–25.

"War Giant Comes Back to Life in Nevada Desert." *Business Week* (20 June 1953): 106–12.

"What Has Wide-Open Gambling Done to Nevada?" *Saturday Evening Post* (20 September 1952): 44–45, 129–30.

"Wounded Lion." *Bluebook* 101 (June 1955): 32–38.

9: GRANT SAWYER

The most important published source for Grant Sawyer is his oral history: Grant Sawyer, *Hang Tough! Grant Sawyer, an Activist in the Governor's Mansion*, a narrative composed by R. T. King (University of Nevada Oral History Project, 1993). Sawyer is candid, humorous, and revealing of personality. The introduction by Gary Elliott is exceptionally well done. Some might prefer to look at the original transcripts, available at the Oral History Project office on the University of Nevada, Reno, campus. These are much longer, contain information not included in the published version, and give an excellent idea of the interplay between interviewer Elliott and Sawyer. Other oral histories housed in the Project that are related to Sawyer are those of James Slattery, Ed Olsen, Clyde Mathews, Peter Merialdo, and John Cahlan.

Sawyer's private papers are held by the Sawyer family and are not yet available to scholars. His public gubernatorial papers are housed in the State Archives in Carson City. Standard works that give important background information on the Sawyer administration include Russell R. Elliott, with the assistance of William D. Rowley, *History of Nevada* (Lincoln: University of Nebraska Press, 1987), Gary Elliott, *Senator Alan Bible and the Politics of the New West* (Reno: University of Nevada Press, 1994), and Jerome Skolnick, *House of Cards: Legalization and Control of Casino Gambling* (Boston: Little, Brown, 1978). An article of unusual interest because of its negative assessment of the future of Nevada gambling is E. F. Sherman, "Nevada: The End of the Casino Era," *Atlantic* (October 1966): 112–16.

10: MOLLY FLAGG KNUDTSEN

This essay is based upon the writings of Molly Flag Knudtsen. See *Here Is Our Valley*, Helen Marye Thomas Memorial Series, no. 1 (Reno: M. C. Fleischmann College of Agriculture, University of Nevada, 1975); *Cow Sense* (Reno: M. C. Fleischmann College of Agriculture, University of Nevada, 1980); *Under the Mountain* (Reno: University of Nevada Press, 1982); *Joe Dean and Other Pioneers* (Reno: M. C. Fleischmann College of Agriculture, University of Nevada, 1985); "The Callaghan House, Grass Valley, Nevada," *Northeastern Nevada Historical Society Quarterly* (1993): 99–104; "Watersheds" (manuscript in author's possession, n.d.); *Toiyabe Song* (Reno: A. Carlisle & Co., 1944); "Notes from a Young Pioneer," *Vogue* (15 September 1953): 117–18; "The Stones of the Blue Sky Magic," *Vogue* (1 April 1954): 62, 176–77; "A Day on the Mountain with the Basque Buckaroos," *Nevada Highways and Parks* 26 (1966): 409; "The Grass Valley Horse: A Baked Clay Head of a Horse Figurine from Central Nevada," *Plains Anthropologist* 11 (1966): 204–7; and "A Report on Perforated Sherds from Central Nevada with a Tentative Suggestion for Their Use," *American Antiquity* (1967): 226–27. In addition, there are more than three dozen historical and topical essays published under the names Molly Flagg Magee and (after 1969) Molly Flagg Knudtsen in the *Reese River Reveille* and elsewhere. Some of them are reprinted in *Under the Mountain*.

For her family history and background, see Frank L. Comparato, *Chronicles of Genius and Folly: R. Hoe & Company and the Printing Press in the Service of Democracy* (Culver City, Calif.: Labyrinthos, 1979); Ernest Flagg, *Genealogical Notes on the Founding of New England: My Ancestors' Part in That Undertaking* (Hartford, Conn.: Lockwood & Brainard Company, 1926); Thyrza B. Fowler, *Harold Fowler, 1886–1957: A Remembrance* (privately printed, 1960); James W. Hulse, *The University of Nevada: A Centennial History* (Reno: University of Nevada Press, 1974); Dara L. D. Powell, *The Flagg Family: An Artistic Legacy and the Provenance of a Collection* (Milwaukee: Burton & Meyer, 1986); Barbara Van Cleve and Molly Flagg Knudtsen, *Hard Twist: Western Ranch Woman* (Santa Fe: Museum of New Mexico Press, 1995), 101–7.

Quotations in the text are from various sources. The description of Mount Callaghan is from Knudtsen, *Under the Mountain*, vi. The quotation from W. Somerset Maugham is from Fowler, *Harold Fowler*, 35. Other quotations are from taped interviews made by Don Fowler with Molly Flagg Knudtsen in December 1995 and January 1996 and are in his possession. Fowler gratefully acknowledges the help of Glenda Powell in transcribing the tapes.

11: Paul Laxalt

This essay is based upon the author's own experiences as a member of Senator Laxalt's staff for ten years and a series of interviews with the senator conducted in 1995. The Paul Laxalt Papers, deposited in the Special Collections of the University of Nevada, Reno, Library, were invaluable. Additionally, the essay benefited from interviews with Senator Harry Reid, Congresswoman Barbara Vucanovich, Robert Aiken, Ed Allison, Pat Dondero, Jerry Dondero, Frank Fahrenkopf, Hal Furman, Warren Lerude, and Wayne Pearson. Also of use were John Dombrink and William Thompson, *The Last Resort: Success and Failure in Campaigns for Casinos* (Reno: University of Nevada Press, 1990); Russell Elliott, with the assistance of William Rowley, *A History of Nevada* (Lincoln: University of Nebraska Press, 1987); Omar Garrison, *Howard Hughes in Las Vegas* (New York: Lyle Stuart, 1970); Robert Laxalt, *The Governor's Mansion* (Reno: University of Nevada Press, 1994); Jerome Skolnick, *House of Cards: The Legalization and Control of Casino Gambling* (Boston: Little, Brown, 1978); and Paul Laxalt et al., *A Changing America: Conservatives View the '80s from the U.S. Senate* (South Bend: Regnery/Gateway, 1980). The author also consulted government documents, including committee reports and hearing minutes.

12: Steve Wynn

Stephen Alan Wynn gave Las Vegas a needed boost during the 1980s. Since then his investments in construction activity have served as a catalyst for maintaining Las Vegas's position as the fastest growing community in America. His properties provide employment for more than twenty thousand people. No one can question these positive results of one man's vision. Yet Steve Wynn does have serious critics. In 1995 *Las Vegas Review-Journal* columnist John Smith went through mountains of records and critical stories about Wynn and painted a very critical account of his history and leadership methods in *Running Scared: The Life and Treacherous Times of Las Vegas Casino King Steve Wynn* (New York: Barricade Books, 1995). I have drawn upon Smith's book, and believe that Smith has based his study upon accurate data. Smith provides the reader with more than just a very negative view of Steve Wynn and the gaming empire he has built. It also provides the perspective of his critics, as well as insights into the nature of contemporary investigative journalism. Wynn's attempts to prevent its publication, however, are characteristic of a charismatic leader attempting to maintain a positive public image. Regardless of the accuracy of Smith's evidence concerning Wynn's associations with people of doubtful reputations, and the relationships of people Wynn associates with, there remains a major question about the ultimate meaning and importance of the information. Smith does not tell us what we should do with the information, even if we were to find it to be completely true. Questions are certainly raised. So too are suspicions. Answers are less certain. The student of the career of Steve Wynn should also consult another critical assault upon his record contained in a five-part series by Max Bauer that appeared in a Las Vegas tabloid, *Casino News* (March 12, 19, 26, April 2, 9, 1993).

More neutral and positive articles also contain quantities of useful materials drawn upon for this essay. Dave Palermo of the *Las Vegas Review-Journal* wrote a cover story on Wynn ("Casino Executive of the Year—1995") for *Casino Executive* (December 1995). Dan Heneghan also published an article ("The Prodigal Son Returns") in the same issue of *Casino Executive* about Wynn's impending Atlantic City project.

The following sources also informed this essay: Glenn Fine, "Steve Wynn: The Re-Founding Father," *Casino Journal* (October 1993): 24–28, and "Wynn's Worries: Exclusive Interview," *Casino Journal* (July 1991): 26–28, 47–48; Neal Karlen, "Mr. Lucky," *Gentleman's Quarterly* (September 1990): 393–97, 439–40; Jonathan Z. Larsen, "Steve Wynn on a Roll," *New York* (16 April 1984): 66–87; Sergio Lalli, "The Wynning Touch," *Modern Millionaire* (February–March 1990): 13–16; Robert Macy, "The Master Planner," *Las Vegas Sun* (17 March 1995); J. Millman, "Can Steve Win?" *Forbes* (28 May 1990): 376–80; Fen Montaigne, "Master of the Game," *Nevada* (May–June 1984): 12–17, 75–79; Priscilla Painton, "The Great Casino Salesman," *Time* (3 May 1993): 52–55; Cy Ryan, "Wynn's Foreign Plans Hit Roadblock," *Las Vegas Sun* (10 October 1991); John Smith, "Image of Wynn, Partner Boosts Foes of Florida Gambling," *Las Vegas Review-Journal/Sun* (6 November 1994); and Pauline Yoshihashi, "In His Biggest Bet Yet, Golden Nugget's Chief Plans a Huge Resort," *Wall Street Journal* (13 November 1987).

The subject of charisma receives its best discussion at the source—Max Weber. The reader is referred to his essays, which appear in H. H. Gerth and C. Wright Mills, eds., *From Max Weber: Essays in Sociology* (New York: Oxford University Press, 1962). Edward Shils offers an excellent summary of the concept in his essay "Charisma" in *Encyclopedia of Social Sciences* (1968), 2:386–90; and Geofrey Parrinder, "Charisma" in *The Encyclopedia of Religion* (New York: Macmillan, 1987), 3:218–22. Other materials that furnished insights on this concept are Barnard M. Bass, "Evolving Perspectives on Charismatic Leadership," in *Charismatic Leadership: The Elusive Factor in Organizational Effectiveness,* ed. J. Conger and R. N. Kanungo (San Francisco: Jossey-Bass, 1988); Joseph Bensman and Michael Girant, "Charisma and Modernity: The Use and Abuse of a Concept," in *Charisma, History and Social Structure,* ed. Ronald M. Glossman and William H. Swatos (New York: Greenwood Press, 1986), 27–56; Douglas Madsen and Peter G. Snow, *The Charismatic Bond: Political Behavior in Time of Crisis* (Cambridge: Harvard University Press, 1991); Dankwart Rustow, ed., *Philosophers and Kings: Studies of Leadership* (1970); and Bryan Wilson, *Noble Savages: The Primitive Origins of Charisma and Its Contemporary Survival* (Berkeley: University of California Press, 1975). Kenneth Snow's quotation is from James L. Fisher, *Power of the Presidency* (New York: Macmillan, 1984).

13: WILLIAM RAGGIO

This essay benefited from the political framework established by Don D. Driggs and Leonard Goodall, *Nevada Politics and Government: Conservatism in an Open Society* (Lincoln: University of Nebraska Press, 1996). The essay, however, is based primarily upon a series of interviews with Senator Raggio and with fifteen individuals who have observed and interacted with Raggio during the course of his public career, several of whom requested anonymity. The author also had access to the extensive Raggio personal files, including an extensive collection of newspaper clippings. The most useful published source is the *Reno Gazette Journal* and opinions filed in the Nevada courts, most notably, *Bean* v. *State,* 398 P. 2ND 251 (1968), and *In re Raggio,* 487 P. 2ND 499 (1971). The Oral History Project of the University of Nevada, Reno, was useful, especially those oral histories of former governors Charles Russell and Grant Sawyer. Robert Laxalt's political novel, *The Governor's Mansion* (Reno: University of Nevada Press, 1994), provides insights into some of the colorful individuals who have made Nevada politics a never-ending drama. Gabriel Vogliotti's popular treatment of prostitution in Nevada, *The Girls of Nevada* (Secaucus, N.J.: Citadel Press, 1975), provides a perspective on the Raggio–Joe Conforte conflict that gives the benefit of the doubt to the brothel owner. See also the files of the political newsletter by syndicated columnist Jon Ralston, who specializes in Nevada politics, *The Ralston Report.*

14: SUE WAGNER

This essay is based primarily upon the Sue Wagner Papers deposited in the Special Collections of the University of Nevada, Reno, Library. The Wagner collection consists of twenty-six boxes of letters, press releases, personal correspondence, speeches, photographs, and other materials covering her legislative years. The Lieutenant Governor Papers are available at the Nevada State Library and Archives and contain eighteen boxes of speeches, correspondence, and the Commission on Tourism and Economic Development files.

Many of the major issues with which Wagner wrestled are placed in historical context by Don D. Driggs and Leonard Goodall, *Nevada Politics and Government: Conservatism in an Open Society* (Lincoln: University of Nevada Press, 1996). Richard Bryan, Jean Ford, Louise Bayard-De-Volo, and Lynn Atcheson provided helpful interviews. The author relied heavily upon the *Reno Gazette-Journal, Las Vegas Review-Journal,* and *Carson City Nevada Appeal.*

15: JERRY TARKANIAN

This essay rests primarily upon published sources, including scores of newspaper and magazine articles. The most important are found in the *Las Vegas Review-Journal,* the *New York Times,* the *Chronicle of Higher Education, Sports Illustrated, U.S. News and World Report, Time,* and *Sport.* The author benefited greatly from learning Tarkanian's values and perceptions of events from two books: Terry Pluto and Jerry Tarkanian, *Tark: College Basketball's Winningest Coach* (New York: McGraw Hill, 1988), and Don Yaeger, with the cooperation of Jerry Tarkanian, *Shark Attack: Jerry Tarkanian and His Battle with the NCAA and UNLV* (New York: Harper Collins, 1992). Walter Byers's autobiography presents an emotional denunciation of Tarkanian, strong on generalizations but short on specifics: *Unsportsmanlike Conduct: Exploiting College Athletes* (Ann Arbor: University of Michigan Press, 1995). Of invaluable assistance was the "Report of the [Nevada] Board of Regents on Jerry Tarkanian's Resignation," a terse 55-page summary report submitted in 1992 to the Nevada State Legislature by the chancellor of the University of Nevada System. This especially frank document is supported by sixty-one exhibits that run several hundred pages, including correspondence, UNLV internal reports, detailed NCAA investigation findings, and legal documents. These materials focus primarily on the history of Tarkanian's relationships with the NCAA and UNLV and on the Lloyd Daniels and Richard Perry episodes. This document is available at the Reno office of the Nevada University and Community College System.

CONTRIBUTORS

Patricia Andrew is director of continuing education at the University of Nevada, Reno. She holds a masters degree in public policy and administration from the University of Missouri, Columbia, and is a candidate for the Ph.D. in history at the University of Nevada, Reno, where she has specialized in western environmental and political history. She is currently completing her doctoral dissertation on the history of Fallon, Nevada, the boyhood home of Alan Bible.

Alan Balboni is professor of history and political science at the Community College of Southern Nevada and a longtime resident of Las Vegas. He received his doctorate from Brown University and has published a number of articles on the history of Las Vegas, and *Beyond the Mafia: Italian Americans and the Development of Las Vegas* (1996).

Richard O. Davies is professor of history at the University of Nevada, Reno, where he teaches courses in modern American history, the history of American sports, and American urban history. He is the author of several books and articles concerned with post–World War II politics and society, including *Defender of the Old Guard: John W. Bricker and American Politics* (1993), and *America's Obsession: Sports and Society since 1945* (1994), and *Main Street Blues: The Decline of Small-Town America* (1998).

Robert E. Dickens holds a Ph.D. in political science from the University of Arizona. He is director of government relations and economic development at the University of Nevada, Reno.

William A. Douglass is a social anthropologist and coordinator of the Basque Studies Program for the University of Nevada, Reno. In that capacity he has authored numerous books and articles. A Reno native, Douglass is part owner of the Comstock and Riverboat hotel-casinos in Reno and serves as president of the Riverboat. He is interested in civic affairs and environmental issues and serves on the board of directors of the Nevada chapter of the Nature Conservancy.

Jerome E. Edwards is professor and former chair of the department of history at the University of Nevada, Reno. A specialist in American foreign policy and Nevada history, he is the author of numerous articles and academic papers and the widely acclaimed biography *Pat McCarran: Political Boss of Nevada* (1982).

Gary E. Elliott is professor of history at the Community College of Southern Nevada, where he teaches constitutional history and civil liberties. He has written a dozen articles and edited several books and is the author of *Senator Alan Bible and the Politics of the New West* (1994).

Don D. Fowler is Mamie Kleberg Professor of Historic Preservation and Anthropology at the University of Nevada, Reno, and a research associate in anthropology of the Smithsonian Institution. His specialties include archaeology of the desert West, western exploration and early photography, and the history of social thought. He is the author of several books and numerous other publications on these, and related, subjects.

Cheryll Glotfelty is associate professor of literature and the environment at the University of Nevada, Reno, where she teaches courses in American literature and environmental literature. She is coauthor of *The Ecocriticism Reader* (1996), has published essays on western American writers, and is currently editing an anthology of the literature of Nevada.

Michael S. Green is a member of the faculty of the Community College of Southern Nevada, where he teaches Nevada and United States history. He is completing his Ph.D. in history at Columbia University. A former reporter and news editor for the *Valley Times,* he is the author of several articles on Nevada history, politics, and journalism, and is coeditor with Gary E. Elliott of *Nevada: Readings and Perspectives.*

James W. Hulse has been a member of the history department at the University of Nevada, Reno, since 1962. He is the author of numerous articles and three books on European history and five on Nevada history. He knew Maude Frazier when he covered the Nevada legislature as a reporter for the *Nevada State Journal* in the 1950s. He held the Grace A. Griffen Chair in History from 1992 until 1998.

Patricia Ferraro Klos specializes in Nevada women's history, and teaches history, geography, and English at McQueen High School in Reno. She also writes about antiques and historical preservation and is active in the Nevada Women's History Project. As an undergraduate at the University of Nevada, Reno, she was president of the Associated Women Students.

Richard L. Spees served on the staff of Senator Paul Laxalt for more than ten years. During that time he held a number of positions, including legislative assistant and staff director of a Senate appropriations subcommittee. He is the general counsel to the Council of American Overseas Research Centers and a legislative attorney. He is at work on his first novel, which will draw upon his experiences living and working in the nation's capital.

William N. Thompson is professor of public administration at the University of Nevada, Las Vegas, where he specializes in studies of public policy and the gambling industry. He has written extensively on the gambling phenomenon, and his works include *Legalized Gambling: A Reference Handbook* (1994) and, with John Dombrink, *The Last Resort: Success and Failure in Campaigns for Casinos* (1990).

Index